SPiRiT™
INTELLIGENCE

Other recent titles published by Richmond

I Need Balance in My Life by James Cowley
The Myth of Nine to Five by Ted Scott & Phil Harker
Captive of the System! by Peter Crawford
The Art of the Long View by Peter Schwartz
Futures for the Third Millennium by Richard Slaughter
Footprints of the Future by Richard Neville

SPIRIT™
INTELLIGENCE

175 practical keys for inspiring your life and business

DAVID R J POWELL

Richmond

CHALLENGING OLD WAYS; BREAKING NEW GROUND

Published in Australia
by Richmond Ventures Pty Limited
8 Ridge Street, North Sydney, NSW 2060, Australia

This edition published July 2003

National Library of Australia
Cataloguing-in-Publication entry

Printed by McPherson's Printing Group Australia

Powell, David R J.
 Spirit intelligence : 175 practical keys for inspiring your
 life and business.

Includes index.
ISBN 1 920688 19 6.

1. Self-actualization (Psychology). 2. Self-realization.
I. Title. II. Title : Spirit intelligence : one hundred
and seventy five practical keys for inspiring your life and
business.

158.1

CONTENTS

ACKNOWLEDGMENTS

This book could not have been written without the help and support of some very special people:

o My parents Reg and Beryl Powell who taught me by demonstration about the vital spirit qualities of enthusiasm, commitment, freedom, inquiry and exploration, vigilance, adventure, truth, honesty, strong morals and ethics, integrity, high standards and above all persistence. My father used to say – "do your best, you can't do more." This book is the best I can do. I hope it helps you do your best to optimise your life endeavours and help those around you. My mother always cares for people in her gentle, loving way. Perhaps this book can help you care more for those you live and work with.

o My wife and friend, Gabriele, whose companionship I value more than I can ever express. Finding a loyal partner to share life's journey has been a very precious gift. Thank you for your unconditional love and support. I love you.

o My sons James, Nicolas and Simon who have grown up to be fine young men. Thanks guys for your encouragement. I am proud of you.

o My secretaries Jan Myers, Jeni Pritchett and Jennie Burhop who slaved over keyboard and dictaphone, always cheerful, always positive and encouraging, unbeaten by the 'aliens' in our computers, researching and working 'unusual' hours! Thank you, you are terrific.

o I would like to recognise some of my early teachers who inspired me by their example — Harold Johnson and David Cohen, our Church Ministers, Paddy Waller and Dai Williams at BP, Garry O'Meally at AGL, Les Nelson at Amoco, Denis Waitley, Wayne Dyer, Tom Hopkins, Brian Tracy, Jim Rohn, Zig Ziglar, Buckminster Fuller, Barbara and Terry Tebo, Robert Prinable, Robert Kiyosaki, Jerry Speiser, Patricia Gillard and Allen Wright.

o My friends and colleagues who have given constant encouragement and hours of time in reading the drafts of this book.

o There are also many unnamed people in these pages who gave of their experience and wisdom to help you. Thank you to them also.

o Finally, my editor, Clare Moss, and my publisher, Oliver Freeman, who had the faith to support this work with his undoubted literary and publishing mastery.

ABOUT THE AUTHOR

David Powell was born in England in 1947 and educated at the City of London School. He gained a first class honours degree in Chemical Engineering from Edinburgh University in Scotland and has undertaken postgraduate studies in Psychology at Macquarie University in Sydney, Australia.

His corporate career spanned 20 years in Oil & Gas with BP, Amoco and AGL, and 10 years in Information Technology with ICL and Tandem where he held General Manager roles.

He is the Managing Director of Corporate Leadership - providing executive leadership facilitation and management development services to corporate, business and government clients across Australia, Asia, the Middle East, Europe and North America.

He is married to Gabriele. They have three sons and live in Sydney, Australia.

Part One

CHOICES

The Red Pill Alternative

In the Wachowski brothers' science fiction film *The Matrix*, the leader of the freedom fighters Morpheus tells the hero Neo that the reality he thought he was living is, instead, an illusion.

Morpheus explains Neo is in fact a victim, trapped in a matrix of delusion and that all the social, political and general living norms he experiences as reality are generated by the computers that have taken control of life on Earth.

Faced with the shock of this rude awakening, Neo is offered a choice of two pills, red or blue.

If he chooses the blue pill, he can go back to sleep, never again aware that he is a victim, living a reality superimposed upon him by others.

However, if he chooses the red pill, he will remain alert and awake with the opportunity to face the truth, reclaim his own reality, fight back for freedom and become the victor of his own life.

You too are now facing a choice – the blue pill or the red pill, life victim or life victor.

The blue pill alternative is to put this book back on the shelf and remain as you are — at risk as a victim, unaware, exposed and vulnerable to the subtle imposition of other people's and society's social, economic, business, political and religious paradigms, visions, agendas, games and rules that are all around you.

The red pill alternative is to take this book, apply the spirit intelligence keys it contains and create your own life as a victor.

This book is dedicated to all those who are looking for the red pill of spirit intelligence, freedom, independence and fulfilment.

ARE YOU?

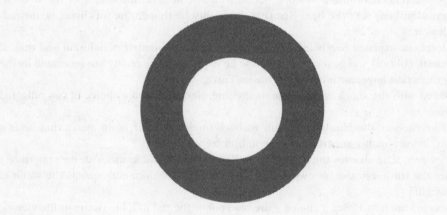

Introduction

SPIRIT INTELLIGENCE

'Wisdom is found in truth.'
GOETHE

Spirit intelligence. What is it? How do you access, develop and optimise your spirit intelligence in order to lead a more fulfilling, purposeful life? Can you also influence the spirit intelligence of those around you at home, in your community and at work to help them?

This book provides you with a set of 175 practical keys to answer these vital questions and shows you how to easily implement and use them.

These spirit intelligence keys will help you choose more effectively between alternative approaches in every aspect of your life, especially at work and at home with your family.

How? By always focusing on inspiring and empowering the whole person – body, mind, emotions and spirit.

The word intelligence derives from the Latin words *inter legere* — to choose between.

o BODY

Clearly our physical bodies are highly intelligent. They know how to grow, digest food, heal and self-regulate, choosing appropriately from a vast range of chemical and biological functions.

How you use your body and what you physically do each day is an activity choice that we will review to improve your sense of fulfilment and your results achieved.

o MIND

Most of us have been tested on our IQ, our Intelligence Quotient, which purports to measure the intelligence of our minds, that inner metaphysical realm of thought. In this book, we explore how your mind works and what you choose to think about — certainly at home and in your community – but especially at work in your business enterprise.

'The key to your universe is that you can choose.'
CARL FREDERICK

o EMOTIONS

Daniel Goleman's very popular and highly recommended book *Emotional Intelligence* has awoken us to another aspect of our inner realms and how we can be strongly influenced by emotional reactions.

Goleman refers to Mihaly Csikszentmihalyi's best selling book *Flow — The Psychology of Optimum Experience* which explores the wonderful emotions experienced when life is lived in 'flow', pursuing self set, stretch goals.

Our emotions are a metaphysical energy flow of feelings. They can range from the slow moving, turgid depths of depression to the free flowing peaks of exhilaration.

Because our emotions are affected by the state of our body and on what we choose to focus the attention of our mind and the intention of our spirit, we will explore powerful tools that will help you choose how you feel.

The last paragraph of Csikszentmihalyi's book states: *'The most promising faith for the future might be based on the realisation that the entire universe is a system related by common laws and that it makes no sense to impose our dreams and desires on nature without taking them into account.'*

This book explores those common laws, the universal generalised principles that allow us to optimise spirit intelligence and thus our emotional enjoyment of life's journey.

o SPIRIT

You can best develop your spirit intelligence by consistently empowering your whole being — body, mind, emotions and spirit.

So who or what is your spirit?

Your spirit is the essence of who you are — the core of your being that brings the breath of life to your body. The emphasis is on the word 'being' — for your spirit is the watcher, the observer, the initiator behind the constant 'doing' of your body, mind and emotions.

The word spirit is derived from the Latin verb *spirare* – to breathe

What you think about and what you do affects the way you feel. It is the experiences gained and the skills developed from everything you have done in your life that develops the qualities and the essence of your spirit being.

Who you are, your spirit being is constantly developing and evolving, reflecting your experiences on the journey of life.

o BE — DO — HAVE

A review of past experience reveals that the formula for success in any sphere of life is :

Be — Do — Have

You have to **be** the person capable of **do**ing whatever it takes to **have** what you want and achieve your goals.

o SPIRIT INTELLIGENCE

Spirit intelligence is thus the ability of your spirit being, the core of you, to make the best life choices. Choices in what you do with your body — your actions; the thoughts you focus on in your mind — your thinking; and the emotions you choose to pursue — your feelings.

Each chapter in this book will give you keys to improve the quality of your **be**ing and your spirit intelligence by providing better alternatives and better choices to **do** what is required at home, in your community and at work to **have** the results, success outcomes and the deep sense of fulfilment that you desire.

o SPIRITUAL INTELLIGENCE

Spiritual intelligence is different to spirit intelligence and concerns your choices, beliefs and practices in relating to Infinite Intelligence whether you call that God, Allah, Jehovah or Brahma. We'll cover this sensitive and very personal subject in Chapter 10 on keys to the spirit within.

o ENTHUSIASM

The word enthusiasm derives from the ancient Greek words — *en theos* — the spirit within. If you want to feel enthusiastic about your life and act enthusiastically, you need to improve the intelligence of your *en theos* — your spirit within.

o SPIRIT INTELLIGENCE KEYS

It's not rocket science. You can simply use the tools and approaches in this book to make better choices about your plans for self-development, how you interact with people, what you do at home with family and friends and how you operate at work.

These spirit intelligence keys are practical, reliable and effective. They are a synthesis of the best ideas and practices, a summary of what is working for people just like you in countries all around the world and the reasons why these techniques and tools succeed and why you can trust them.

We'll explore approaches that will inspire you and those around you to higher and more satisfying levels of performance.

○ ACCELERATED LEARNING

You may have come across the techniques of accelerated learning — using colour, music, questions and activities to increase the speed and effectiveness of the way you learn. Einstein said we use about 3 per cent of our minds. In our busy world, could you use an extra 97 per cent of mental firepower? Wouldn't you like to wake up the sleeping part of your mind?

Although this book can't play music, we have included many illustrations because as we all know, a picture is worth a thousand words. And we have asked many questions which will stimulate your mind and activate your latent 97 per cent of mental firepower.

If you really want to reach your full potential in life and succeed, you must surround yourself with people who demand more of you than you do. In other words, people who will stretch you and test you and force you out of your comfort zone into your growth zone.

You may find some of the questions challenging, even confronting. That's okay because I plan to call it straight down the line — to stretch you to achieve your full potential.

The keys to spirit intelligence are relevant to every aspect of your life — at work and play, at home with family and friends and in your community.

FIND THE KEYS.

UNLOCK YOUR POTENTIAL **NOW.**

One

POWERING UP THE WHOLE PERSON

'Make the most of yourself, for that is all there is of you.'
RALPH WALDO EMERSON

The first key to optimising spirit intelligence is to focus on inspiring and empowering the whole person — body, mind, emotions and spirit.

To demonstrate spirit intelligence and reach our full potential, we need an awareness of how to bring into play all our human attributes.

As a public speaker, I had struggled for years to simply explain the hidden power of the unseen realms of mind, emotions and spirit. In 1991 during an extended period of fasting and deep meditation on this challenge, the following metaphor literally just popped into my head — as they say, out of the blue. I imagined people as engines — powerful 16 cylinder engines. The metaphor has subsequently been greeted as very helpful by many people of all races and creeds in explaining our untapped potential.

o 16 CYLINDERS

To pursue this metaphor, let's consider that the body, mind, emotions and spirit all contribute 'fire power' to the engine but not in equal amounts. In my experience working with thousands of people around the world, the contribution of people's empowered emotions and enthused spirits are far greater than that of a fit body and mind. In our 16 cylinder whole person (body, mind, emotions and spirit) model, let's consider the components of the engine.

 Body

Everyone has a physical body, as does every living creature. That's why the body only contributes three cylinders of the engine. Of course you have to look after your body. You know not to eat too much junk food and not to drink too much coffee or tea. You know you are supposed to exercise aerobically three times a week for 20 minutes. How well do you care for your body?

Mind

A second source of 'fire power' is the mind. The mind is a formidable, non-stop bio-computer. It works seven days a week, 24 hours a day. I am sure you have woken up in the middle of the night and found a personal or work problem running or a solution to a tough problem suddenly appearing. Or perhaps you have been to a barbecue or social gathering on a weekend, supposedly relaxing, yet somewhere in background mode, there is a problem running. Has that happened to you? All the time, you say!

Other animals have minds capable of thought. Despite the fact that the bio-computer of the human mind is so relatively powerful, it is only equivalent to another three cylinders of the engine. Why? Because we have two other sets of qualities that deliver tremendous 'fire power' when properly inspired.

Emotions

Like our family pets, we all experience feelings and emotions. Dogs and cats make it abundantly clear when they feel happy or content or scared. But the tremendous additional range of our human emotions represents another five cylinders of potential 'fire power' in our 16 cylinder whole person engine.

Many work environments seem designed to disregard how people feel. Have you worked in one of those organisations? Almost everyone has — it's amazing. Because of the mistreatment we feel, our emotion cylinders tend at best to clog up or at worst shut down. So many people get to the point of thinking — *'Oh no, time to go to work. Put the iron plate over the heart.'* Expressing feelings at home, in the disco or at the pub is usually okay but expressing strong feelings at work is not.

We can so easily lose the tremendous, latent 'fire power' of the five emotion cylinders in many organisations and even at home.

Spirit

If that wasn't bad enough, there are then the challenges faced by our spirit. The enthused spirit represents the remaining five cylinders of potential 'fire power' in our 16 cylinder engine metaphor. Strength of spirit is demonstrated in such qualities as integrity, honesty, ethics, enthusiasm and commitment. These qualities define the essence of our being and differentiate us most strongly from the animal kingdom.

You probably know someone who clearly possesses strong spirit qualities. The sort of person whom if they rang you at two o'clock in the morning saying, *'I'm terribly sorry to wake you up, but I'm stranded 20 kilometres outside town. I've just had my second puncture, it's pouring with rain and nobody will come and help me'*, you would unhesitatingly jump out of bed and go and help them.

You might have also had the misfortune of meeting or working with someone who could not spell the word 'integrity' if their life depended on it. Their approach to ethics is at best, dubious and they believe honesty is for fools. They don't care, they don't nurture. If you saw them tomorrow over in the corner with their trousers on fire, you would really have to make an effort to put the fire out!

We know when these spirit qualities are present and we know when they are not. Too often spirit qualities are suppressed. Politicians and business leaders bend the truth to suit their ends. Our response may appear muted. We may feel powerless but we know what's going on and the cancer of cynicism develops. The precious five spirit cylinders clog up and at worst shut down entirely.

○ 16 CYLINDER PERFORMANCE

In the following chapters, we will explore a variety of tools and approaches for you to use to fire up the 16 cylinders in your family and business enterprise by making the most of your spirit intelligence.

Sustained high levels of fulfilment and performance are elusive until you recognise and inspire the latent passion and enthusiasm of the emotions and spirit in yourself and those around you. You will find the goal of 16 cylinder empowerment to be well worth the effort and very rewarding.

Someone once asked me, 'How do you know there are 16 cylinders?' Of course as I explained, the 16 cylinders are just a metaphor to reflect my experience of the relative 'fire power' contributed by body, mind, emotions and spirit. This has proven to be a very effective metaphor that people all around the world can readily relate to. See if it makes sense to you.

○ PHYSICS VERSUS METAPHYSICS

Consider your 16 cylinders of body, mind, emotion and spirit. How many of the cylinders are physical — you can reach out and touch them? The body cylinders are physical. Can you physically touch the mind, the emotions or the spirit? No. Only three of the 16 cylinders, those of the body, are physical — less than 20 per cent.

The other 80 per cent are metaphysical — unseen and untouchable. If you are to master motivating and enthusing yourself and other people, where should your focus be — on the physics of people or their metaphysics?

Clearly the leverage lies in the metaphysics because 13 of the 16 cylinders are metaphysical. So you must master the metaphysics. This is the major challenge for us all.

From the ancient Greeks through the great period of scientific discovery of Isaac Newton and his peers on to the industrial revolution and beyond, we have refined and worked on our understanding of the laws of physics. Yet the laws of metaphysics are not as widely understood. Certainly not in the Western education system which seems to place more emphasis on the logic of facts and data.

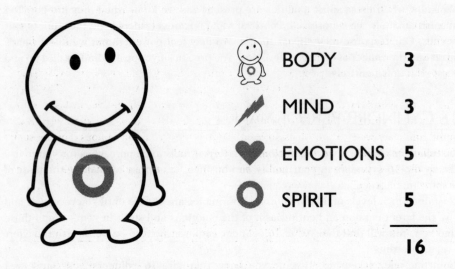

	BODY	3
	MIND	3
	EMOTIONS	5
	SPIRIT	5
		16

'We do not need more intellectual power, we need more spiritual power ...
We do not need more of the things that are seen, we need more of the
things that are unseen.'

CALVIN COOLIDGE

We will explore a range of metaphysical laws in this book so your spirit intelligence
choices are based on reliable laws and not someone's opinion or theories.

o 16 CYLINDER TEAMS

Living in a 16 cylinder family is clearly a challenging and exciting concept.

Organisations are now beginning to look for 16 cylinder whole-of-person (body, mind,
emotions and spirit) performance. Would you like to live and work on 16 cylinders?
Of course, it's more fun.

Would you like to be part of a 16 cylinder team? Absolutely. 16 cylinder teams give
better service and achieve better results. Good people are hard to find and there are many
out there who are fed up with working on five (on a good day!) cylinder teams and would

jump at the chance of working on a team firing on 16 cylinders. Customers like dealing with 16 cylinder staff, therefore 16 cylinder staff attract more customers.

An executive recruitment specialist told me that 85 per cent of the executives he contacts are prepared to talk to him about alternative positions and that 65 per cent are significantly dissatisfied with their current jobs. He has been in the executive search game for a long time. If those are the statistics for executives, imagine what the dissatisfaction statistics must be like for high quality workers and potential team members. If you set up a 16 cylinder whole person (body, mind, emotions and spirit) enterprise, you will have them knocking down your door.

The problem is that most people and organisations want the 16 cylinder performance but only understand how to work with their six cylinders of body and mind. They don't seem to have a clue how to inspire the passion of the emotions or the enthusiasm of the spirit. They are trying to achieve 16 cylinder performance from their six cylinders of body and mind and they wonder why it is so hard. That is why you find famous slogans such as – *'Retrenchments will continue until morale improves!'*

This book gives you the spirit intelligence keys to fire up and sustain you and the people around you on all 16 cylinders.

o UNIVERSAL GENERALISED PRINCIPLES

Buckminster Fuller, the brilliant American scientist and philosopher had a passion. It was working to understand the generalised principles that are the organising laws of the universe. He believed that these generalised principles give us a direct insight into the mind of Universal Intelligence.

Because so much of the universe is invisible, his interest lay in both the universal laws of physics and metaphysics — the seen and the unseen.

If we understand how the universe is organised, we can trust and work with these generalised principles and access power and success. If we work against these universal generalised principles, we are in trouble.

That is the problem with following other people's fads and trends, theories and opinions. They may align with the universal generalised principles and bring you success. However, they may work at right angles or be diametrically opposed to the universal generalised principles or be specialised or localised cases. They may be inapplicable to your situation and will cause you to fail.

To empower the whole person — body, mind, emotions and spirit — the seen and the unseen, we need to explore these same universal generalised principles — the laws of the physical and metaphysical universe.

These laws are generalised principles — they are true in all cases and will not let you down. You can trust them and rely on them.

Regrettably our education system does not currently emphasise the unseen realms of the metaphysics of mind, emotions and spirit. Fortunately many of the laws of metaphysics are directly linked to laws of physics so they can be simply explained.

This book gives you an understanding of the laws of metaphysics to improve your understanding of the people around you and inspire them to higher performance.

We will do this by reviewing specific laws of physics and see how understanding the laws of physics can give you insights into the relevant laws of metaphysics.

As spirit intelligence optimises the three physical cylinders of body and the 13 metaphysical cylinders of mind, emotions and spirit, these insights are fundamental.

'I know this world is ruled by infinite intelligence ... Everything that surrounds us — everything that exists — proves that there are infinite laws behind it. There can be no denying this fact. It is mathematical in its precision.'

THOMAS A. EDISON

o THE LAW OF PHYSICAL AND METAPHYSICAL LEVERAGE

A simple example of the correlation between a law of physics and its metaphysical equivalent is the law of leverage from Archimedes.

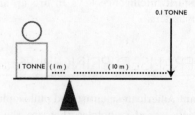

The diagram shows that to move a physical object, it is best to step back from the task and introduce a lever and fulcrum to assist you. So instead of directly applying a force of 1 tonne to lift the 1 tonne weight, the lever and fulcrum allow you to stand back 10 metres and apply a force of 0.1 tonnes to lift the same weight.

The job is done with ease - utilising the physical law of leverage.

Employing a team in an enterprise can utilise physical and metaphysical leverage. The capabilities of the team, correctly harnessed and focused on a task, means they can do the work faster than you can on your own.

If digging a hole takes ten days for one person, introducing a team of ten people, providing they can work effectively together, means the job can be done in one day. Here we see the generalised principle of physical leverage in action. If the task was creating a complex computer program working with the metaphysics of thinking, the law of metaphysical leverage could be utilised to harness the power of more than one mind to do the job more efficiently.

Strong organisational culture and systems can significantly improve the leverage obtainable from the team by providing a reliable fulcrum to support and enhance individual and team performance. Conversely, poor culture and sloppy systems greatly undermine performance and thus reduce the available leverage from the team. We will cover this in Chapter 12 on building passionate teams.

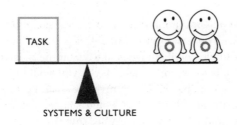

SYSTEMS & CULTURE

o THE WOO-WOO FACTOR

To help you further in mastering the metaphysics and enhancing spirit intelligence, let's introduce the concept of the 'woo-woo factor'. The 'woo-woo factor' is the weirdness or strangeness factor, the off-the-wall factor of any subject that we need to discuss.

If we are reviewing the practice of mowing the lawn, there is no weirdness involved. There is nothing worrying or frightening about mowing the lawn. The 'woo-woo factor' on a scale of 0 to 10 of mowing the lawn is zero.

However, what if I told you that one of the secrets to increasing spirit intelligence and achieving high performance is the ability to listen telepathically to the quiet voice of guidance from a Tibetan Buddhist monk, who is now dis-incarnate and living in spirit form on the planet Mars. All of us, including me, would find that would have a very high weirdness or 'woo-woo factor' — definitely a 10. It is off the wall, totally weird, X-Files material!

The 'woo-woo factor' prepares us to expect strange things in the realm of metaphysics. Yet if you wish to master inspiring people, enhancing spirit intelligence, developing team spirit and consistently achieving outstanding results, you must be prepared to harness the 13 metaphysical cylinders of mind, emotions and spirit.

The 'woo-woo factor' in this book may sometimes climb the scale.

o THE SHELF

A useful device to help you with potentially high woo-woo ideas and to help you in mastery of the metaphysics of inspiring and motivating people is the shelf. We had a family friend, Colonel Alan Hanbury-Sparrow. He was so old he could remember the relief of the siege of Mafeking in the Boer War. He was made a Colonel in the First World War after surviving the machine gun attacks of Passchendaele. He is dead now, but when he was in his early nineties, I asked him what was the secret of becoming so old and so wise, as he was both.

He said to me, *'David, the secret is simple. It is the shelf.'*

I queried, *'The shelf?'*

He replied: *'Yes. In your life you are going to hear many ideas and concepts that you are tempted to simply reject as preposterous. But the key is not to reject ideas because they seem unacceptable.'*

'Everywhere you go, carry an invisible metaphysical shelf that you can put up on the wall of the room you happen to be in at the time or in your car or on the bus or wherever you are. Because if you file the outrageous 'high woo-woo factor' ideas on your shelf, then a day, a week, a month, a year, ten or even 25 years later, you will glance up at that shelf and take down that seemingly silly or strange idea. Because of the experience you've

gained on your life journey in the intervening time, suddenly the idea does not seem so silly, nor so high woo-woo as it did at the time.'

The key for you to handle possibly high woo-woo, off the wall metaphysical ideas as we pursue spirit intelligence is to create a shelf. Maybe you would like to pause now, look up in the room where you are and just create an invisible shelf. From now on, take it with you everywhere that life's path may lead you. I would suggest you make it fairly strong and robust because you may find that as we go forward into the new millennium and the speed of change picks up, your shelf may have to carry some fairly heavy ideas that you personally, at the time, find too way out to handle.

o MODELS FOR EMPOWERMENT

These are our fundamental models to empower the whole person and build spirit intelligence:

- o 16 cylinders of BMES — body, mind, emotion and spirit — three physical cylinders — 13 unseen yet powerful metaphysical cylinders.

- o An understanding of the laws of metaphysics as well as the laws of physics as they effect high performance.

- o Because metaphysics are not so well understood, you need to be able to tolerate relatively higher woo-woo factor ideas than maybe you would have done.

- o Anything that is too much, put it on your shelf.

With these models in place, let us now look at your life to date.

Two

THE LIFE JOURNEY

'I will prepare and some day my chance will come.'
ABRAHAM LINCOLN

o YOUR LIFE JOURNEY

Before we move forward to help you develop and hone your spirit intelligence, let's first review your life journey and experience to date. This will reveal to you the skills you have already gained as part of your spirit intelligence growth.

Let me ask you some personal questions. Where were you born? Where did you go to school? What was your first paid job? Maybe it was delivering newspapers in your early teens or perhaps you worked part-time after school at a supermarket? Or maybe you packed shelves in a warehouse, were a part-time gardener, drove a tractor at harvest time or worked for McDonald's?

Since that first paid job, how many different organisations have you worked in? If you've been with the same organisation for many years, how many different departments have you worked in? Just pause and add them up. The number may surprise you.

o APPRENTICE / JOURNEYMAN / MASTERY

If you had been born a thousand years ago in the Middle Ages, long before the industrial revolution, and you were not lucky enough to be born up in the castle or in the palace with the kings and queens, emperors or war lords, and you didn't want to be like your parents and grandparents, living in a mud hut and working in the fields as a serf or peasant, then in those days, your only chance of upward mobility was to join a craft or a guild and learn a trade.

You could have worked in gold or silver, leather or silk, or as a stonemason or a carpenter. As an example, let's assume that you decided to work as a potter, or to be more precise, your parents decided you would work as a potter. When you were about eight or ten years old, they took you along to the local pottery so you could become an apprentice. That's how your working journey through life started out, as an apprentice.

Your parents introduced you to the master potter, someone of very great importance, to be respected and even feared. The master potter would explain that your job as an apprentice was to do everything around the pottery that needed to be done to help the potters. You had to get up early in the morning, chop the wood, fire up the kilns, mix the glazes and prepare the clay so when the potters started work, everything was ready.

During the day you would assist the potters making plates on the wheel. You would fetch the clay and tools and glazes. As they worked they would let you practise, show you different techniques, and teach you the skills of their trade – how different clays required alternative techniques and different glazes at various heights in the kiln produced different effects.

In the afternoon, you would perhaps work with potters who were making vases. As they worked, they too would let you practise, gradually building up your skills. The master potter was always at a distance, working with and advising the potters.

Each day you were up early, working and learning, finally falling asleep each evening, exhausted. The days, weeks and months passed. Potters came and went from the pottery. You learned a range of skills. Then one day the master potter approached you and explained that your apprenticeship was over and now was the time for you to become a journeyman.

You would leave the pottery and journey all over Europe, the Middle East or the Far East – working at different potteries, under different masters, using different clays, glazes and kilns as you broadened your skills on your journey towards personal mastery of your trade – developing the skills to consistently and elegantly produce outstanding results.

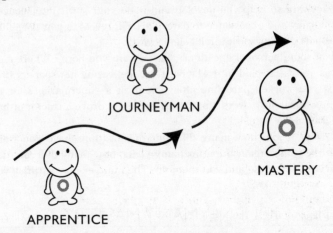

Why introduce this metaphor? Because, despite the progress of the last millennium, nothing has really changed. We may live in nice houses, drive fancy cars and go on holidays to exotic destinations, but all of us start out as apprentices. We are all journeymen on a journey through life, on the road to mastery and the achievement of outstanding results — at home with our family and at work with our organisation — by optimising spirit intelligence.

The aim of this book is to help you enhance your spirit intelligence skills on your road to personal mastery — the ultimate destination — if you accept the challenge.

o REVIEWING YOUR LIFE JOURNEY

How are you progressing on your life journey? If you counted the organisations or the departments within one organisation where you have been employed, how many 'potteries' or places have you worked in? Count all the part-time jobs you had when you were at school too.

How many? Two, half a dozen, more than ten?

As I mentioned in the Introduction, it is the experiences gained and the skills developed from everything you have done in your life that develop the qualities and the essence of your spirit being. Who you are, your spirit being, is constantly developing and evolving, reflecting your experiences on the journey of life.

Life skills inventory

To help you appreciate just how much spirit growth you have already achieved, list all the skills that you have gained on your life journey.

Take a sheet of paper, divide it up into blocks of five years for your life so far (1–5 years, 6–10 years, etc) and list all the skills you have learned in each phase of your life. You can start from the infant skills of learning to walk and talk, through childhood skills of making friends and riding a bicycle and then list your adult life skills such as problem solving, planning, relationship management, etc.

I bet it is an impressive list.

This book will provide you with an array of practical keys and tools to develop your skills further in all aspects of your spirit development by helping you improve your spirit intelligence and thus make better life experience choices.

Life masters

On your journey through life, how many masters have you had the privilege of being apprenticed to – people you might describe as your mentors or role models?

Who has really inspired you in the way they handled other people? Who has shown you the way to realise the full potential of yourself and the people around you, the way to bring up an inspired family and, at work, develop the team spirit which leads to high performance and excellent results?

Think about it and note down their names. It may be a short list.

Were there any anti-masters along the way? People whom you've watched and thought, 'I'm never doing it that way!'

People's journeys are fascinating. Some of us have had the privilege of meeting and working with a number of masters, some have worked for one or two and others have completed their journeys so far without ever meeting a single master — that person capable of developing high performance people and demonstrating consistently excellent results.

Many people working together are so busy that they have never even taken the time to find out about each other's life journeys. Powerful team building at work can be exactly that – taking the time to give everyone five minutes to tell the story of their journey through life. Try it with your team. I guarantee you'll have some real surprises, finding out where some of your people have been before they joined your organisation.

Irrespective of where your journey through life has taken you, irrespective of whether you have had the privilege of being apprenticed to masters, the purpose of this book is to give you the mastery keys, so that you can continue to improve your performance and the performance of those around you by optimising spirit intelligence.

o MY LIFE JOURNEY

It might help if you knew something of my life journey, both my working life and my personal experiences.

My working journey

I was born in Loughton in the south of England in 1947, went to school locally and then to the City of London School. My working journey started with my first paid job in 1960. I was 13 and selling flowers in Miss Barnes' flower shop. Holiday jobs included stints at Du Pont and ICI, then I worked for Stone and Webster Engineering and Sainsbury's after leaving school.

In 1966, British Petroleum hired me as an apprentice. They paid for me to study Chemical Engineering at the University of Edinburgh in Scotland where I gained a first class Honours degree. I worked for BP in Europe in various refineries and in their Head Office in London in shipping and supply.

However, before I started my apprenticeship, I had driven a Bedford van with six other young people to Greece and Turkey. In 1966, driving through Europe and across communist Yugoslavia and Rumania was an exciting adventure. When we reached Turkey, we met hippies coming back from India and Nepal. It was then that I had a dream to drive some day to India and beyond.

An engineering colleague and I jointly purchased an old Land Rover which we bought in a scrap yard in Glasgow for 50 pounds. We proudly towed it all the way back to Edinburgh and spent a couple of years rebuilding and refurbishing it.

In 1971-72 we spent a year driving overland from London to India and Nepal and then on to Australia, where I have lived and worked ever since, initially working for the Australian Gaslight Company and then Amoco, Standard Oil of Indiana.

In 1984, when BP bought out Amoco in Australia, I made a major journey shift and moved into the computing industry, joining ICL, the British computer company.

In fact it was as a general manager for ICL that I first became interested in corporate education. By 1987, the mainframe computer industry was facing significant revenue issues. Downsizing and retrenchments were becoming common. I took over a group of 200 people who had suffered two rounds of retrenchments. Sales targets for my group were extraordinarily high, morale was equally low!

Something had to be done. As the new general manager, I decided to introduce some motivational team building, leadership and sales training. Well you can probably guess what else ICL had cut besides the head count. The training budget! So I was immediately forced to take off my general management hat and put on the training manager's hat because if I didn't do the training, it clearly was not going to happen. The results we produced were excellent and we exceeded our budget targets.

ICL reorganised again with another round of retrenchments. I inherited a new group of demoralised people, this time spread out all across Australia. Once more, if I did not do the training, nobody would. We produced outstanding results, 200 per cent of budget target!

In 1990, I moved as a general manager to Tandem Computers, a Californian computer company. Training budgets were tight. I ran the dual role of general manager and training manager for my people. Again, we performed well.

By 1993, I realised my true passion lay in corporate education. So I left Tandem and formed my own executive training and facilitation company — Corporate Leadership.

My personal journey

Driving overland to Australia from Europe through the Middle East, India, Nepal and Thailand was a very powerful experience. The spiritual focus and teachings of the Eastern religions of Islam, Hinduism and Buddhism were so different from the Protestant Congregationalism of my family in England.

My father, Reg Powell, was a true Protestant Christian – a free thinker with not much time for orthodox dogma. Already possessing an extensive knowledge of the Bible, he spent most of the Second World War in Palestine and the Middle East. For him the Bible became living geography. I remember countless Sunday lunches after church as he involved us in his grappling with the New Testament scriptures. What happened at the feeding of the 5000; the water into wine; walking on water? What is the significance of a miracle? Is it supernatural power or a deep metaphor or both? If we had the faith, could we really move mountains? What does faith mean for our lives? What's the message? Questions and more questions.

Now you know this sort of thinking is not a priority for any teenager but my father's deep questioning must have given me that zest for challenging what's presented, especially dogma.

When I arrived in Australia in 1972, I set out on what could best be called a personal journey of discovery and development — learning yoga and meditation, studying psychology at university, reading book after book on Eastern philosophy and mystic Christianity, attending many different personal development courses and listening to hours of audio cassettes on every aspect of self-development. In 1975 my wife and I even went to live with a yoga teacher in Sri Lanka for several months. I was always searching for the keys to personal spirit intelligence.

The journeys merge

In the early days, my experiments in bringing my personal development experience into the environment of corporate training were judged as unusual and strange, but had some powerful effects. These days the gap between discovering personal potential and culturally acceptable organisational norms is slowly closing.

With product life cycles becoming shorter and shorter, with the speed of change accelerating, corporate leaders are coming to understand that the real power in any organisation lies in its people. Restructuring organisations and cost cutting have had their day as 'the solution', as have the quality processes and business process re-engineering of the 1980s. Are they useful strategies? Sometimes. Are they the complete answer? Certainly not.

The focus in business today is on customer value and customer loyalty. The keys to achieving and sustaining outstanding results in any organisation are in the potential of the staff and their creativity and innovation, in their ability to respond to the customer in new and value enhancing ways.

Thus developing and enhancing spirit intelligence and whole person — body, mind, emotions and spirit (BMES) – empowerment are vital skills. Because 13 of the 16 BMES cylinders are invisible, you will have to become a metaphysical engineer. This book will show you how.

My journeys have merged. I don't pretend for a moment to be a master but I am an experienced journeyman. I have raised a family and managed many teams at work where we've had some fun, powered up and got the job done with excellent results. Now it's time for me to share my spirit intelligence with you.

o THE GAME OF LIFE

If understanding people is such a vital key to success, let's first look at all the people on the planet. At the moment our population is six billion. The United Nations estimates that the population grows by over 80 million every year and will be over eight billion by 2030.

This means 250,000 extra people are showing up every day. Every second of every hour of every day, roughly ten people die and 13 people are born. So every second, three extra people arrive. The question is – what's the life game? What are all these people doing here?

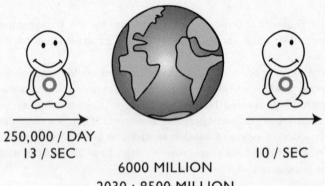

250,000 / DAY
13 / SEC

10 / SEC

6000 MILLION
2030 : 8500 MILLION

Many people, it is true, are living in sub-standard conditions and their life game is survival, worrying only about today's food. Two billion people don't even have access to electricity. But more and more people are playing a game called business. Look at what is happening in China, where over one billion people are taking part in a major business revolution.

o THE GAME OF BUSINESS

The game of business can be played in many ways, at many levels – from large corporations to small family businesses, in government and in non-profit organisations. It is a game of providing the benefits of goods and services at a competitive price or cost to consumers and customers.

Almost everyone is involved in the game of business. In any business, money comes in and money goes out, goods and services are provided. The army is a business, local government is a business, the Roman Catholic church is a business, the local kindergarten is a business, even your household is a business.

○ PLAYING TO WIN

The game of business can be a tough game. Many people see it in terms of 'winners' and 'losers'. What is the difference between the game of football and the games of life and business? The game of football is optional but the games of life and business are compulsory. If you have to play the games of life and business, you might as well be good at them and aim for mastery.

The game of business increasingly requires people to be organised in teams. The general principle is that the 'A' Team is the winning team. Are you involved in the game of business offering goods and services to customers? Do you need the help of an 'A' team to improve your results and win?

Are there enough masters of life and masters of business developing high performance people and demonstrating outstanding results out there for us all to apprentice to and learn from? No. They are in short supply. So we journeymen, working to optimise our spirit intelligence, raise 16 cylinder families and build our own 'A' teams at work are often on our own. That's why this book is designed to collate the best of spirit intelligence enhancing, whole person (BMES) high performance techniques and approaches.

○ WORKING IN TEAMS

Some problems are convergent – the more we work on them, the more the answers seem obvious. But many of the challenges that await all of us in achieving tomorrow's results are divergent problems. We simply don't know what to do.

What worked yesterday may well not work tomorrow. What worked for somebody else may not work for you. You are the journeyman. It's your journey and your experience.

Few of us work entirely alone. Most people need the help of others to succeed. Your team can either be a formally organised group or a loose network of inter-dependent associates. The word 'Team' itself is an acronym. It stands for:

TOGETHER
EVERYONE
ACHIEVES
MORE

○ THE WINNING TEAM AND THE LEARNING TEAM

There are only two types of teams — the winning team and the learning team. If you want to consistently be on the winning team, you first have to be on the learning team. That's why the metaphor of the journey through life is important. The learning team learns by making mistakes. There are no short cuts: masters have simply made more mistakes than we have.

We learn by mistakes. Look at how we walk. We don't walk in a straight line. We make a mistake to the left with the left foot, corrected by a mistake to the right with the right foot. Left, right, left, right, always correcting. You've probably heard the statistics. They say a jumbo jet en route from Sydney to Singapore is only on course about 3 per cent of the time. For 97 per cent of the flight, the plane is slightly off course with the inboard computers correcting — left aileron, right rudder, continually adjusting.

Thomas Edison, in his search for a light bulb that worked, reported over 10,000 light bulb experiments that failed before he succeeded. You have to have the courage and tenacity to make and admit your mistakes, extract what you can learn and move on. It's only when you deny your mistakes that you don't progress on your journey to life mastery.

'I am not discouraged, because every wrong attempt discarded is another step forward.'
THOMAS A. EDISON

At school, we were all given a tick for being right and a cross for being wrong. We are penalised every time we make a mistake and conditioned to believe that mistakes are bad. Getting it right is good. Getting it wrong is bad, a failure.

Well of course getting it right is good, but making a mistake should be a — *'Whoopee, a mistake, a mis-understood. What is it I can learn from this mis-understood?'* Because if you leave a 'mis-understood' unhandled, it clogs your mind. It slows you down and stops you learning. A mistake needs to be admitted and learnt from.

Look at the progression:

o Success is a function of good judgment.

o Good judgment is a function of experience.

o Experience is a function of poor judgment and making mistakes.

o Mistakes come from taking action, getting feedback and learning.

The only real mistake is to deny the mistakes and thus their lessons.

Most organisations that I have known are not very tolerant of mistakes. However, there is a brilliant story of Tom Watson Snr in the early days of IBM. A major blunder was made by a middle-ranking executive. He was hauled into Watson's office expecting to be fired on the spot. To the executive's amazement, Watson said: 'No, of course I'm not going to fire you. You have just had a very, very expensive learning experience. What we are going to do now is use that learning experience. If I fired you, I would have wasted that money.'

'Would you like me to give you a formula for ... success? It's quite simple really, double your rate of failure ... You're thinking of failure as the enemy of success.

But it isn't at all … You can be discouraged by failure — or you can learn from it. So go ahead and make mistakes. Make all you can. Because, remember that's where you'll find success. On the far side of failure.'

THOMAS J. WATSON

o YOUR COMMITMENT TO SUCCESS

What do you want to learn from reading this book?

Do you simply need some new approaches to improve your spirit intelligence? Are there particular angles on family or business success, enthusiasm, motivation, management or leadership that you are searching for?

List the areas that interest you. Writing these down will give you clarity and clarity is one of the keys to power.

o THE POWER OF COMMITMENT

Let me help you towards your success by asking for your commitment. You may be familiar with the story of the bacon and egg breakfast. In the bacon and egg breakfast, the chicken is participating and the pig is committed. In other words, the chicken gets to enjoy another day and lay another egg and the pig does not. The pig is on the plate as bacon — committed!

It is important to understand the power of commitment. Nothing really happens until you make a commitment to do something differently in your life, your family or in your organisation. This is best achieved by keeping a Commitments Register of your planned changes as you learn these new spirit intelligence tools and approaches.

The definition of insanity is to keep doing everything the same way and expecting things to magically improve. As my grandmother used to say, *'If you do what you've always done, you'll get what you've always got.'*

To improve your ability to reach your full potential and achieve outstanding results, you must commit to change. The road to mastery and optimising spirit intelligence is a road of continuing growth and change. It requires commitment and courage. As you read and work through this book, ideas will appeal to you that you can use on your journey towards mastery.

So use the Commitments Register at the back of this book to record your commitments to change and to integrate the new ideas into your life and work.

'The individual who wants to reach the top in business must appreciate the might of the force of habit — and must understand that practices are what create habits. He must be quick to break those habits that can break him — and hasten to adopt those practices that will become the habits that help him achieve the success he desires.'

J. PAUL GETTY

Just remember: for things to change, first you must change.

'Sow an act and reap a habit, sow a habit and reap a character, sow a character and reap a destiny!'
ANON

o HARD VERSUS EASY

You have a choice as you read this book — to play hard or easy. Are you prepared to play hard — to tackle the spirit intelligence ideas in this book and the actions that flow from them? If you are prepared to play hard and go for it, then the road ahead will become easier.

If you want to play easy now, read the book, think about changing and then wait until you 'get around to it', the road ahead will stay hard.

How are you going to tackle this book? Is your focus on just you or are you also working to improve the performance of your family and your team or organisation? Are you going to cruise along? Or are you going to play hard and commit to go for it?

Three

KEYS TO SUCCESS

'He who has done his best for his own time has lived for all times.'
SCHILLER

We are all journeymen on the road to increasing spirit intelligence, learning how to realise our potential, how to inspire the people around us, and how to achieve high performance and outstanding results.

There aren't enough masters of the games of life and business currently around to teach us what to do and how to do it, so the best thing to do is to look first at the work of past masters. What have they done? How did they achieve enormous success?

o THE FOUR KEYS TO SUCCESS

There have been many people in the past who have produced outstanding results. There have been many masters of the games of life and of business and many books written by or about them.

One of the most famous books that can guide us as individuals, in our families and most certainly at work, is called *Think and Grow Rich* by Napoleon Hill.

It is very well known. Over 20 million people have read and benefited from this work. The story behind the book is both fascinating and pertinent. In 1908, an old man, Andrew Carnegie approached a young man, Napoleon Hill.

Andrew Carnegie was a Scotsman who made a great deal of money from steel, oil and gas. He went to the United States when he was 12 years old. He started work in a cotton mill and never went to school. When Andrew Carnegie died in his nineties, they found in his desk drawer a piece of paper he had written on when he was very young. On that piece of paper he had written, *'I will spend the first part of my life making more money than anybody else ever has. The second part of my life, I will give it away to who I want to'*.

That was what he did. Andrew Carnegie made a lot of money and then gave it away.

In 1908, Napoleon Hill was a young journalist. Carnegie said to him that he believed he had discovered the secrets of success and mastery of the games of life and business. He asked Napoleon Hill to write a book to pass on these secrets to the generations to follow.

Carnegie's request was that before writing the book, Napoleon Hill should talk to a few of Carnegie's friends. Twenty years and 504 in-depth interviews later, he eventually published what was to become a landmark text.

Among Andrew Carnegie's friends were Henry Ford, creator of the modern car, Thomas Edison, inventor of the light bulb, Alexander Graham Bell, who developed the telephone, Rockefeller, Roosevelt, Kodak's Eastman, Woolworth, Firestone, Gillette, the Wright Brothers and JP Morgan: people who helped structure the foundations of much of our social, commercial, corporate, government and financial world today.

They certainly did not succeed alone. To achieve success, all of them had to understand the fundamental principles of working with other people.

Why listen to their advice from a century ago?

As we will see in Chapter 14 on the power of the mind, these people were masters of spirit intelligence. They explored whole person empowerment. They speak to us from an era untainted by the so-called New Age, with its bewildering array of theories and approaches. Their four keys to success are timeless, elegant and simple to comprehend.

THINK AND GROW RICH

A Definiteness of **Purpose**

A Burning Desire to Succeed — **Passion**

Clear **Plans** of Action

Persistence

o A DEFINITENESS OF PURPOSE

The first key to success is a definiteness of purpose. It is vital that you, everyone in your family and the people at work around you are clear about what they are working to achieve. What is the purpose of your endeavours? Where are you heading? What are you supposed to be doing and achieving?

A good demonstration comes from Henry Ford. His original model T car was built with an in-line four cylinder engine. In 1929, after the car had been in production for over a year, he called his engineers together and explained that he now wanted a larger motor with the eight cylinders cast in a V in one single engine block for cost-efficient production. This had never been done before. Cadillac had produced a V8 in 1914 but their engines were complex and expensive, involving multiple castings.

His engineers were adamant that it could not be done. Ford was equally adamant that there must be a way. He held firm over many, many months. He had a definiteness of purpose. He knew what he wanted and why and, in the end, his engineers succeeded.

Having a definiteness of purpose is the first key to any success in life. Knowing where you are heading, what are you working to achieve and why is vital. You must have a sense of direction.

Do you have a definiteness of purpose within your family and at work?

We'll focus on these key questions shortly. Defining your sense of purpose is the first vital key to enhancing spirit intelligence.

○ A BURNING DESIRE TO SUCCEED - PASSION

The second key to success in achieving exceptional results in any field of endeavour, at home or at work, is to have a burning desire to succeed — passion.

As Yoda tells Luke Skywalker in Star Wars — *'There is no try, only do or do not'*.

A good example of a burning desire to succeed and passion is the story of the conquest of Mount Everest. Everest was finally conquered in 1953 by Edmund Hillary from New Zealand and Sherpa Tenzing from Nepal. The leader of the expedition was John Hunt, an Englishman.

The British had held a burning desire to succeed in conquering Everest since the early years of the 20th century. My family was acquainted with Dr Somervell who was doctor to the 1920 and 1924 British Everest expeditions. In 1924, Everest mountaineers Mallory and Irvine were last seen by him and other observers, climbing just below the rock wall, about 600 feet from the summit at 2.30pm. They were dressed in tweeds, a pullover and leather boots. Mallory had primitive oxygen equipment. When they set off, the weather was good and they were last seen heading into light cloud, close to the summit. They would have known at that point that there was no way that they could reach the summit and get back, because as soon as the sun sets on the top of Everest, the temperature goes down and down and down. You don't really fare too well at minus 60 degrees in tweeds and leather boots!

Mallory and Irvine had a burning desire to succeed. It was so strong that they made the trip up Everest a one-way trip. Did they reach the top? Dr Somervell told my father he thought they did. We will never know.Hillary and Tenzing searched the summit unsuccessfully for any signs of them in 1953, almost 30 years later. Recently Mallory's body was found high on Everest with both his legs broken from a fall. Did they make it? Irvine had the camera — but they didn't find him!

Your personal 'Everest' does not have to be a one-way trip. But the experience of those such as the Wright Brothers and Thomas Edision show us that a burning desire to succeed and passion is critical. Clearly for you to achieve outstanding results, you must fire up passion in yourself and in the people around you. This is vital to optimising spirit intelligence. We examine this in later chapters.

○ CLEAR PLANS OF ACTION

All successful people have a clear purpose and a strong passion. They also have the third key to success – clear plans of action. They know what they are going to do to get the result they desire.

Do you, your family members and the people at work have well documented, clear plans of action on how to achieve the definiteness of purpose – plans that are good enough to sustain the passion and achieve results through thick and thin? Good planning skills and tools are critical to spirit intelligence.

○ PERSISTENCE

In his 20 years of interviewing Andrew Carnegie's friends, Napoleon Hill said he met many people with a definiteness of purpose, a strong passion and clear plans of action. Yet they failed, because there is a fourth key to success. The fourth key separates the men from the boys, the women from the girls and is found in one word – persistence.

Sometimes looking at the origin of a word can tell us more about the meaning of the word than we understand from everyday usage.

The word persistence is derived from the Latin *per sistere* to stand firm throughout

All successful people say persistence is the real key. Are you and your team able to — *per sistere* — to stand firm throughout, no matter what tries to stop or block you or insidiously eat away at your morale and determination?

There is an enemy to success and it is called resistance, from the Latin — *re sistere* — to stand against you.

You may have seen the *Aliens* movies. The Aliens were nasty and they grew really big, really quickly by eating humans! In the first *Aliens* movie, Sigourney Weaver was the heroine and survived the alien menace encountered on a distant planet. In *Aliens 2*, she was persuaded to go back to that dreadful planet with the marines. Just when they were about to radio back to Earth that the base was secure, what jumps out of the air conditioning ducts? You've got it – aliens!

That is how life, and especially work, can be:we encounter aliens of resistance

Just as you are about to savour the sweet taste of victory, what comes out of your office air conditioning ducts? The aliens. They are the problem, the resistance — primed to snatch defeat from the jaws of victory just when you least expect it. The weak quit, the strong — *per sistere* — stand firm throughout and persist. This is the true essence of demonstrating spirit intelligence and independent (whatever it takes) action.

How does Sigourney Weaver kill aliens? Tickling them with a feather? No, with a big powerful flame thrower. So in later chapters on persistence, we are going to equip you with flame thrower strategies so you can identify and eradicate the resistance aliens as they come after you, your family and your work team.

You've probably heard of examples of persistence. Thomas Edison and his team made 10,000 light bulbs experiments that failed before they finally succeeded and changed our night-time world forever.

Colonel Harland Sanders had long experimented with chicken recipes in the tiny restaurant of his gas station in Corbin, Kentucky. Finally in 1954, at the age of 65, he made tentative attempts at franchising his now famous brand name — Colonel Sanders Kentucky Fried Chicken. His behaviour in driving across the country, calling on restaurant owners who were potential franchisees, and often sleeping in his car, showed incredible persistence. By 1963, aged 74, he had established over 300 outlets.

*'I made a resolve then that I was going to amount to something if I could.
And no hours, nor amount of labour, nor amount of money would deter me from giving the best that there was in me. And I have done that ever since, and I win by it. I know.'*

COLONEL HARLAND SANDERS

Walt Disney, founder of animated pictures, was often challenged in his early years. He started business in Kansas in 1919 and after initial success, he went broke. Undeterred, he moved west and restarted in Hollywood in 1923. He was successful there until the resistance aliens again showed up. His creation of the popular cartoon series Oswald the Lucky Rabbit was sabotaged by his distributor, Charles Mintz, due to a contractual clause which saw Mintz cut Disney out and lure away Disney's best animators to start a rival business.

Christopher Finch, author of The Art of Walt Disney, writes that: *'Disney was shocked and hurt. He had trusted Mintz and he had trusted his employees. He was disgusted but not discouraged. Walt Disney had faith in his own abilities. He had reached the age of twenty-six after touching many of the bases of hardship that had come to seem archetypal of America in the first quarter of this century. His personal creed must have included the notion that success does not come easily'*.

Disney went on to create with his partner, Ub Iwerks, the legendary cartoon character Mickey Mouse and the rest, as they say, is history. None of it was easy. It was Disney's persistence through all the tough times that shines through his life story and his creations that have entertained millions.

'All our dreams can come true — if we have the courage to pursue them.'
WALT DISNEY

The fourth key to success is persistence. The ability to stand firm when all around us want to give up.

Churchill in his later years gave a famous speech at an Oxford University graduation ceremony. He stood up, walked slowly to the lectern and looked at the audience for a long time. Those that were there said it felt as though he made eye contact with everyone in the hall, over a thousand people.

He said slowly – *'Never give up. Never give up. Never give up.'*

Then he sat down. That was the speech!

The well-known motivator, Zig Ziglar, sums it up well – *'failure is the line of least persistence.'* And then there's the wonderful quote from Calvin Coolidge.

'Nothing in the world can take the place of persistence. Talent will not, nothing is more common than unsuccessful men with talent. Genius will not, unrewarded genius is almost a proverb. Education will not, the world is full of educated derelicts. Persistence and determination alone are omnipotent.'

○ GREAT LEADERS AND THE FOUR KEYS TO SUCCESS

Think of great leaders in history, people who have achieved results by motivating individuals, teams and nations. Alexander the Great conquered the known world in his late twenties. He led an army of men across vast deserts and mountains from Northern Greece to India and back to Babylon. Did he and his men have a definiteness of purpose? Absolutely. A burning desire to succeed, a passion? Yes. Clear plans of action? Yes. Did they have persistence? Yes. They beat Darius the Persian King and overcame extraordinary odds.

Consider Winston Churchill. His purpose was to rally the Allied forces in the darkest hours of the Second World War against the Nazi's Third Reich. Did he have a definiteness of purpose? Passion? Clear plans of action? Persistence? Yes he did. He stood firm through some very grim times when many of Britain's ruling class wanted to appease Hitler. You may have heard his great speech, *'We'll fight them on the beaches'*. Determination and commitment were the message — I'll do it on my own if I have to. Join me.

Were John F Kennedy and his brother Robert men of purpose? Were they men of passion, wanting to change the wrongs of their society as they saw them? Did they have plans of action? Yes. And they demonstrated persistence until the 're sistere' — the resistance — stopped them with bullets.

Did Martin Luther King have a definiteness of purpose? Remember his famous speech: *'I have a dream.'* Yes, yes, yes!

What about Nelson Mandela? During all those years of incarceration, did he have a definiteness of purpose? Yes – a united South Africa, free of the scourge of apartheid, with one man equalling one vote. The passion sustained him through all those years of imprisonment. His persistence was undeniable.

o PURSUING THE FOUR KEYS TO SUCCESS

These are the four keys to success that have been passed on to you – the current journey man – by people who have demonstrated extraordinary life and business success, often in the face of tremendous adversity: true masters of spirit intelligence and of the metaphysics of mind, emotions and spirit, as we shall explore in Chapter 14 on the power of the mind.

You too have to explore these four keys to success in pursuit of your own spirit intelligence and to inspire your family members and your colleagues, helping them and you in achieving outstanding results.

For you and the people around you, what does it mean these days to have a definiteness of purpose?

How are you going to fire up the passions, the 16 cylinders of body, mind, emotion and spirit?

How are you going to develop clear plans of action so that every day your family and your colleagues know exactly what it is that they have to do?

How are you going to demonstrate persistence so that when the enemy, the resistance aliens, show up, you are victorious?

As you continue reading and working with this book, you will see that we tackle each of these four keys to success comprehensively. In so doing, you will become a metaphysical engineer, skilled in working with the unseen forces of mind, emotions and spirit.

Only then will you be armed to demonstrate spirit intelligence mastery.

Part Two

PURPOSE

A Sense of Direction

You can choose to live your life to your own agenda with a sense of personal purpose that gives your life ventures meaning and a feeling of fulfilment.

This is called being *at cause* — living from the inside out, creating the life and reality you want.

Or you can choose to be purposeless and be *at effect* — where you drift through life, constantly at the mercy of external forces, pressures and demands, living life as a potential victim to whatever comes next over the elusive horizon of your tomorrow.

How do you choose to live your life?

That is the first spirit intelligence question we need to explore.

Four

A DEFINITENESS OF PURPOSE

'A man without a purpose is like a ship without a rudder.'
THOMAS CARLYLE

The first key to success is a definiteness of purpose. Do you feel your life has a sense of purpose? What's important to you? Where are you heading and what are you trying to achieve?

Do you have a sense of purpose in raising a family or running your home? At work, where is your organisation heading? What is the purpose of your enterprise? What is it you are working to achieve?

A strong sense of purpose is vital to your health. And it is the fastest way to increase spirit intelligence. Exploring personal, family and organisational purpose has to be our starting point.

o A PURPOSE OR MISSION STATEMENT

Many people report feelings of disorientation and confusion when faced with the speed and complexity of modern life. It can be challenging to find much meaning from what happens around us. Many companies spend significant time developing a purpose or mission statement.

The question of mission is – what have you been sent to do?

Your purpose is like a marker peg placed up ahead to guide you, your family or your work team on the journey. What is up ahead for you in each aspect of your life? What are you aiming for?

The word **mission** derives from the past participle of the Latin verb – *mitto* – having been sent.

Purpose derives from the past participle of the Latin verb – *ponere* – having been placed forth.

o LEADERSHIP AND PURPOSE

Although much of the English language is derived from Latin or Greek, the word leadership derives from a very old Anglo Saxon verb — *laedan* — to show the way.

If you are to be a leader, there has to be 'a way'. You have to know what you have been sent to do and what you are aiming for. If you are to show 'the way', you must know 'the way', where the marker pegs are on the journey to success. Thus having a clear mission or purpose is a critical leadership trait.

This applies to leadership in any field of endeavour — with your family, in your community or at work.

During the French Revolution, as the mob rushed past Robespierre's door in the suburbs of Paris, carrying off some poor nobleman to be beheaded, he was heard to utter the immortal quote: *'I must follow them, I am their leader!'*

Leadership implies knowing where you are heading. As they say at the start of *Star Trek*: *'These are the voyages of the Starship Enterprise. Its five year mission ... to boldly go where no man has gone before'.*

o DEVELOPING YOUR PURPOSE

Where are you, your family and your people at work boldly going? What's your purpose?

> *'You must be single minded. Drive for the one thing on which you have decided.'*
>
> GENERAL GEORGE PATTON

Here are some concepts that will help you with your personal, family and organisational purpose development.

o COURAGE

One of the keys to purpose development and leadership is courage.

There are three components to courage:

The word courage derives from the French word *la coeur* — the heart.

o Commitment
Nothing really happens unless there is a commitment to a purpose.

o Action
The leader of any group or team takes the initial action to achieve the purpose. Courageous thoughts don't really cut it!

o Fear and doubt
In my early days of management and leadership, I didn't realise this. I thought I was the only one hearing that little voice of fear, that feeling in the guts, the doubt – what happens if things go wrong? What happens if this is the wrong direction?

Now I realise that fear goes with the territory of leadership and purpose responsibility. If you have to lead 'where no man has gone before', then it's not whether the fear and doubt will arise that is the issue. The only issue is how you handle it.

'Courage is resistance to fear, mastery of fear — not absence of fear.'
Mark Twain

o THE COMFORT ZONE

In leading people and handling the fear and doubt that goes with the leadership challenge of defining and achieving the purpose, you may be outside your comfort zone.

DISCOMFORT
OR
LEARNING
ZONE

COMFORT
ZONE

The word management derives from the Latin *manus* — the hand.

You are probably familiar with the concept of the comfort zone. All of us are surrounded by a space in which we feel comfortable.

In management

If you have management responsibility, you may find some of your management challenges can be handled within your comfort zone. Why? Because management know-how comes from journeyman experience. You know what to do because you have been there before and have done it before. You are experienced.

Management is defined as 'the ability to handle, control and organise with authority and skill'. You gain that skill from your life journey experience. Your comfort zone expands to encompass that database of experience.

In leadership

Outside the comfort zone, there is the discomfort or learning zone. That is where purpose development and leadership often lie: nobody knows what to do and it's up to you to lead them. The great truth of life on this planet is that nobody anywhere really knows what is supposed to be happening. Six billion people wake up each day and then make it up as they go along. There is no grand plan!

Leaders clarify the purpose and 'show the way.' They handle fear as part of the job.

> *'Far better it is to dare mighty things, to win glorious triumphs, even though checkered by failure, than to rank with those poor spirits who neither enjoy much nor suffer much, because they live in the grey twilight that knows neither victory nor defeat.'*
> THEODORE ROOSEVELT

o RESPONSIBILITY

If we return to the journeyman in the Middle Ages – who was responsible for defining the sense of purpose in the 'pottery'? The answer is the leader, the master potter.

Whether leading a family or any other group of people, the leader is responsible for the sense of purpose of those on the journey.

Once the definiteness of purpose has been established, your responsibility as leader is then to be in service to the people to support, empower and inspire them to get the job done. This book will show you how.

'And whosoever of you will be the chiefest, shall be servant of all.'
MARK 10:44

o YOUR PURPOSE STATEMENT

Optimising spirit intelligence makes it essential to write down as concisely as possible your personal purpose and the purpose of your family, team or organisation.

Purpose gives meaning to playing the game of life and the game of business. Your purpose or mission statement gives you direction and meaning – we are here to conquer the known world, build a new V8 engine, develop a new alloy.

So stop reading and write your personal, family, work team's and organisation's purpose statements now.

o My purpose is …

o The purpose of my family is …

o The purpose of our work team is …

o The purpose of our organisation is …

o FLUFF / SUPERFLUFF / SPECIFIC

To ensure your purpose is focused, we must introduce the concept of fluff. If you listen to the way people communicate in day-to-day language, it is usually very imprecise and fluffy, open to all sorts of interpretation.

'How's the weather George?'
'Oh, it's great.'

'How was your weekend Mary?'
'Just wonderful!'

'Is that order on track John?'
'George, have we ever let you down?'

If you analyse these words, they are fluffy and imprecise. It's hard to understand exactly what they are talking about. We imagine what the words mean. The specifics or the reality of the situation are lost in fluffy communication.

Many people drift through life surrounded by an imprecise, fluffy sense or lack of purpose. Often when people are unclear about where they are going, their dialogue drifts into what is known as 'superfluff.'

'Where are we heading Michael?'
'Onwards and upwards as usual, Simon.'

'How was your holiday Dianne?'
'Amazing!!'

We think we know what that means, but it's 'superfluff'. The communication means nothing. What is needed for clarity and mastery are specifics.

'What's the weather like Helen?'

'Glad you asked — it's 26 degrees, 54% humidity, the wind is from the North, North East at 5 knots and the pressure is 1001 millibars and holding.'

Be specific.

o STATE YOUR PURPOSE

So take a moment to re-read the purpose statements you have just written. Is there any fluff or superfluff in the language you have used? If so, be more specific.

Whether you call it a purpose statement, a mission statement or a vision statement, it really does not matter. Some people argue that the purpose statement defines the destination and the mission statement defines the daily activity. Spirit intelligence simply needs a sense of why? For our needs, the purpose statement defines the chosen game, be it in life or business. What's your chosen game?

By writing your purpose statement with specifics, you achieve clarity and clarity is one of the major keys to power.

o STAKEHOLDER SUCCESS CRITERIA

In our corporate planning workshops, before finalising a purpose statement, we find it is critical for the work team to review its stakeholders and their success criteria. Who has a stake in the results from your work efforts? What are the success criteria of each of your stakeholders?

A purpose statement must optimise the needs of the stakeholders. Otherwise they might withdraw their support.

Many organisations are influenced by a number of stakeholders. For example:

o Senior management
o The board of directors

o Customers
o Staff
o Families of staff
o Suppliers
o Distributors
o Government
o Banks
o Taxation department
o Industry bodies
o Environmental protection agencies

The word reconnaissance derives from the French verb connoitre — to know.

The success criteria of different stakeholders can vary significantly. Senior management may principally want to achieve business targets, hold operating expenses under budget, increase revenue. Environmental protection agencies may have very different success criteria, for example, lower pollution and emission levels.

Only when you have listed all your stakeholders and reviewed their success criteria, can you then be assured your purpose statement will satisfy them.

Write a list of all the stakeholders that have a stake in the success of you, your family and your work enterprise; then for each stakeholder, write down their success criteria. When you and the people around you have achieved their purpose, how will these various stake holders judge your success?

The army have a saying — *time spent in reconnaissance is never time wasted*.

You have to reconnoitre — to know your stakeholders and their success criteria. In a war, if you charge over a wall without reconnaissance, you can run into machine gun fire. Don't hurry your purpose statement only to run into the 'machine gun fire' of criticism from dissatisfied stakeholders.

So take a moment now. Having completed the list of your stakeholders and their success criteria, re-check your purpose statements to ensure they satisfy those criteria.

o A PURPOSEFUL BEGINNING

How effective is your purpose statement? In our experience, a purpose statement in the written word alone may be a waste of time. Why is that? The problem in only writing a purpose statement lies in the way we process information and make decisions.

We are all guided by our sensory inputs:

o Our visual input — sight — how we see the world

o Our audio input — sound — what we hear

o Our kinesthetics — feelings — which includes touch and how we feel about the world

Researchers have shown that on average, when we make decisions, 45 per cent of the decision is based on our visual inputs, 40 per cent is based on our gut feelings (kinesthetic) and a mere 15 per cent of our decision making is based upon what we hear.

VISUAL = 45%
AUDIO = 15%
KINESTHETICS = 40%

If you, with the people around you, develop a purpose statement expressed only in words, it will only impress the 15 per cent of their audio senses, what they hear. 85 per cent of their senses, their visual and kinesthetic (feeling) processing power will be making up individual pictures and feelings of what the words mean. They are imagining and hallucinating. The medium of words is a very poor medium for defining or communicating a sense of direction and purpose to other people.

Your purpose statement will help you clarify your thinking, but it's not enough to inspire you and the people around you. Optimising spirit intelligence requires something more, an additional tool.

Some people might argue that a framed purpose statement can be seen and thus involves the 45 per cent visual sensory channel. You may have been in your local auto dealer recently to have your car serviced and behind the check-in desk, up on the wall, there was a framed purpose statement:

Our purpose at Fix-it Autos
Sir or Madam. Relax. The purpose of this motor dealership is to ensure that no matter how many problems your car has when you check it in this morning, when you pick it up this afternoon, they will all be fixed. And your car will have five new problems that you never had before. That's the way we ensure continuous cash flow in this business!

Just kidding!

You could say that as the statement is framed and up on the wall, you can see it. So it is visual input. However, we process that written information as we read by talking to ourselves. We use our internal audio channel. 'The purpose of this motor dealership is ...'

Thus the problem of communicating with people in words alone is that they hear the 15 per cent of the words of the purpose statement and 85 per cent of their visual and feeling senses are hallucinating about what the statement means.

o ACTIVATING YOUR PURPOSE STATEMENT

To enhance spirit intelligence, you have to move from a purpose statement to something much more powerful. You have to give your team a picture of success, a picture of the purpose achieved — because a picture is worth what? A thousand words.

Writing a purpose statement helps you to clarify your thinking. Some senior management teams spend days, weeks or months, word by word, crafting the perfect statement.

I have worked with clients who insisted on doing the same thing. The truth of the matter is that within a week, they cannot remember the words. They may remember the essence, but the words just don't stick. So you have to move on from purpose to something infinitely more powerful — vision.

Five

THE POWER OF VISION

'Where there is no vision, the people perish.'
Proverbs 29:18

The discipline of creating a purpose or mission statement helps you, your family or team members achieve clarity on what it is that you want to do and achieve. However, words alone are not enough to fire up those vital 16 cylinders. Everyone interprets words differently – a sure-fire recipe for confusion.

All over the world, you will find organisations with mission and purpose statements up on the wall in board rooms, in corridors, foyers and meeting rooms. But I would guarantee, that if you took a million dollars into your office, placed it on the table and said to the staff — 'Without referring to the company's mission or purpose statement, repeat it word for word' — your money would be perfectly safe.

o WHY HAVE A VISION?

The word **vision** is derived from the past tense of the Latin verb *videre* — having been seen.

People don't remember words. That is why it is critical to embrace the power of vision by illustrating what success looks like. Vision is best shown as an iconic representation of the success that you are envisaging.

The vision must be seen by the people.

Have you contracted someone to build a house or a house extension for you? How did you do that? Did you just order bricks and timber, roofing tiles and cement, dump them on the front lawn and say to the builder, 'There you go. Just knock it up.'

No of course not. That would be a recipe for disaster. You engaged the services of an architect or draughtsman who drew up a set of plans and pictures (cross-sections and elevations) of how the completed house would look from all angles. When the builder and his sub-contractors showed up for work, they could clearly see what it was they were constructing.

In an organisation, staff are exactly like the builders and sub-contractors. They work to build the picture of future success — the vision. We need to know 'why we are showing up' before moving on to knowing 'what to do' and 'how to do it'.

Vision is the first critical key to developing spirit intelligence and making better choices, to empowering and inspiring people and building high performance teams.

Every person, family and enterprise needs a vision, a picture of the success to be achieved, a brightness of future. I am amazed at how many organisations bumble along on the six cylinders of body and mind without involving their people or communicating to them a clear sense of direction or vision.

o WHAT IS A VISION?

A vision is a pictorial or iconic representation of future success. What will that success look like in 12 months, three or five year's time?

In a relatively slow-moving business such as the oil industry, the vision could easily be five or ten years in the future. In the high-speed world of telecommunications, a vision of two years might be a tremendous stretch. It depends on the pace of change in your industry, or circumstances. Families with young children can build 25 year visions to see the kids launched successfully into adulthood.

o VISION AND FOCUS

The difference between a purpose statement and a vision is like the difference between a light bulb and a laser beam. The average wattage of a light bulb in your lounge room ceiling is between 60 and 100 watts. If you look at a 100 watt light bulb close up, it is very bright. It hurts your eyes. But a 25 watt light bulb glows relatively dimly. However, if you look at a 25 watt laser, not only would it burn a hole in your eye, it would probably blow a hole in the back of your head – it is the same power, but focused.

If you communicate purpose or mission using only words, you are making a light bulb, because the diversity of interpretation of each member of the team spreads the team energy in all directions.

A vision is like a laser beam. Everybody sees the same future – the vision creates the focus.

'Concentrate all your thoughts upon the work at hand. The sun's rays do not burn until brought to a focus.'
Alexander Graham Bell

o DEVELOPING VISIONS

No single individual has copyright on all the good ideas potentially available in defining your family or work team's vision. The whole team should create an iconic representation of future success.

At work, break your team into groups of four or five people, give them large sheets of paper and coloured pens. It doesn't matter if some of them haven't drawn pictures since they were in kindergarten. Their only brief is to draw what success will look like in the future.

After an hour, ask each group to present their vision of success. You will be surprised how each group develops excellent iconic concepts to represent the envisioned future.

When you review the themes, it will be clear that some people have better artistic gifts than others. The team can then ask the more gifted artists to produce a composite vision incorporating the best ideas and icons. Sometimes the artists return with a composite of the original iconic representations from the groups. Sometimes they develop a synthesised vision with new icons. It doesn't matter. The important point is that the vision constructed is more powerful and comprehensive than any one person on the team could have achieved by themselves. As everyone has been involved, ownership and enthusiasm increase.

○ LEADERSHIP IN VISION DEVELOPMENT

Occasionally when working on organisational vision, people can be over-enthusiastic. Some years ago, Peter Lee was the Managing Director of Financial Products Research Group (FPRG) in Australia. Peter's staff were so excited about the financial services markets across the world that their synthesised five-year vision was world wide and much larger than Peter's view of what was possible or practicably achievable in that time frame. His very sensible counsel to his team was their global vision might be on the ten-year horizon: a realistic three to five year horizon would be to expand into Asia first.

Over-reach

There is nothing wrong with ambitious visions, but a dose of reality is always helpful. A key leadership role is to find the fine line between an enormous stretch and challenge, or over-reach and potential failure. Peter knew that and worked to maintain team enthusiasm without setting up an over-reach that could have led to disappointment and loss of motivation.

Creating a two or three step vision works well in dealing with over-zealous visions! In fact, seven years later, Peter and his team subsequently achieved their global vision sooner than anticipated by joining forces with Greenwich Associates, a company with global representation.

Under-reach

Garry and Allyn Beard, directors and owners of AH Beard — makers of quality beds — had exactly the opposite problem. They were keen to involve their team in creating a comprehensive vision for their company. In fact, their vision workshop was held over a weekend so that manufacturing and delivery staff could attend the session. Allyn and Garry's challenge was that their leadership vision of expansion for AH Beard was larger than their staff dared to think. They had been involved in protracted and confidential negotiations to significantly expand their business. At that time, they were not in a position to share those discussions with their staff.

To encompass this undefined potential and avoid under-reach, their iconic vision contained an unspecified expansion path, backed up by excellent work from their people on what it would take to become the 'A' team – supported and prepared for major (as yet not detailed) growth opportunities both in Australia and overseas.

Should Allyn and Garry have waited till the expansion negotiations were complete before involving their staff in a vision workshop? No. They needed to galvanise their whole team into a spirit of 'getting organised.' So when the negotiations were successfully concluded and the call to expansion came, the expansion would sit easily within the vision and they would be ready to meet the challenge.

A lack of team consensus

Teams do not always achieve total consensus on the future vision. You may find there is significant divergence of views about the way ahead among the people around you.

The vision exercise will draw out these disagreements. As the leader, you may need to work with your people to hone the potentially divergent views into a focused consensus of future vision.

Remember spirit intelligence requires tools to help the spirit 'choose between' alternatives. Development of a comprehensive vision does just that.

Team reactions

During a vision creation exercise, the family or work team may become highly motivated and excited, because a picture is, indeed, worth a thousand words. The quality of dialogue, of communication between the people improves because you have made the effort to build a vision picture.

Is the vision perfect? Maybe. Could it change? Possibly. Is it photographic? No. It is iconic and gives people a common language. With a verbal purpose statement, people interpret what the words mean differently. When you draw an iconic vision and the visual and kinesthetic senses are engaged, there is far less likelihood of misunderstanding occurring.

o ICONS

Icons convey a sense of positive feeling and enthusiasm. What sort of icons show up? In business, maybe there are smiling faces for happy customers, telephones ringing red hot, bags of gold to represent profit, shaking hands for relationships. Depending on your venture, there might be mine shafts, environmentally clean waters, sleek high speed railway engines. The icons must appeal to your team.

In a family, it can be a new house or car, great holidays, university degrees and world travel.

Capturing the vision

Emperor Gold Mines operate an underground gold mine at Vatukoula in Fiji. Their challenge is compounded in a number of areas. First, underground mining is a tricky game. They pit their wits, skill and experience against the vagaries of Mother Nature who in the past has laid down narrow veins of gold in the rock of an extinct volcano.

Secondly, the population of the mine site is made up of South African, Australian and European ex-patriots, together with local Indian and Fijian nationals; a multi-cultural, multi-racial group of men and women. When I first met them, the mine was troubled by a lack of capital and high operating expenses. There had also been some very divisive labour disputes under previous management.

They worked on a new vision. People on the management and supervisory teams had varying artistic abilities. Using the techniques we have reviewed — dividing their people into groups, explaining to them the concept of the power of vision, giving them large sheets of paper and colour pens, the groups developed a number of visions that were remarkably similar.

It must be said that some groups limited their vision to the existing volcano crater, the Vatukoula Basin, where the current gold mine is situated. Other groups developed a vision that expanded out to develop other potential gold areas on the islands of Fiji. And some developed a vision to take their narrow vein, underground gold mining experience overseas.

The visions developed by the various groups certainly generated much discussion. In spirit intelligence terms, there were many ideas to choose between. The vision development exercise facilitated that discussion.

In the end it was clear. If the management team were to fire up the employees with enthusiasm and opportunities in the future, the vision needed to be expansive. They developed a tremendous sense of the mine as not only a commercial operation but also socially by putting something back into the Fijian and Indian communities on which the mine depends for success.

Some organisations employ a graphic artist to capture the essence of the team's vision. Charlie Barclay, the General Manager at the time took his teams' vision efforts to a Fijian artist in Suva because he needed icons that would appeal to his 2000 Fijian and Indian mine workers.

There are no words included in the vision because the people on the mine site speak different languages. Is the picture literal or photographic? No, the vision is always iconic. Did it greatly improve dialogue about potential futures for the mine and the community around the mine? Absolutely!

A moving demonstration of the power of vision was when the son of one of the

underground miners asked for a large ladder and money to buy some paint. He then painted a copy of the vision on a 25 by 30 foot wall of the miners' changing hut, there for all to see. A second giant size vision was erected at the entrance to the mine site as a continual reminder of their game – Get the Gold!!

Vision development with families is equally powerful. Some of the Fijian mine workers were so impressed by working on the company future vision that they hired a bus to take their own young children right across the island to Suva, the capital of Fiji so they could start to envision future life journey possibilities beyond working in the mine village of Vatukoula.

○ TAKING UP THE CHALLENGE

Most of us share the common experience of seeing someone we recognise — on the street, or at the airport for example — but not remembering their name. Or being introduced to a number of strangers at a cocktail party and while acknowledging their faces, not remembering their names beyond a minute or less!

Why is it that we have so much trouble with names? It is because the face accounts for the visual 45 per cent of our sensory input. When people talk and smile that involves 40 per cent of our kinesthetic senses. The name and the words only account for 15 per cent of our sensory input.

It is the same challenge with iconic visions and verbal purpose statements.

This recent Mitsubishi advertisment really makes the point beautifully. Which communicates more to you, the picture or the words?

Do not underestimate the power of vision. It is one of the most powerful tools for increasing spirit intelligence, especially when you involve the people around you in developing the vision. You now have a tool to fire up their relatively elusive ten cylinders of emotional passion and spirit enthusiasm at home and at work.

So I challenge you to:

○ develop your personal, family and work visions now

○ collect pictures of the ideal new home or car or bike, holiday destinations, etc o involve the people around you

o use colour pens and large sheets of paper

You will not regret the investment.

Later in this book, in Chapter 14 on the power of the mind, we will further explore why every individual, family and organisation would do well to develop a positive, challenging graphical vision.

We will review how reality is created from our thoughts and goals, how to use the power of graphical vision with the deeper parts of the mind and why individuals, families and organisations without graphical vision are so vulnerable to mediocrity and failure.

Six

WORKING WITH VISION

'Dream no small dreams for they have no power to move the hearts of men.'
GOETHE

Developing a vision is the first essential key to improving spirit intelligence and setting any individual, family or organisation on a positive and inspiring path to growth and success. But people also need to know how to use that vision key to unlock their full potential.

o THE ABILITY TO MAKE A DIFFERENCE

Joel Barker, author of *The Power of Vision*, emphasises the importance of acting on our vision to bring it to reality. He reminds us that we have all been gifted with the ability to make a difference and our challenge is to find our particular gifts and then work to make that difference through our vision for the future.

This is equally true for individuals, families and business enterprises. Joel Barker reminds us that:

VISION WITHOUT ACTION
MERELY A DREAM

ACTION WITHOUT VISION
JUST PASSING THE TIME

VISION WITH ACTION
CAN CHANGE THE WORLD

○ VISION WITHOUT ACTION MERELY A DREAM

If you have a vision of the future and do nothing about it, it remains a dream. While studying at Edinburgh University and working with my friend rebuilding our Land Rover, we would 'occasionally' wander to the pub — as students do! We would talk to people about our vision of driving overland to Australia and even round the world. Many of them said, 'Oh yes, driving around the world. What an incredible idea. One day I'm gonna do that.'

Now, 35 years later, where do you think those 'gonna do's' are? That's right. Still back in the pub in Edinburgh. Vision without action is merely a dream, which is why Chapter 13 on clear plans of action is so important.

> 'To be always intending to live a new life, but never find time to set about it — this is as if a man should put off eating and drinking from one day to another till he be starved and destroyed.'
>
> SIR WALTER SCOTT

o ACTION WITHOUT VISION JUST PASSING THE TIME

Action without vision is just passing the time. Nothing could shut down the spirit faster than action without vision. This is clearly true for individuals who feel purposeless. It is especially relevant for individuals working in organisations.

On your life journey, have you worked in organisations where the vision was not clear? Have you worked in places where there was no sense of achieving anything other than '*ship the product*' and continual quarterly pressure to make the budget numbers. It's not very fulfilling or inspiring, is it?

At the end of the year, even if you achieved the budget numbers, you are at best in David Bowie's words – *heroes just for one day*. The counters go back to zero and you start again. It feels more like a grind on a treadmill than being part of an inspired team building and living a vision.

The problem is that numbers are not the critical part of the vision. There is no 'spirit within' who will bounce out of bed every day just to achieve numbers for someone else.

Numbers can be useful, and can help us develop our vision, but they are not critical in themselves. For example, in the game of football, we keep the score by the number of goals. The only important score is at the end of the match. In the game of business, we keep the score with the revenue, profit and balance sheet. But the numbers are merely a record of progress towards the vision. Where an organisation is just chasing numbers, there is a great danger of action without vision, just passing the time. This sort of boredom leads to a spirit shut-down.

If you look around our towns and cities, many people are wandering without a vision. Their lights are on but nobody is home. Their spirit seems to have checked out and they are just going through the motions. Have you seen them? They appear to be victims of action without vision, just passing the time with no visible sense of passion or enthusiasm about their lives. That seems so wrong, such a waste of talent.

Would you tell me please, which way I ought to go from here? That depends a good deal on where you want to get to, said the Cat. I don't much care where — said Alice. Then it doesn't matter which way you go, said the Cat.

LEWIS CARROLL, ALICE'S ADVENTURES IN WONDERLAND

o VISION WITH ACTION CAN CHANGE THE WORLD

Vision with action can change the world. As Joel Barker reminds us, we have all been gifted with the ability to make a difference and when we are really clear about our gifts and we work together, vision with action can indeed change the world.

Would you like to work in an enterprise where there was a real sense of making a difference? Would that be inspiring and motivating?

○ ACTING FOR POSITIVE CHANGE

We can act on our visions in all areas of life — from the personal to the global, from the corporate to the public. The power is in the vision and the ongoing committed action that brings the vision into reality.

'You see things: and you say — Why?
But I dream things that never were, and I say — Why not?'
GEORGE BERNARD SHAW

○ VISION WITH NATIONS

In his book *The Image of the Future*, Fred Polack's question, in studying the history of nations, was *did a nation's success follow the nation's vision of the future or was the nation's vision created as a result of the nation's success?*

Polack found that time and again in successful nations, a significant vision precedes significant success.

The Greeks had a vision of how they wanted their society to be. The British had a vision of a large trading empire. The USA had a vision of freedom for the individual both in business and belief. Singapore under Sir Stamford Raffles and later Lee Kuan Yew had a vision of a South East Asian trading centre.

What's the current vision for your nation? Do you know how your country will look in the year 2030? In Australia many people think we'll eventually become a republic but beyond that it's a little vague. It's probably the same in many other countries.

Remember the word 'leadership' derives from the old English verb *Laedan* — to show the way.

Who should show the way and supply an inspiring vision of a nation's collective future for the people to embrace — royalty, the president, the church, politicians, elder statesmen, the common people? This is a good question. (We'll talk more about this in Chapter 18 'Change in a Changing World'.)

Whatever the answer, the principle stands:

SIGNIFICANT
VISION
PRECEDES
SIGNIFICANT
SUCCESS

o VISION WITH INDIVIDUALS

What is the significance of vision for individuals? Viktor Frankl wrote his book *Man's Search for Meaning* as a result of his experiences of surviving the Auschwitz concentration camp during the Second World War.

Frankl found that although millions died, the ones who survived were not necessarily the young or the healthy or the fit or the wealthy. The people who survived the hell on earth of the Nazi concentration camps were those who had 'something significant yet to do'. They had a vision beyond the war that they absolutely had to achieve. Having a personal definiteness of purpose and a vision taps deep sources of strength. And it is the vision that gave them the passion for life, the will and persistence to survive against the odds.

For maximum 16 cylinder performance and to exercise spirit intelligence in making the best life choices, it is essential that you ensure that you and each member of your family and work team has:

SOMETHING
SIGNIFICANT
YET
TO DO

How do you do that? By co-creating with them a powerful vision of what can be achieved in their future.

o VISION INSPIRES ENTHUSIASM

Would you like more enthusiasm from the people around you?

I know of no more powerful method of talking to the *en theos* – the spirit within, than ensuring the relevant people have been involved in creating a powerful vision so at all times they have 'something significant yet to do'.

Our thesis and experience is that everyone has an *en theos* – a spirit within.

The word enthusiasm is derived from the Greek words *en theos* the spirit within

Most people's spirits are a bit battered and bruised from life's journey. How's yours? Spirits can also be cheeky. They like playing games. They also get bored.

A leader of any team always faces a critical spirit intelligence choice. Either give the team a challenging game called 'Let's work together to achieve the vision', or risk the spirits getting bored and making up their own games – 'Let's cause trouble', 'Let's play politics', or worse still, 'Let's get the boss!'

Have you worked in an organisation where there was politics? Did it have an inspiring graphical vision of challenge and growth which everyone supported? I doubt it. That's why politics develop — there is no big game to engage the spirit.

At work, if you provide an 'A' grade vision, you are setting up an 'A' grade game that will attract an 'A' grade team. Why? Because in our experience, no one is looking for just a job, everyone is looking for a game.

Creating a vision encourages innovation, creativity and diversity of thinking because the spirit is free to envisage a more exciting and challenging future. Once the vision is created, people can work together to win the game and achieve the dream.

o VISION WITH YOUNG PEOPLE

The power of vision has special poignancy for young people. Helping them develop positive visions of their future can influence their performance. This is a crucial component of spirit intelligence in the home.

In Australia, we lose almost 500 young people every year to suicide. Ten to 20 times that number attempt suicide. That means every hour of every day, a young person somewhere in Australia tries to quit and leave the game of life.

Every day, 365 days a year, at least one young person succeeds in checking out — permanently. Behind all the grief and anger, pain and sorrow, the vision of their own future is so uninspiring and negative, it's simply not worth hanging around. And they call Australia the lucky country. In many countries, youth suicide statistics are pretty depressing and getting worse.

o VISION ACHIEVEMENT

A vision is metaphysical because it exists in the future.

We will now explore additional laws of physics that will help explain the laws of metaphysics that you need to make the best spirit intelligence choices and optimise vision achievement.

Remember, the laws of metaphysics are important because 13 of the 16 cylinders of body, mind, emotions and spirit are metaphysical. The generalised principles of physics give us a guide to the more challenging realm of metaphysics.

○ THE LAW OF COMPRESSION AND TENSION

The generalised principle relevant to the power of vision concerns the relationship between compression and tension in the physical universe.

Wherever forces of tension exist in the physical universe, you will find forces of compression acting at right angles to the tension. Equally wherever compression exists, you will find tension acting at right angles. Tension and compression co-exist at right angles in the physical universe. It is a generalised principle.

If you take an inflated balloon, or better still a rubber cylinder full of gas, sealed at each end with a flat plate (as shown in the diagram) and you apply compression to the balloon or to the two ends of the cylinder, then the generalised principle predicts that the tension will act at right angles so the walls of the balloon or cylinders bulge outwards. The tension pushes them out.

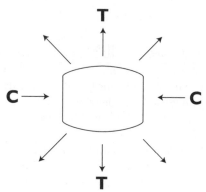

If, conversely you take hold of the top of a balloon and the neck of the balloon where the knot is tied, and place the balloon under tension, or hold the two ends of the cylinder and pull them apart, placing them under tension, then the forces of compression act at right angles and the balloon or cylinder becomes thinner.

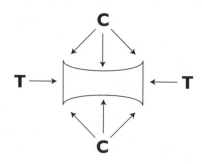

If you take a piece of elastic and stretch it, does the elastic become thicker or thinner? Thinner, because the forces of tension stretching the elastic mean the forces of compression act inwardly at right angles.

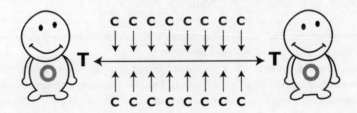

The compressive forces act at right angles to the tension applied and vice versa.

Armed with an understanding of the physical generalised principle or law of compression and tension, let's now review the law of metaphysical compression and tension in the workplace.

o A COMPRESSIVE MANAGEMENT STYLE

Demonstrating spirit intelligence involves making better choices. This is well illustrated by considering alternative management styles to motivate people.

A compressive style of management is illustrated by phrases such as:

'Look Michael, if you don't do that now, I can't guarantee your job by the end of the week.'

'Jennifer, tell the workers to improve performance or lay-offs are inevitable. That should get their attention.'

'George. That is the most stupid idea I have ever heard of. If you people can't do better than that we will be looking for a new team of architects.'

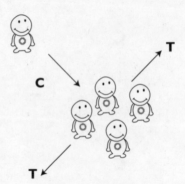

We've all met managers who use a compressive management style, pushing down on their team, suppressing their spirits. They would call it assertion and discipline. If the compressive force of this style of management is applied on the team, at what angle will the tension appear? At right angles. Tension always acts at right angles.

Will the tension act inwards or outwards? As you can see from the diagram, the tension acts outwards.

Now, here is the key question. Is this force of tension arising as a result of the compressive management style, serving to pull the team together as a cohesive whole or pushing them apart?

It is clear from the diagram that the forces of tension are pushing the team apart. These tension forces will show up in the team as absenteeism, sickness, irritability, complaining, gossiping. Finally, people will leave.

I have come across compressive managements that are losing over 30 per cent of their skilled workforce every year. Imagine that cost against the P&L!

'Force is all conquering, but its victories are short lived.'
ABRAHAM LINCOLN

o A POSITIVE TENSION MANAGEMENT STYLE

Conversely, you can choose to use this generalised metaphysical principle of compression and tension to improve motivation and team work. Together with your team, you can co-create a powerful vision in the metaphysics of the future, a vision the team is inspired and excited to achieve with passion.

The vision sets up a force of tension, a force that is exciting the people to move forward toward the future to bring the vision into reality.

Your team are 'called out to' and attracted towards that future vision.

**The word excite
is derived from
the Latin
ex ciere
to call out to**

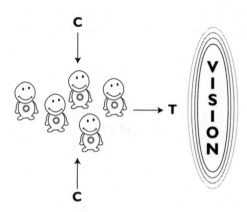

As the tension of the exciting vision pulls them forward, moment by moment, the compressive forces show up inwardly at right angles.

These compressive forces are thus acting inwards and are binding your team together.

A vision is not only the most powerful way of speaking to the spirit within, it also is the simplest way of using a generalised principle of metaphysics, tension and compression – to bind the team together.

Enlist people to help you build the vision and in doing so you will enlist the help of not only positive tension, but positive compressive forces. This is a clear example of spirit intelligence in action.

o VISION STABILITY

There is another generalised principle that needs to come into play – the need for stability. You must ensure your vision is stable because it is hard to hit a moving target.

How can you stabilise a vision?

o PHYSICAL STABILITY

If a physical sphere is to be rendered totally stable in three-dimensional space, the minimum number of restraints to limit the sphere's degrees of freedom of movement is 12. The sphere is held rigid at a point in space if it is secured by 12 restraints.

In our workshops, we give teams wooden spheres covered with hooks to which they attach strings. Each string attached represents limiting or stabilising a degree of freedom of movement. Five or six restraints can achieve a certain level of stability of the sphere in three-dimensional space, 12 restraints produces total stability.

o METAPHYSICAL STABILITY

In the same way, defining the success criteria of each stakeholder acts to stabilise your vision in metaphysical space.

This is because each stakeholder is 'pulling' to ensure their success criteria are met and their often opposing needs provide the dynamic tension and thus the vision stability.

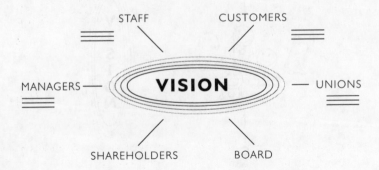

For example, shareholders want maximum return on shareholders' funds and employees want maximum wages. The two opposing success criteria provide the dynamic tension.

Dissatisfied stakeholders will either pull harder to get their needs met which will destabilise the vision or they will quit and 'let go' of the vision which again destabilises it.

Most visions have nine or ten stakeholders as we have discussed and so can be stabilised quite well, ensuring the vision achieved meets all the stakeholder success criteria.

Ensuring your vision represents a balance of often conflicting stakeholder success criteria is another example of spirit intelligence in action — aligning with a generalised principle of physics and metaphysics.

o METAPHYSICAL GRAVITY

How do you find the right people to activate your vision? It is said that when the cause is just, the right people show up. Time and again I have seen this happen.

Why? Because the metaphysical vision, once created, involves another generalised principle, the law of gravity.

In physics, Newton showed that there is a force of attraction between two physical masses. A physical body such as an asteroid, when equidistant from the sun and the Earth will be pulled towards the sun because the sun has bigger physical mass.

Similarly, once you have established your vision as a metaphysical entity, it too will attract other metaphysical entities or bodies. The right people and resources tend to show up. Faced with choice, an 'A' grade person will gravitate to a powerful vision rather than a job or position description. The vision has more metaphysical mass than the job description. It is a bigger idea and thus has more pulling power.

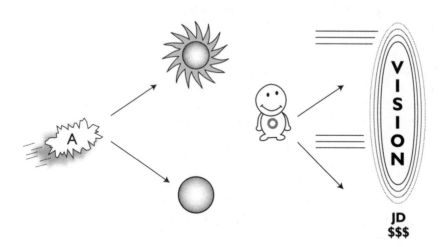

We will review using this generalised principle of metaphysical gravity to attract 'A' grade people to your team in detail in Chapter 15 on managing people.

o UNCLEAR VISION

To conclude this discussion on vision, I will mention my experience with the Arab Bank. This single conversation has been pivotal in helping many senior managers in other organisations around the world.

Jim Liu, the Executive Vice President and Chief Executive Asia Pacific of the Arab Bank plc in Singapore said to me, *'David. It is not possible for us to have a detailed vision of our future because we are an opportunistic commercial bank. We don't know what the opportunities are going to be tomorrow. We just know that we will be there to give better service than our competitors.'*

After some discussion, we talked about the Hollywood movie *Congo*. In the film, there is something mysterious going on around a mist enshrouded mountain in the Congo in Africa. A fully equipped team flies in to investigate and their plane crashes. The surviving heroes salvage their equipment from the wreckage and set out to explore the misty terrain, equipped with all the latest in weaponry and laser surveillance. They need it!

I said to Jim that his challenge was probably similar to many opportunistic organisations. Rather than prescribing an exact desired future, the vision is the future mountain of opportunity shrouded in mist and uncertainty.

The key vision question is therefore: Is your team prepared for all eventualities? Do you have an 'A' team trained and equipped with world's best practice support systems and culture – prepared and facing the future? So when the mist clears, as it will, your team can kick into action and succeed.

o LINKING THE PRINCIPLES

Whether you see the future of your enterprise clearly or whether, like Jim, you need to be opportunistic, the power of working with vision can be tremendous.

Have we strayed far from the words of wisdom of the Wright Brothers, Henry Ford and Thomas Edison? No. Definiteness of purpose is still the fundamental theme. All we have done is to link that theme to the principle that a picture is worth a thousand words and developed a vision, which in turn calls into play the generalised metaphysical principles of compression and tension, stability and gravity.

Now we must move on to the second of the four success keys from *Think and Grow Rich* — passion — a burning desire to succeed. You must have the keys to motivate yourself, your family and the people around you at work to perform on 16 cylinders — body, mind, emotions and spirit — to achieve your vision.

Part Three

PASSION

16 Cylinder Performance

What do we all have in common? Body, mind, emotions and spirit.

You have 16 cylinders of power available to you. So does every member of your family. At work, your organisation is paying for 16 cylinders in every employee. The key question is – how many cylinders are currently firing? Vision without action is merely a dream. It's people that will make it happen. So let's turbo charge you and those around you. Start your engines. The keys are over the page.

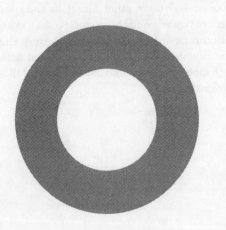

Seven

YOUR LEADERSHIP PASSION

'Few men during their lifetime come anywhere near exhausting the resources dwelling within them. There are deep wells of strength that are never used.'
ADMIRAL RICHARD E. BYRD

Developing a vision is inspiring but because your vision exists in the metaphysics of the future, the challenge is to achieve results in the physics of now. And to do that you will need inspired, motivated people to enact your clear plans of action with passion and persistence.

○ A BURNING DESIRE TO SUCCEED

The second of the four success keys is a burning desire to succeed — passion.

In this chapter, we will review your leadership role and passion. Whether or not you hold a formal position of leadership in an organisation or your community is not the issue. True leadership is not about being the boss. It is about your own passion keys and the image and influence you are projecting. In the next chapters, we will review how to develop rapport with the individuals around you and how to inspire them to 16 cylinder performance. Finally, we will cover the keys to inspiring passionate teams. Optimising spirit intelligence requires the keys to turn on the 16 cylinders of everyone involved in your enterprises.

○ PASSION – THE UNREASONABLE CHAMPION

Being a leader is not always comfortable or easy. In my experience, if you really want something to happen in life, you have to find 'an unreasonable champion' — somebody who is so passionate that they simply refuse to take no for an answer.

The unreasonable champion is prepared to persist and suffer repeated setbacks to achieve whatever it is they believe in and care about. In the early phases of trying to achieve your vision, that unreasonable champion may have to be you.

The word passion derives from the Latin verb *patir* to suffer.

77

'The reasonable man adapts himself to the world, the unreasonable one persists in trying to adapt the world to himself. Therefore all progress depends on the unreasonable man.'

GEORGE BERNARD SHAW

THE WOO-WOO FACTOR AND THE SHELF

As leadership passion is principally expressed in the unseen realms of metaphysics, let's recall the woo-woo factor and the shelf from Chapter 1. The woo-woo factor measures the weirdness or strangeness of anything we discuss. The shelf is where you can file concepts that are too 'far-out' to accept right now. Leave them on your shelf for a later time of possible re-evaluation instead of rejecting them outright.

PASSION

Look at the word passion:

PASSION

PASS-I-ON

PASS-I-ON

PASS-   -ON

As a leader, what is the quality of the 'I' you are passing on? This will have a profound influence on your leadership capabilities. Increasing your self-knowledge and self-awareness is a critical spirit intelligence step on the journey to becoming a passionate leader.

o BODY LANGUAGE

You may be aware of the concept of body language – our bodies talk and pass on tacit messages all the time, many of them below our conscious awareness.

You may have observed that when people are not open to ideas, they sometimes fold their arms. Whatever the reason, they feel threatened by the idea or simply disagree with it. They don't want to 'let it in.' By folding their arms, they are blocking the flow of information.

People often fold their arms when they feel insecure.

o POWER CENTRES

In the East where people are much more comfortable with metaphysics, Indian philosophy postulates that our physical body is sustained by seven metaphysical energy or power centres. These are positioned through the body and sustain our metaphysical energy and life force.

The first energy centre is at the base of the spine, the second in the region of the sex organs, the third in the solar plexus with the fourth at the heart. The fifth energy centre is in the area of the throat, the sixth on the brow and the seventh on the crown of the head. The Indians call these energy centres chakras.

You may have seen an Indian person with a spot painted on their forehead or a Jewish person with a small skull cap on their crown. The religions of the world understand the metaphysics of the body.

For an Indian philosopher, people fold their arms to cover their solar plexus and heart centres. They feel less exposed or less threatened, safer and more comfortable when these energy centres are covered.

At a cocktail party full of strangers, we usually accept a drink, which we hold in front of our heart centre so we feel less exposed and more comfortable. If you have trouble with this concept, take the challenge. At the next cocktail party you attend, decline the glass, go and talk to people empty handed and see if you find yourself feeling slightly less confident and more exposed.

The body language of the people you interact with will speak volumes to you if you can read it. They too will be subconsciously scanning and reading your body language. If you fold your arms while they talk to you, they will perceive (at a subconscious level) that you are not totally open to their ideas or you feel vulnerable.

If you cover your power centres in front of other people, they will scan you and read that. A devious senior manager I know often holds his hand over his throat or mouth as he talks. The subconscious message is that his communication is not straight forward — and it rarely is!!

Interpreting body language is an art, not an exact science. People also fold their arms when they are cold! Just be aware of the way you behave with your body and how and when you may be covering your power centres with your arms. These behaviours affect the quality of the 'I' you are passing on.

When you start to watch people, you will be amazed how even senior business people and politicians give so much away by insecure body language. Reading body language is a vital spirit intelligence skill.

o CHARISMA

The ancient Egyptians believed that each person has a spirit or Ka that survives beyond death. This Ka is the core of your being. The Greeks postulated that at the base of the spine, you have what they called a Kharis pump. Your fitness and the way you hold yourself, your posture, defines how much Ka you project, how much Kharis or charisma you pump out. In other words, your posture affects the quality of the 'I' you are passing on.

Rounded shoulders and a stooped posture straighten the base of the spine and shut down the Kharis pump. Head up, shoulders back, chest out puts a curve at the base of the spine that turns on the Kharis pump. Charisma is in the realm of the unseen but sensed — the metaphysics shining out of the physics.

Good body posture can project strong charisma. What is your body posture like? How much charisma are you projecting and passing on to inspire other people?

o PHYSICAL APPEARANCE

Physical appearance is important in influencing other people. A powerful game in our training workshops is called 'Choose the Leader'. I ask for three volunteers, task unknown! They line up at the front of the room and I ask the workshop participants whom they would choose as their leader. They vote by standing in front of their chosen candidate. I then ask them why they chose their candidate.

The answers are always intriguing and emphasise that the 'choosers' have taken note of physical appearance, posture, clothes. Grooming and personal posture are all critical leadership features.

o METAPHYSICAL APPEARANCE

Workshop participants always struggle to put into words how they are sub-consciously reading the metaphysics of what the leadership volunteers are projecting. They may say the person projects confidence. When we ask them to be more specific, words do not come easily, they just have a sense or a feeling. We have feelings about someone that are hard to put into words but those feelings are very powerful.

o ZONES OF EMPOWERMENT

As 13 of the 16 BMES cylinders are metaphysical, the power of leadership passion projection is in the invisible metaphysics. There is something much more powerful than your physical stature or your body language.

o YOUR EXTERNAL ZONE OF EMPOWERMENT

We all have in front of us something that we might call the external zone of empowerment.

This zone of empowerment is invisible and can best be understood by imagining that you have a metaphysical slide projector in your navel. Your external zone of empowerment shines out from this projector telling the world what you are really like. You can't see it or touch it, but it is there.

Other people will be subconsciously scanning and reading your external zone of empowerment because it is on, shining out there in the invisible metaphysics, seven days a week, 24 hours a day. You can't switch it off and you can't pretend it's different from what it really is.

In the business world, most people see themselves as practical, sensible people and they can be uncomfortable talking about scanning anything metaphysical, least of all something as personal and intangible as a metaphysical zone of empowerment. That is definitely high woo-woo!

In our training workshops, I often ask people if they have been in an old cathedral or temple. Some of the temples in the East are over a thousand years old and many of the cathedrals in Europe are at least 600 years old.

When you walk through those large studded wooden doors into an old cathedral or mosque, you can't see or touch 600 years of worship. But you do have a sense that inside that house of worship, there is a different atmosphere, a different feeling. It feels very different in the cathedral, mosque or temple from how it feels in the market place or the street.

We have a feeling that there is something different about the metaphysics in a place of worship, the unseen feel of the space. As the poet Lord Byron once observed, when you go into a cathedral your soul expands as if to 'fill' the space.

It is exactly the same with your external zone of empowerment. It is in front of you, shining out from your navel, telling the world what you are like. We scan each other at a subconscious level and 'read' the invisible metaphysics that we project.

You may have seen Arnold Schwarzenegger's *Terminator* movies. Just as the

EXTERNAL
ZONE
OF
EMPOWERMENT

Terminator is scanning across all frequencies, other people are also scanning you on all frequencies. They may be doing this subconsciously, but the feelings of comfort or distrust that result are real enough. You can't fool the Terminator and you can't fool other people.

The Germans talk of the Ausstrahlung, the rays that shine out from someone. The reason that the sudden death of Princess Di was such a shock to people was that her Ausstrahlung, her external zone of empowerment was special. There was more to her than her physical beauty and she fascinated us.

John F Kennedy also had a special Ausstrahlung.

We are all projecting an external zone of empowerment. It is an important part of the 'I' you are passing on. You can't hide it or fake it. The key question is — what powers it?

This is a vital question if you are in a leadership position at work or in your community. Spirit intelligence reflects in a strong external zone of empowerment.

o YOUR INTERNAL ZONE OF EMPOWERMENT

Your external zone of empowerment is powered by your internal zone of empowerment. Your external zone is a reflection of your internal zone and your internal zone is a function of your fitness – not just your fitness of body but your inner-self fitness of mind, emotion and spirit.

We all understand the need for physical fitness. Even if you have never regularly exercised, when you have done so you may have experienced that afterwards your mind was clearer. A fit mind is a clear mind with a strong sense of purpose and focus.

Fitness of your inner-self means that you are able to develop a wide range of feelings and, for example, can feel empathy for your family, other people in the community and for your colleagues and your customers at work.

In other words, you can make a 'heartfelt' connection with them. The quality of your heart shines out in your external zone of empowerment for all to see.

Inner-self fitness means you are playing the game of life and the game of business with the spirit qualities of integrity, morals and ethics. How you assess that is up to you. Some people have a strong spiritual or religious set of beliefs to guide them. Others rely on their instincts. Are you working from integrity? Clearly there are many people with no sense of integrity, ethics or honesty. The quality of your integrity, ethics, morals, will power and tenacity shines out in your external zone of empowerment.

In examining the quality of your external zone of empowerment, the 'I' that you are passing on, what level of fitness do you have on the inside? How is your fitness of body, mind, emotions and spirit? These questions are vital when you enter a nexus of influence.

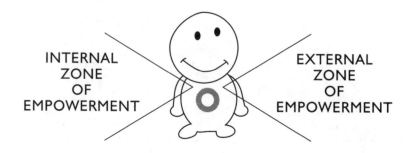

'The beauty of the soul shines out when a man bears with composure one heavy mischance after another, not because he does not feel them, but because he is a man of high and heroic temper.'
ARISTOTLE

○ YOUR NEXUS OF INFLUENCE

Why is the concept of the nexus of influence important? Because as the diagram shows, you enter such a nexus many times a day .

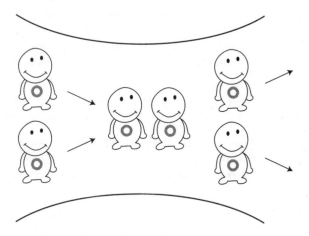

Someone enters a nexus of influence with you, for example, during a formal, arranged meeting, a chance meeting in a corridor or a meeting over the phone. When the meeting is concluded, you will have influenced the way that the other person will behave during the next hour, day or week.

When do you have maximum influence on them? Before, after or in the nexus? Clearly in the nexus of influence, itself.

Look at the nexus of influence. When two people meet they bring their external zones of empowerment into the nexus. If your zone is strong, — you are fit in body, mind, emotion and spirit and you have strong vision, passion, plans and persistence — people are more likely to follow your lead.

Most people's heads are full of problems — relationship problems, teenage children problems, mortgage problems, cash flow problems, car problems, health problems, pet problems. They will probably not be thinking as clearly as you nor have such a strong sense of purpose — and their external zone of empowerment is weakened by their internal state. If you are clear and strong, the chances are that they will follow your lead. It's so much easier to be a follower than a leader.

However, what happens if your internal zone of empowerment is weak? — because physically you are unfit; mentally you are slow and unimpressive; emotionally, as John Lennon said, you are 'crippled inside' — you can't reach out with empathy to other people's feelings and in spirit fitness, you lack integrity, honesty, ethics and morals. Everyone will read your external zone of empowerment and will know the weakness of the 'I' you are passing on. Your leadership ability will be correspondingly weakened.

o ZONE OF EMPOWERMENT CHECK LIST

Check the strength of your internal zone of empowerment. Run a zone of empowerment audit by scoring yourself across the following nine questions. Answer each question in the range 0–10. This is a classic spirit intelligence optimisation activity for you and those around you.

The point of power

Be honest with the questions. It is not about being Superman or Superwoman but how you find yourself at the moment. Facing the truth of a situation is another key to power. The truth forces you into present time and your point of power is always in the present. The past is gone, history. The future is still in the metaphysics. The point of power is now, so you need to assess the strength of passion you are currently projecting because you cannot fool other people. At a deep level, they know it and so do you.

Question 1 — Personal Purpose

How strong is your definiteness of purpose? How clear are you about what it is that you as an individual, a leader or team member are working to achieve and why?

0 is very unclear. 10 is crystal clear.

Question 2 — Personal Passion

How strong is your burning desire to succeed? How strong is your personal passion? Assess your feelings and views about what you are doing. How strong is your passion to succeed? Is your heart in your work?

0 is very weak. 10 is red hot and burning.

Question 3 — Personal Plans

How clear are your personal plans of action? Do you know what you will be doing over the next day, week, month or year? Are you organised?

0 is no plans. 10 your plans are all clearly defined.

Question 4 — Personal Persistence

How strong is your personal sense of persistence? How strong is your determination to stand firm throughout? Do you have a flexible, adaptive 'What Ever It Takes' (WEIT) attitude?

0 is very weak. 10 is outstandingly strong, unstoppable.

Question 5 — Physical Fitness

How good is your personal physical fitness? Do you aerobically exercise three times a week for 20 minutes? Are you fit enough to run a mile? Are you eating sensibly? Are you looking after your body?

0 means you are a physical slob! 10, you are in really good physical shape.

Question 6 — Mental Fitness

How sharp are you mentally? Are you on the ball and with it? Are you feeding your mind with a constant stream of educational books, cassettes and videos? How alert are you?

These are subjective judgments and hard to quantify. Do you have trouble thinking clearly and concentrating? Assess your mental fitness.

0 is very dull. 10 is mentally sharp as a tack.

Question 7 — Emotional Fitness

How is your emotional fitness? Can you feel joy and sadness, elation and despair, fear and anger, compassion and love? How good are you at emotionally reaching out and creating empathy and understanding with other people? Do you have the emotional reach to feel what they are feeling? Can you establish rapport and empathy?

How broad is your emotional bandwidth? (We can all achieve some degree of emotional rapport with some people, often with people who are like us. We will cover that in detail later in Chapter 9.) How good are you at achieving emotional rapport with a broad bandwidth so you can relate to everybody around you?

0 is very poor. 10 is outstanding.

Question 8 — Spirit Fitness

How is your fitness of spirit? Do you consciously work to maintain integrity and honesty and operate from the strength of ethics? This has nothing to do with religion or spirituality, it is about how you choose to play the personal game of life.

Do you bend the rules on your tax return? Do you claim for expenses you didn't spend? If a waitress brings you your bill in a restaurant and they have undercharged you, do you draw the undercharge to their attention? What standards are you playing to?

'Sooner or later everyone sits down to a banquet of consequences.'
ROBERT LOUIS STEVENSON

Again this is a very personal question but it is one that must be faced because if your score is low, it is going to affect your external zone of empowerment that other people are scanning at that deep subconscious level. So look at yourself in the mirror.

0 is a very weak attitude to integrity, trust, ethics, morals, responsibility and accountability. 10 is a high level of personal integrity and strength of character.

Question 9 — Life Journey Experience

What sort of journeyman experience do you bring to the current challenge? How many organisations have you worked in? Have you been around a bit? Are you experienced in the game of life and the game of business? Are you awake or asleep? Life journey victor or victim? Score your overall experience from your life journey so far.

0 is a very shallow, short journeyman experience. 10 is a significant journey mixture of life experiences.

Your zone of empowerment score

From these very personal, subjective nine questions, there is a possible score of 90 if you score 10 on each. Just add up your scores.

How are you doing? Is this science? No, it is art. Is your score below 40? If so, you have significant work to do. Fifty to 60? Passable. Sixty to 80 and on towards 90 is clearly the aim for a strong zone of empowerment. Spirit intelligence asks for you to make better choices in your life and to work on increasing your scores.

This book is designed to help you improve the external zone of empowerment, to improve the 'I' in your passion, the 'I' that you are passing on. You may already have gained some distinctions, some areas for personal improvement to list in your Commitments Register after completing this zone of empowerment audit.

o YOU AS LEADER

The ultimate question for any leader is why would anyone follow you? Management operates significantly from positional power but leadership is much more about personal power.

If people are going to follow you 'over the wall into battle' to achieve a vision, you can try mandating that using your managerial positional power but the truth of the matter is, to be a leader, people have to choose to follow you because of the qualities you project.

o SUMMARY

You have reviewed your personal level of passion and your burning desire to succeed. You are aware that you are projecting your zone of empowerment and the charisma of the 'I' you pass on.

Now we must explore a range of spirit intelligence tools to ensure that the people around you also have a burning desire and the passion to succeed.

To achieve your vision, you need them all on 16 cylinders.

The next step is reconnaissance and mapping the territory that surrounds you.

Eight

MAPPING THE TERRITORY

'Time spent in reconnaissance is never time wasted.'
  BRITISH ARMY

With a clear vision established and your personal leadership passion optimised, the next step is to inspire the passion — the burning desire to succeed — in the people around you. Without their passion it will be very hard, if not impossible, to achieve the vision.

Mastering the keys to inspiring people's passion is an exciting spirit intelligence journey.

o LEADERSHIP NON-EXISTENCE

The first key to firing up passion in those around you is to gain an understanding of the general operating environment. You need to map out the territory, especially if you have not worked or been involved with the people before.

When you take control of a team as a new leader, you are in a phase known as non-existence. You have no profile with the team. They may know of you vaguely or even intimately, but they cannot know how you will behave as their leader.

Experience says the best initial strategy is to curb the desire for immediate action and listen. Spirit intelligence demands that as leader, you make the best choices. So first you must engage in reconnaissance.

Ask a lot of questions and find out what is going on. Ask people about their current vision. Some say that leadership is about asking the 'right' questions, not finding the 'right' answers. Calibrate the current level of team passion, the clear plans of action they are working with and their approaches to ensure persistence.

If you are joining a new team as a team member, the same territory mapping principles apply. Ask them about their team culture and as you listen, map out what you are hearing. Once you have an initial map, then you can begin to make changes to fire up their passion.

These initial mapping principles hold true every time you are involved with new people or a new team and will work for you even with an existing team that you want to take to higher levels of passion and performance. They are just as relevant in assessing the current status in your family or local community.

A while ago in Australia, one of our large banks ran into profitability and balance sheet problems and the board brought in a new CEO from the US. From a distance, in his first weeks in the new job, all he seemed to do was wander around talking to people from senior management right down to people in the staff canteen.

What was going on? He was asking questions and listening. He was mapping the territory, figuring out what he had inherited before developing a new vision and clear plans of action.

o CONTRIBUTION CONTRACTS

One of the early steps of mapping is to find out if each person in the team has a clear contribution contract. Do they understand what is expected of them? Do they know the criteria by which they will be judged and the performance standards to which they are expected to perform? Do they have a clear understanding of the work to be done? (We will cover this extensively in Chapter 15 on managing people.)

o INDIVIDUAL EMPOWERMENT

If members of the team know the contribution expected from them, are they supported and empowered to achieve the results? As you scan your new team members, use these three key questions to check out their individual level of empowerment:

1. Are they *able to* do the job? Do they have the ability and the skills?

2. Do they *want to* do the job? Are they motivated?

3. Have they been given the *chance to* do their job with supportive systems and culture?

In Chapter 15, we will use these keys to help you manage people, because clearly you are not going to fire up sustainable passion in other people unless the contribution contract and the three empowerment keys of *able to*, *want to* and *chance to* are addressed and handled.

o ABLE TO = SKILLS AND CAPABILITIES

As you probe, work to calibrate your team member's apparent level of skills compared to what you would expect in the circumstances. You can't ask people to rise to the challenge of achieving a stretch vision if they are not up to it. No one can sustain passion in the face of being inadequately skilled for the task. Asking someone to play on a team when they do not have the right level of skill is unfair and de-motivating to their spirit within. (We'll also cover this further in Chapter 15.)

Spirit intelligence requires that you carry out this skills audit so that later on you can make the right task delegation and training choices to optimise passion and thus results.

o WANT TO = MOTIVATION

Ask questions to calibrate your team member's level of *want to* — their motivation.

Find out what has been motivating them to move and perform before you arrived.

Ask them to describe their vision, plans and budget targets. Calibrate the level of personal and joint ownership of these plans. Have they been properly enrolled in the game of 'let's achieve a vision'? You need to know this before attempting to move forward with them.

o EMOTIONS

If you want your team's emotion cylinders to fire up, you need to ascertain whether they have a reason to get going? What has been motivating them to date?

Have they been subjected to management by the motivation of fear? Fear can be a strong emotional motivator, but is it a tool to achieve long-term 16 cylinder high performance? No. It is at best a short-term motivator.

The simplest way to make sure they 'move out from' where they are today is to give them something to move towards — a vision.

> The word **motivation** derives from the Latin verb *movere* — to move
>
> The word **emotion** derives from the Latin — **ex movere** to move out from.

o ENTHUSIASM

You will need to encourage enthusiasm in your new team. Find out if anyone has previously addressed the spirit within.

Have they been asked to co-create a team vision and a comprehensive set of action plans to achieve the vision – thus defining 'a game to play' and 'something significant yet to do' for every member of the team?

SOMETHING
SIGNIFICANT
YET
TO DO

Have they all worked out a personal vision for their lives so they know why they are working with you and where they are heading? Have they clarified their life journey ahead of them, their aspirations, dreams and personal goals?

o CONFIDENCE

The word confidence derives from the Latin *con fidele* with faith.

Finally, is the team full of confidence?

For people to step forward with motivation and enthusiasm and a desire to perform, they must have faith in their leader. Has this been the case in their recent past?

Consider this quote from Kahlil Gibran —

'Faith is an oasis in the heart that can not be reached by the caravan of thinking.'

Developing faith is a heart matter. You can't command faith or prove it logically. What you can do is speak to people's hearts by clearly defining the definiteness of purpose and the vision, ensuring that clear plans of action are visible to all and by providing the tools for persistence.

When the resistance enemy shows up, if the people around you have the faith and passion, they can overcome all opposition and succeed.

How has this been managed before you arrived? You can't make the best spirit intelligence choices unless you know what you have inherited.

o CHANCE TO = CULTURE AND SYSTEMS

As you keep talking to your team you will start to get a feel for the prevailing culture and whether they feel they have the *chance to* perform and succeed. Resilient culture is built on trust and assertion. You need to find out which activities have been building trust and where trust has been eroding.

You also need to calibrate whether people have previously felt confident enough to speak up and assert their point of view. It is treason to the spirit within to ask someone to enrol in the game of 'let's achieve a vision' and then not give them the *chance to* win the game by denying them supportive culture and systems.

In most organisations, many crucial support systems are far from adequate and deny the chance to achieve consistent outstanding performance. Most people are remarkably resilient in working around poor systems, but they do significantly corrode enthusiasm.

Spirit intelligence will require you to 'choose between' and decide which of the poor systems are upgraded — to stop the treason to the spirit within and to optimise passion and performance improvement. (We'll cover this in detail later in Chapter 16 on persistence.)

Nine

ACHIEVING RAPPORT

'No man is an island.'
JOHN DONNE

You need to achieve rapport with the people around you if you are to empower them, inspire their passion and gain their help in achieving the vision.

The skill of achieving and sustaining rapport with a wide range of people is a fundamental skill of spirit intelligence because indeed 'no man is an island.' You cannot achieve a significant vision on your own.

A bridge carries traffic across a river or canyon. Your job is to build bridges of rapport with the people around you to achieve communication and understanding and optimise cooperation and passion.

The word rapport derives from the French verb *rapporter* to carry across.

Only when the bridge of rapport is established with each person, can you reach out and consistently fire up their 16 cylinders.

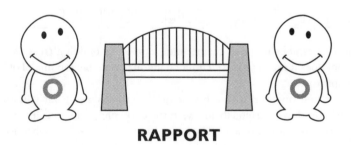

RAPPORT

o THREE KEYS TO RAPPORT

There are three principle keys to establishing and maintaining rapport with people.

o RAPPORT KEY ONE — SINCERE INTEREST

The first rapport key is simply one of sincere interest. Are you showing sincere interest in the people around you?

This is such a simple spirit intelligence key that we don't need to spend much time on it. To optimise cooperation with anyone, you have to understand where they are coming from and what they want from their association with you. How else will you achieve that unless you show sincere interest?

I am sure that you have personally experienced incidences of insincere interest. For example, talking to someone at an office party but their eyes are wandering around the room trying to spot when the chairman of the board is free; or being served by staff at a discount retailer who only go through the motions of customer service; or being in a meeting with someone who keeps glancing at their watch or answering every phone call while you sit there.

People pick up insincere interest in a flash. You may have highly sophisticated skills that you think will fool anybody but you don't. Either you choose to be sincerely interested in helping the people around you to fire up on 16 cylinders or you don't. Do you have sincere interest in them?

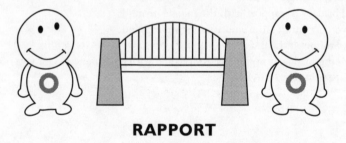

RAPPORT

o RAPPORT KEY TWO — BUILDING TRUST

The second key to establishing and maintaining rapport is building trust. An interesting word, trust. What does it mean to you? Think about our whole person model of body, mind, emotions and spirit.

When you are first involved with other people, do they sense what you are thinking? No, of course not. Do they consciously know, in the early phases of your interactions, what your heart and spirit qualities are like? They may have an idea as they subconsciously scan your external zone of empowerment but they can't yet know from personal experience, whatever they have heard from other people. The only way that they can establish a level of trust with you is by the way you behave.

Four behaviours of trust

There are four behaviours that build or destroy trust

RELIABILITY
OPENESS
ACCEPTANCE
STRAIGHT-FORWARDNESS

Let's review and audit your trust building behaviours.

Reliability

Do you always do what you say that you are going to do? Do you keep commitments? Do you show up when you say you will? Can people rely on you?

Reliability is a vital spirit intelligence quality. You either choose to be reliable or unreliable. Which is it for you?

Openness

Are you open with people? Rapport is a bridge between you and those around you. Is it a one-way or two-way bridge? To build rapport, clearly you need a two-way bridge in order to be open to both give and receive feedback.

Are you open to receiving feedback? Listening is a tough skill to master. You know what they say – one mouth, two ears – that's the required ratio!

Acceptance

Do you accept people for who they are? There is clearly a difference between accepting a person and accepting their behaviour. If you have experience with children, you will know the distinction. Little Jimmy's habit of throwing breadcrumbs around the kitchen is simply unacceptable behaviour. Jimmy is okay and acceptable as a person, but his behaviour is not.

It is your choice to accept each person for who they are — that is a trust building behaviour. Most people genuinely do the best they can in the circumstances in which they find themselves.

Everyone has a spirit within. Even if their flame went out years ago, you have to rekindle the spark. (We will have more to say about this later in the next chapter on spirit keys.)

Are you accepting people for who they are or are you judging them?

'He's dumb.'
'What a jerk.'
'Who hired this bimbo?'

Even if you don't say it, your judgment emanates from your invisible zone of empowerment. Be careful. There is more to trust and acceptance than just smooth patter.

Straightforwardness

Do you say what you mean? Do you do what you say? Integrity, honesty and telling the truth are fundamental spirit intelligence choices. People won't trust you when the going gets tough if they are not sure they are getting the truth from you.

Trust summary

Trust is thus built up by behaving reliably, being open to giving and receiving feedback, accepting people for who they are and being straightforward. This is spirit intelligence common sense.

Try building rapport by being unreliable, closed off to feedback, judging everyone around you and constantly bending the truth. You won't get far.

The third rapport key is incredibly simple, powerful and easy to learn and use.

o RAPPORT KEY THREE — SATISFYING NEEDS

By ensuring you remain sincerely interested in the people around you and by focusing on your trust building behaviours, you can establish a bridge of communication and rapport with each of them. It is now time to cross that bridge and fire up their passions.

The challenge is that each person is different. This third rapport key enables you to read people and modify your approach to satisfy their deep needs – at home, in your community and at work. How is it that we are all so different? That is one of the great mysteries. How is our micro-code wired up? Where do our personalities come from? Why do people behave as they do?

To explore these questions, we will work with a model initially developed by Dr William Marston and expanded upon more recently by Dr John Geier to explain what motivates and affects people's behaviour.

Marston was a psychologist. While others such as Freud and Jung were deeply interested in pathology and mental illness, Marston was more interested in the normal, healthy parameters of body and mind. His book *Emotions of Normal People* was published in the 1920s. In it he developed a two-axis, four-dimensional model that is a very powerful tool for achieving rapport — by understanding and satisfying the deep needs and thus, the passions of the people around you.

Other psychologists have developed powerful personal analysis tools. In my experience as an international corporate trainer and facilitator, Geier's is the best tool for rapidly reading people and achieving rapport. It is simple and practical. It works across continents because it speaks directly to the spirit within.

Geier's analogy is that the drivers of behaviour can be viewed like an iceberg. About 70 to 90 per cent of an iceberg is below the surface of the water. Only 10 to 30 per cent is visible. In the same way, we see people's physical behaviour but underneath that behaviour, is the 70 to 90 per cent that internally drives them. Geier explained that our behaviours are influenced by three major areas:

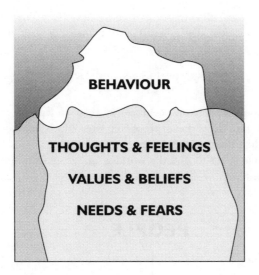

Our behaviour is clearly influenced by our thoughts and feelings. We feel hungry so we eat. We think we are late for a meeting so we hurry. (We will explore the power of values and beliefs and how they influence our thoughts and feelings and thus motivate our behaviour in Chapter 11.)

o NEEDS AND FEARS

Marston's and Geier's work illustrates that we are all driven by very fundamental needs and fears that critically affect our levels of passion and our behaviours.

If you are to build strong bridges of rapport with other people, fire up their passion and motivate them, it is critical that you can read and understand their deep needs and fears so that you can, respectively, meet and alleviate them.

We are dealing with deep, universal needs and fears that affect all of us in our daily lives. If you have a tool that will enable you to observe the behaviour of everyone around you, and from that understand the deep needs that drive them, then you can adapt your own behaviour towards them so that you build the bridge of rapport. You can consistently help them meet their needs and avoid their fears. Does that sound like a powerful passion key?

How are these deep needs and fears formed? You must understand this if you are to motivate people. This is a vital spirit intelligence skill.

o WHY DO PEOPLE BEHAVE AS THEY DO?

Marston's and Geier's principal quests were to answer the question 'Why do people behave the way they do?' As people can react so differently to the same external environment, presumably their perceptions of the environment and what behaviour is appropriate must be different.

Two questions

Early in life, in the first few days, weeks and months, we all have to answer two fundamental questions for ourselves.

Question One — is the world favourable or unfavourable to me?

Some people's early experiences of life seem to lead them to feel the world is a favourable place. You can always recognise these people in later life because they become more people oriented. They like the world and they enjoy people.

However some people seem to find the world is more unfavourable. In later life they become more task oriented.

PEOPLE

TASK

So the first behavioural axis derived from an analysis of people is: Is this person more people oriented or more task oriented?

Question Two — how am I going to act in the world?

The second question that we answer, irrespective of how we feel about the world, favourable or unfavourable is — how am I going to act in the world?

Some people take the decision to become more active in their approach to life's challenges. Other people take the decision to be more cautious, a little more reserved before they act.

Thus the second axis of behavioural analysis is: Is this person more active or more reserved?

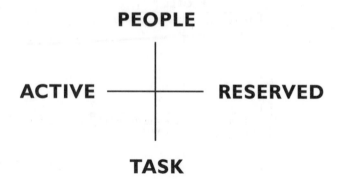

These early perceptions and decisions reflect our deepest needs and fears. So reading people's behaviour — more people or more task oriented in focus, more active or more reserved by disposition — gives you a very powerful tool to understanding their deep subconscious needs and fears.

The reason that this is so important to you as a spirit intelligence analysis tool is that Marston and Geier found in their research that people would do anything to get their fundamental needs met. Equally, they would do anything to avoid having their fears triggered. If they can't get their needs met overtly.

Working with the people around you at home, in the community and at work is challenging enough without having them working covertly to get their deepest needs met. Thus it is a far better spirit intelligence choice to ensure you are achieving rapport and helping them get their deep needs met overtly even if they may be unaware as to what you are doing.

By employing this basic four way grid – people / task : active / more reserved — let's explore how you can use this information to improve your understanding of other people and then achieve rapport and motivate them to peak passion and performance to achieve the vision and get the results.

o UNDERSTANDING PEOPLE USING THE FOUR BEHAVIOURAL STYLES

When I first came across this tool many years ago, it initially surprised me to realise that people are driven by needs that are different from mine. Surely everybody is motivated to succeed and achieve results? At a deep level, people can be driven by very different basic needs. In the past, you've probably been surprised by how some people react to a situation. Their response to a deadline or problem may have been different to your view of what needed to be done. Why is that?

Geier categorised four basic types of people with different behavioural responses to explain the differing needs and fears that drive us all, regardless of nationality or culture. This is a universal tool for understanding people and achieving rapport and a fundamental spirit intelligence key to turning on individual motivation and passion.

Geier nominated the four groups of people for the behaviours they displayed:

PEOPLE

	INFLUENCER	STEADINESS	
A C T I V E			R E S E R V E D
	DOMINANT	CONSCIENTIOUS/ CAUTIOUS	

TASK

This diagram will help you to review four very different types of people. You need to know what motivates them and how to achieve rapport and fire up their passions.

Clearly we are all mixtures of these types to varying degrees. This is a tool of empowerment, not categorisation. We can change according to circumstances but spirit intelligence requires you make better choices in dealing with the people around you. This tool helps you with those better choices because it is so simple, awesomely powerful and effective on your road to mastery of inspiring passion in others.

Influencers

There are people who are by nature wamly more people oriented and active. Geier called them Influencers. They are interactive. They like people. They are always out there, talking a lot, moving around and meeting people. They are active by nature. The more people they meet, the better.

PEOPLE

	INFLUENCER	STEADINESS	
	NEED: social recognition looking good		
A C T I V E	**FEAR:** rejection		R E S E R V E D
	DOMINANT	CONSCIENTIOUS/ CAUTIOUS	

TASK

The fundamental need that drives the Influencers is one of social recognition. They want to be recognised, to be liked, to be involved. They want to look good. Their greatest fear is social rejection. They don't like being ignored. He called them high 'I's because of their strength in influencing others.

Using our 16 cylinder BMES (body, mind, emotions, spirit) model, it is as though each of us has two buttons, one on each lapel of our shirt or blouse.

On one lapel we have a needs button. In the case of an Influencer, a high 'I' active, people oriented person, their need is for social recognition. If our needs button is consistently activated as our needs are met, what do you think will happen to the 16 cylinders? Will they fire up or shut down? If the needs are consistently met, the 16 cylinders will fire up.

However, if the fears button on the other lapel is consistently pushed, the 16 cylinders start to shut down and people become less motivated. For a high 'I' who needs social recognition, pressing the fear button would involve some form of social rejection such as criticising them in public or shouting at them.

Remember that people will do anything to get their needs met. Thus to achieve rapport and motivate active, people-oriented people, ensure they are given social recognition and praise and not subjected to public rejection or correction.

You may have been exposed to this rapport tool in the past. If you have not, you will be amazed at its power and effectiveness as you practice and hone this vital spirit intelligence skill.

Dominant

There are some people who are more coolly task oriented and active by nature. They can appear very focused on the result with not a lot of time for small talk. They can appear assertive, even pushy. Geier called them Dominant people — high 'D'.

Their principle need is for control and results and they have a strong fear of loss of control because in their own minds, if they lose control, what is jeopardised? The results.

PEOPLE

	INFLUENCER	STEADINESS	
A C T I V E	**NEED:** social recognition looking good **FEAR:** rejection		**R E S E R V E D**
	DOMINANT **NEED:** results control **FEAR:** loss of control	**CONSCIENTIOUS/ CAUTIOUS**	

TASK

A high 'D' active, task focused Dominant type of person needs control. If people will do anything to avoid triggering their fears and a high 'D' fears losing control, then guess what they do — they keep control.

Do you have people around you who are active and more focused on the task, maybe a little less sensitive to people? Do they push hard to get the job done and sometimes ruffle a few feathers in the process? Their task focus can be a great asset in a crisis or when you have to meet a deadline.

Clearly the way you achieve rapport with these people is different to achieving rapport with high 'I's.

Steadiness

There are some people who are also people oriented but have a more reserved approach to life. You can always recognise these people because they have a Steadiness to their character – high 'S'.

They are generally quieter by nature. They are fabulous people on a team as they are always aware of and care for the well being of those around them. They are like oil between the cogs, a calming influence. They have a strong need for acceptance and stability. They are team players. Their great fear is loss of stability and sudden, unplanned change.

Although these people are marvellous on teams because of their inherent team building natures and the fact that they care about team members, they are really being challenged now.

PEOPLE

	INFLUENCER	STEADINESS	
	NEED: social recognition looking good	**NEED:** acceptance stability team	
A C T I V E	**FEAR:** rejection	**FEAR:** rapid change	**R E S E R V E D**
	DOMINANT	**CONSCIENTIOUS/ CAUTIOUS**	
	NEED: results control		
	FEAR: loss of control		

TASK

What is happening all round us? Change. As we move into the 21st century, the pace of change seems to be speeding up.

Originally we sent communications at the speed that somebody could walk or run. The Marathon race celebrates the famous run by Pheidippides in 490BC from Marathon to Athens, a distance of 25 miles (40 kilometres), to bring the news of the Athenian victory over the Persians. Having delivered the news, he dropped down dead. The Industrial Age heralded inventors such as Samuel Morse who developed the telegraph in 1837 and Alexander Graham Bell who invented the telephone in 1877 — passing information using electricity down copper wires. Now we are passing information across massive distances, down glass fibres at the speed of light.

With high speed information transfer and product life cycles growing shorter, change is happening more frequently.

So for 'S' people who are more people oriented and reserved by nature, whose great need is for team and stability and whose great fear is sudden or unplanned change, which of their buttons is being pushed more and more? That's right, their 'fear' button.

'S' people are very valuable as team members. You must look after them, plan the necessary changes – step by step – and help them maintain 16 cylinder empowerment.

Conscientious / cautious

There are some people who are more task oriented and yet tend to be more reserved by nature. They work long hours and are very detail oriented and conscientious. Geier called these people Cautious or Conscientious — high 'C'.

These people have a high need for accuracy, quality, detail, and getting it right. Their great fear is criticism because criticism makes them wrong and they have a strong need to be right.

PEOPLE

	INFLUENCER	STEADINESS	
A C T I V E	**NEED:** social recognition looking good **FEAR:** rejection	**NEED:** acceptance stability team **FEAR:** rapid change	**R E S E R V E D**
	DOMINANT **NEED:** results control **FEAR:** loss of control	**CONSCIENTIOUS/ CAUTIOUS** **NEED:** accuracy quality, detail get it right **FEAR:** criticism being wrong	

TASK

To meet their needs, high 'C' people will work back long hours to complete the work. They are detail aware. They will do almost anything to be right. They are very conscientious in their approach to life and work, setting high quality standards on themselves and the rest of a team.

A mixed team?

Successful teams need a mixture of these different types of people.

The high 'C' Conscientious people are the guardians of the detail and the quality, while the active, task focused Dominant high 'D' personalities are out there doing almost anything for the result, knocking down the Berlin wall, taking no prisoners, whatever it takes to succeed. You also need the optimists, the high 'I' Influencers. They are active and enthusiastic, always up and bright, always out there. They can always see that the bottle is at least half full. They see the world in positives — you can't keep them down. Sometimes their attention to detail is not always their strong suit. That's why you need the high 'C's.

The more reserved high 'S' — Steadiness — people, as we have said, are the team guardians. Because they really appreciate being on a good team, they will work to preserve and enhance teamwork even when the pressure is on.

DISC as an analysis tool

This DISC tool gives you the clues to other peoples' needs. You can start to see the power of the tool in meeting needs and thus optimising passion. The diagram summarises the needs and fears of the four types of people we have looked at.

PEOPLE

	INFLUENCER	STEADINESS	
A C T I V E	**NEED:** social recognition looking good **FEAR:** rejection	**NEED:** acceptance stability team **FEAR:** rapid change	**R E S E R V E D**
	DOMINANT	**CONSCIENTIOUS/ CAUTIOUS**	
	NEED: results control **FEAR:** loss of control	**NEED:** accuracy quality, detail get it right **FEAR:** criticism being wrong	

TASK

DISC graphic equalisers

It is essential to emphasise repeatedly that we are all mixtures. This tool is not intended to categorise anyone. Imagine people having four DISC graphic equalisers like on a stereo system. They can change their DISC emphasis but have a preferred setting.

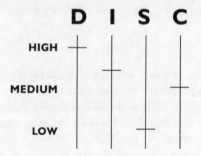

You will find that most people will have tendencies towards being more people or task oriented in the way they approach a challenge. You will also find that some people are more active and some more reserved by nature.

To make the best choices, spirit intelligence demands that you understand how to relate and achieve rapport by adjusting your DISC graphic equalisers to match those of the person you are dealing with.

Your own preferred DISC setting is not important, but rather being flexible, achieving rapport and thus motivation and firing up passion.

People analysis

List each of the key people around you at home, in your community and at work. Ask yourself — is their orientation by nature more warmly people or more coolly task? Are they more active by nature or more reserved? How have they set their four DISC graphic equalisers?

Then think about their needs as we have discussed them and see if you can discern those needs and fears through in their behaviour.

If you are in a relationship, think about your partner and see if the model holds for them too. Are they more people or task oriented by nature, more active or more reserved? Can you see how they get their needs met in your relationship? If you help them get their needs met more, your relationship will improve. What about your kids?

o VARIABLE RAPPORT STYLES

To achieve a vision and get results, you need all the people around you consistently fired up on 16 cylinders. It will greatly help if you can establish and maintain rapport with each of them in good times and when under pressure. This is equally true at home or with close friends and relatives.

Now we will explore how you can you modify your rapport approach to ensure you consistently meet each person's needs especially when under pressure, firing up their 16 cylinders and passion. We will also cover what behaviours are appropriate to avoid triggering their fears and shutting down their cylinders.

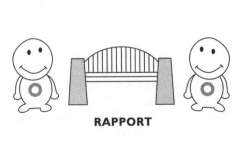

RAPPORT

PEOPLE

	INFLUENCER	STEADINESS	
A C T I V E	**NEED:** social recognition looking good **FEAR:** rejection	**NEED:** acceptance stability team **FEAR:** rapid change	**R E S E R V E D**
	DOMINANT **NEED:** results control **FEAR:** loss of control	**CONSCIENTIOUS/ CAUTIOUS** **NEED:** accuracy quality, detail get it right **FEAR:** criticism being wrong	

TASK

Rapport with active 'D's

When you are dealing with active high 'D' Dominant people, speed up and keep it moving. The task oriented 'D's will want to cut straight to the chase, with no time for chit-chat or small talk. In, talk, decide, act — preferably their way!

Let's take an example. John is a young man on your team. He is very enthusiastic, keen, even pushy, always opinionated. Some people find him cold and abrasive. You like him because he can be relied on to get the job done. Our model would indicate that young John is active and task-oriented. He has a high 'D' Dominant graphic equaliser. This helps you motivate his passion in two ways — first, it gives you clues to the speed of your approach to him in building rapport. Secondly, it influences the way you phrase the needs of the challenge to play to his needs and to avoid his fears.

With someone who is task focused and active by nature, your rapport style must necessarily be active. Avoid the chit-chat and move straight to the point.

'John, this task will need to be done over the next few months. Like you, I am only concerned with one thing. Getting it done. How you go about this is entirely up to you.'

Now what have you done? You have just passed control to John and pressed his needs button. You have emphasised the need for results. You have steered away from any sense that he might have been losing control. You have avoided his fears. Give John the control he is looking for and he will be on 16 cylinders.

When we come to Chapter 15 on managing people, we will look at John's level of experience. Discovering his ability for the task helps you to decide whether you delegate with loose or close supervision and check points. For now, John is active and task-oriented and your rapport approach presses his needs button.

'D' under pressure

High 'D', active task people like John will become more dominant, aggressive and domineering if a stressful situation threatens their control needs fulfilment. Under extreme pressure they can tend to become dictatorial — *'Just do it. It's my way or the highway. Got it?'*

In order to ensure that you keep them motivated under pressure with their passion fired up, make sure that you leave a sense of control with them. Make sure that they have a clear path forward with a set of action plans to achieve results.

Rapport with active 'I's

Mary is also an active person but much more outgoing, friendly and people-oriented. She is always organising trips to the pizza restaurant at lunchtime, always knows where the best parties are. She is friendly and optimistic. Mary has a high 'I' Influencer graphic equaliser.

To establish rapport, Mary will want some time for a preliminary chat. If you use the same task oriented approach as you have just done with John, she will find you cold and unfriendly. High 'I's need to talk. Try and shut them up or push the task too hard and the rapport bridge weakens. People with an Influencer high 'I' in their nature like some preamble.

> 'How was your weekend Mary?'
> 'Oh, it was wonderful, let me tell you about it.'

High 'D's couldn't give a damn about the weekend. That's past. They went sky diving or bungee jumping and it's past and doesn't affect today's result. So why waste time talking about it!

High 'I's, however, like the social interaction and in talking to Mary, your initial rapport approach must provide time for talking about how her weekend was and how she is feeling. Then in talking about the vision and the work plans, your approach could be:

> 'Mary, if you and your group can do the work in this area, you will really be very popular with the whole team. We need this done well and you can do it.'

Appealing to her need for social recognition by giving plenty of praise and recognition and a chance to shine is the way to ensure Mary is highly motivated and in action, with her passion cylinders fired up.

If you have to, always correct high 'I's, in private to avoid perceived social rejection.

'I' under pressure

Under pressure and stress, the high 'I' Influencer like Mary tends to become more excited and talkative as they fear social rejection and loss of face.

If the tension really mounts, they may throw a tantrum in order to receive attention and have their recognition needs met. So under pressure, when things are not looking so good, make sure that you reach out to give your high 'I' Influencers the recognition they need.

Don't ignore them and don't bring in negativity. Keep it positive and optimistic. You need the high 'I's on 16 cylinders. especially in the tough times.

o RAPPORT WITH MORE RESERVED PEOPLE

People who are more reserved also tend to have much higher acuity. They are, in general, far more observant and perceptive than the more active 'D' and 'I' personality types. However, because they are reserved by nature, they won't necessarily speak up.

They are also more sensitive. This can cause problems when we consider the external zone of empowerment of the high 'D's and 'I's.

We discussed the external zone of empowerment that we all project in front of us in Chapter 7 on leadership passion.

The external zone of empowerment of the active high 'D's and 'I's goes before them like a metaphysical shock wave. I'm sure you've seen the large bow wave in front of a power boat. These people don't mean to project it so strongly, it is just their nature, their natural active energy. They don't notice it because by nature they are active. When cautioned they'll say — *'I had no idea I had that effect on people'.*

To understand the likely reaction of a more reserved and sensitive high 'S' or high 'C' person to the shock wave preceding the high 'D's and 'I's, we can use a metaphor from the science fiction series *Star Trek*.

In *Star Trek*, who are the baddies? The Klingons. The Klingons have spaceships that can be made invisible to the USS Enterprise scanners of Captain James Kirk and his *Star Trek* team. However, the Klingon spaceship can't fire its weapons until the invisible device is de-activated. So it uncloaks itself just prior to attack and thus appears on the Enterprise scanners before firing. When that happens, the USS Enterprise puts up shields to protect itself from attack.

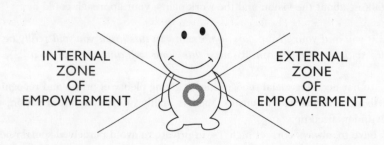

INTERNAL ZONE OF EMPOWERMENT   EXTERNAL ZONE OF EMPOWERMENT

It is exactly the same with these more reserved and sensitive people. As the high 'D's and 'I's power around, external zone of empowerment shock wave ahead of them, the high acuity 'S's and 'C's see them coming and say to themselves — *'Oh no, here come the Klingons, those dreadful, pushy 'D's and loud 'I's'* — and up go the shields!

It's no surprise the 'D's and 'I's wonder why they have trouble communicating with more reserved people, if they notice at all! You can't build rapport or communicate through a shield!

Rapport with more reserved people requires calm.

Rapport with more reserved 'S's

To build rapport with a more reserved, people oriented person with a high 'S' graphic equaliser, slow down. Because they are people oriented, they also need some preliminary rapport building talk – *'Hi. How is it going? How is the team? How is the family?'*

Nothing too exuberant. Nothing too long. You just need some basic, friendly introduction.

George is a nice, friendly guy but he is quieter and not quite as animated as Mary. George has a high 'S' Steadiness graphic equaliser. He is people focused by nature. There is a warmth in his eyes and in his voice, but he is definitely more reserved. He has high sensitivity and acuity and often sees more than the active people. However, he tends to hold his counsel and not speak up.

After the initial people oriented chat, frame up your discussion about the vision, the plan and the other team members in terms of George's needs —

'George, I need your help in involving the whole team. It is critical that during this

project we maintain an air of stability and teamwork.'

George will be very concerned about sudden or unplanned change. What would look like a crack in the floorboards to a high 'D' like John or a high 'I' like Mary would look like jumping the Grand Canyon to George. He will tell you that what you are proposing is absolutely impossible. It just involves too much change. So for George, crossing the Grand Canyon requires stepping stones:

'George. I appreciate your concerns, and I've thought through a 14 step plan of action. What I suggest is we go over the 14 steps and when you are comfortable, then I would like you and your team to initiate the plan.'

You show the high 'S' person how to deal with the change necessary to bring your vision to life.

'S' under pressure

Under pressure, people with a high 'S' Steadiness graphic equaliser like George, who are more retiring and more reserved, will tend to withdraw. They are looking for stability and pressure brings instability and change.

If you push them beyond what is a tolerable limit to them, watch out. They literally explode. When they go, it is spectacular. Why is that? Because in their need for stability and acceptance, they often suppress personal frustrations. These can build up over time, till one day under stress and pressure these suppressed frustrations and emotions build up and blow like the Mount St. Helen's volcano.

Boom — you trigger it all — a five year backlog of pent-up frustrations! When you see a more reserved, people person high 'S' blow their stack, it is very impressive!

So plan any required changes step by step and keep calm with them. (The graphical planning tool introduced in Chapter 13 is excellent for step by step planning).

You see how vital this skill of DISC rapport mastery is — to subjugate your own needs, alter your DISC graphic equalisers to match those of others to meet their needs so they stay on 16 cylinders, even under pressure.

Rapport with more reserved high 'C's

Susan is more reserved by nature and also more coolly task oriented in focus. She has a Conscientious or Cautious nature — a high 'C' graphic equaliser.

The high 'C's around you will bring great strength because they are so concerned with getting things right. They need detail, accuracy and quality and will work back late, even taking work home until the task is done 'right' to their own, self-imposed high standards.

The commitment to quality that people with a high 'C' Conscientious graphic equaliser like Susan bring to a team means they will often want more information.

Faced with a challenging situation, the active 'D' task people like John will usually be keen to take action. High 'C's like Susan will often argue, *'But we don't have enough information. To get this done well, we must do more market research.'*

They are usually right, but you don't always have the time in rapidly changing environments to gather all the details. Sometimes you will have to manage the over enthusiasm of the active high 'D' and 'I' graphic equaliser Johns and Marys. Often you may have to tackle the reticence of the more reserved nature of the people with a high 'C' Conscientious graphic equaliser like Susan in order to get them involved with less data than they deem necessary.

In establishing rapport with a high 'C' like Susan, don't be pushy. Calm it down, be precise and specific. Put more of a task edge in your voice:

'Susan. I would like your considered opinion. We need to discuss this in detail.
Then I need you and your team to draw up and initiate a comprehensive
action plan.'

High 'C' people who are more reserved and task focused, need detail, so give it to them. If you yourself have a high 'I' graphic equaliser, this rapport flexibility to bridge to a slower paced, task oriented high 'C' can be really challenging and tiring.

'C' under pressure

Under pressure the high 'C's like Susan can have a tendency to fall silent, because they have a need to be right and it is harder to be right when everything is swirling under pressure. If you really pile up the pressure on a high 'C', they may well withdraw because it is easier to withdraw and remain right than it is to stay and argue and risk the possibility of being wrong which is their greatest fear.

So they usually fall silent and then leave – 'You lot simply don't know what you're talking about.' What will people do to get their needs met? Anything. So to stay right, the high 'C' withdraws.

o YOUR DISC GRAPHIC EQUALISER SETTINGS?

Are you now clearer on your preferred DISC graphic equaliser settings? Are you by nature more people or more task focused, more active or more reserved? Where have you set your four DISC graphic equalisers?

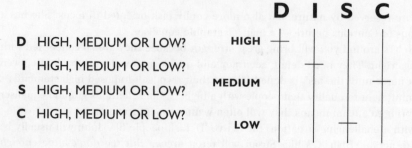

D HIGH, MEDIUM OR LOW?

I HIGH, MEDIUM OR LOW?

S HIGH, MEDIUM OR LOW?

C HIGH, MEDIUM OR LOW?

Clearly it depends on the circumstances. That was Marston's point: we behave in a way that reflects our perception of the environment and is best suited to get our needs met and avoid our fears being triggered.

This DISC rapport tool is a critical spirit intelligence key to firing up 16 cylinder passion and performance because if people will do anything to get their needs met, you have to make the right rapport choices and meet those needs.

John Geier developed some outstanding tools for helping you analyse the preferred DISC graphic equaliser settings of you and the people around you. They are currently produced by Inscape Publishing, Inc in Minnesota.

If you are attracted to an in-depth exploration of these tools, I strongly recommend you contact the authorised distributor in your country. (In Australia, contact Integro Learning Company Pty Ltd.)

o RAPPORT FLEXIBILITY AND DISC MASTERY

It is not possible to attain mastery of rapport skills in a day. It is part of life's journey. You may wish to include this skill on your spirit intelligence Commitments Register. If we are to play hard, I would suggest mastering this skill is a spirit intelligence necessity.

Mastery of rapport implies having the maturity to meet others' needs instead of your own. For a high 'D' needing control, the very act of delegating a task to a subordinate can be challenging. Because while the employee has the task to do, the high 'D' manager has temporarily lost control, activating their fear button.

It is unlikely other people will see you as insincere if you change your natural style to achieve rapport with them. They will welcome the bridge of rapport you are building.

You can do this with each individual in a meeting. The key is rapport flexibility, moving your DISC graphic equalisers. If you slow your pace down for the more reserved high 'S' and 'C' members of the team, you will gain their involvement. Then you can speed up to keep the 'D' and 'I' members alert. Your aim is to keep everyone fired up on 16 cylinders to achieve a vision and the results you are after.

To further enhance passion and enthusiasm, we now need to explore a range of tools and approaches that speak directly to the spirit within the people around you.

Ten

KEYS TO THE SPIRIT WITHIN

'We know what we are, but know not what we may become.'
WILLIAM SHAKESPEARE

To reach out to the people around you across the bridge of rapport and inspire their passion and enthusiasm, to make sure they are totally motivated and turned on, you need to know how to directly address their *en theos* – the spirit within.

Remember the word enthusiasm derives from the ancient Greek — en theos — the spirit within.

We have already found that one key to enthusiasm is to ensure that the people around you have 'something significant yet to do'. They must have clear vision and know what their role is, so they can relate to the effort they are being asked to make. Remember the spirit within is not looking for a job. The spirit within is looking for a game.

SOMETHING SIGNIFICANT YET TO DO

To raise the spirit intelligence in another person, you must equip them to make better life choices. What does that mean specifically and how can you use that as a passion key to fire up their spirit?

To explore this, we will initially review the life of Winston Churchill. As we discussed earlier in Chapter 3, he will always be remembered as the man who held the line for freedom and successfully led the Allied forces in the Second World War.

Not all of Churchill's activities could be termed wonderful, outstanding successes. He had his share of failures and challenges. He had a tough time at school at Eton and later, as

First Lord of the British Admiralty, he was closely involved with the disastrous invasion at Gallipoli in the First World War.

o LIFE IN TRAINING

In later life, when asked how he found the strength to take on the leadership challenge of the Second World War, he replied that he had experienced a long and varied life. He said that when he looked back on his life, he could see that he had actually been in training. At the time he didn't realise it, but it was the training he had received on life's journey that gave him the skills, experience and ability to tackle the leadership challenge, hold the line and turn the course of the war around.

'The farther backward you can look, the farther forward you are likely to see.'
WINSTON CHURCHILL

Field Marshall Montgomery, who successfully lead the Allied forces to defeat Rommel's Afrika Corp in North Africa, made similar comments about life as continuous training.

Churchill said of Monty – *'Indomitable in retreat; invincible in advance; insufferable in victory!'*

Clearly Monty was not the easiest person to get on with but he demonstrated great powers of leadership and motivational ability when the call to action came. With the wisdom of hindsight, he too viewed his life as training and preparation for that call.

o THE JOURNEY OF LIFE

If Churchill and Montgomery felt that life could be viewed as a journey on which we are being trained for challenges ahead of us that we may not even glimpse today, let us see if we can use that metaphor to help you to motivate the people around you and fire up their deepest passions – those of the spirit within.

As we noted earlier, all of us start out somewhere in life as an apprentice. We are all currently on a journey – working in a 'pottery' – at home, in the community or at work. We probably have worked previously in other 'potteries' and may move on in the future. So we could view life as a series of chapters, a series of 'potteries' that make up life's journey.

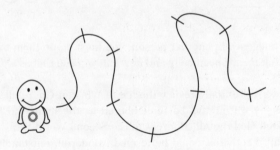

If we follow Churchill's metaphor that during our journey of life we are in fact in training, then the key question is what are we being trained for? The fastest way to help people become personally motivated is to speak directly to their spirit within and give them a wider, longer-term perspective on their life's journey by playing a game called the $25 million game.

o THE $25 MILLION GAME

The game is run in two parts and is specifically designed to help someone get in touch with their life purpose, what they really came here to do. Its ramifications usually extend far beyond their current role or occupation and current organisation.

The game can be a very powerful experience — literally a life-changing event. The game only works if approached with great personal honesty and courage. I invite you to take this opportunity and play the game.

Part One

Imagine yourself the recipient of a $25 million cash cheque which you deposit in your bank account. This enables you to pay all your credit cards, mortgage, school fees, car loan and any other debts.

Now imagine purchasing ten million dollars worth of residential real estate to be rented out to tenants. You can buy houses or apartments – the choice is yours.

Assume you would receive a rental return of about 5 per cent. For the rest of your life, you would receive an income stream of about $500,000 a year and as the years roll by, the rentals would increase roughly in line with inflation.

The balance of the $25 million goes to the bank for a rainy day.

The question for Part One of the game is then:

If you found yourself with an income stream of $500,000 a year and no debt and you did not have to go to work for the money any more, what would you do with the rest of your life?

For many people, this is a really jolting question. Some people initially say 'Well, I don't know' or 'I would travel the world' or 'I would play golf every day'. As they think over the question, they write down all the things they would do if they did not have to go to work for the money.

When running workshops, after about ten or 15 minutes have elapsed, participants are writing out all the things they would do, I say to them:

'Let us assume ten years have gone by. If you were keen on travel, you've travelled the world from the North Pole to the ice cliffs of Antarctica, from the great pyramid of Cheops to the Grand Canyon, from the Iguassu Falls in South America to the incredible lakes of Band-e-Amir in Afghanistan. When you have done it all and seen it all, what are you going to do with the rest of your life?

For the people who have been out and played sport, ten years have gone by and you have played every famous golf course in the world, you know every blade of grass at Pebble Beach. You have even played at St Andrew's 257 times. When you have done them all and played them all, what are you going to do with the rest of your life?'

For those people who say 'I don't know what I would do', I simply say to them — 'I appreciate that you don't know, but what would you do if you did know?' It is amazing how that little phrase can un-jam their logical left-brain and they start to articulate what it is they really want to do with their life.

If you did know, what would you do, now you don't have to work for the money? What is important to you? What are you passionate about? Who would you do it with and where and why?

The interesting thing for me, having played this game now with thousands of people — Australians, Europeans, Americans, Asians, Arabs, Fijians, Indians — is that regardless what part of the planet they come from, over 90 per cent come to the conclusion that they would like to spend part or all of their life helping either their fellow man or the planet or both.

That's what they'd really like on their tombstone — that they made a difference. Not that they made sales quota or drove a Porsche or got to be General Manager. Why? Because this exercise speaks directly to the spirit within. And we have already discussed that the spirit is not motivated by a job, the spirit is searching for a game — achieving life purpose.

> *'How strange is the lot of us mortals! Each of us here for a brief sojourn, for what purpose he knows not, though he senses it. But without deeper reflection one knows from daily life that one exists for other people.'*
>
> ALBERT EINSTEIN

Part Two

Clearly right now, for most people, the money is not out of the way. So the second part of the exercise, if we follow Churchill's example and map out our lives as a training journey through a series of 'potteries', is to then ask a second question:

> *'From the first part of the game, you may have a better understanding of your longer term goals in life, possibly your life purpose. What is it that you are receiving from the experiences and challenges in your current home and work environments*

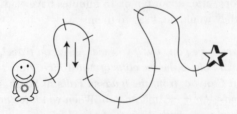

WHAT IS IT THAT I AM GETTING FROM WORKING IN THIS CURRENT "POTTERY" THAT IS TRAINING ME, DEVELOPING ME, STRETCHING ME, GROWING ME FOR THE BIGGER JOURNEY THAT LIES AHEAD TO ACHIEVE MY LIFE VISION?

that is training, preparing, expanding and growing you in preparation for the achievement of your longer term life goal or purpose which you may have glimpsed by playing this $25 million game?'

Part Two of the game emphasises what you are gaining from your current life roles at home and at work. Most people give a lot to their home life and especially their work. It is important to recognise that. This game is about the balance of giving and receiving, the principle of exchange.

What are you gaining from your home life and your work that is training you for your longer-term life journey and goals?

o SPIRIT EXCHANGE

For long-term motivation and enthusism, there must be a reasonable exchange between giving and receiving. This is not to emphasise anything selfish but to recognise a basic principle of spirit health.

Spirit intelligence means choosing to live in balance — giving and receiving. When the spirit within is chronically out of balance, usually giving far more than receiving, the enthusiasm dies and eventually the spirit disengages.

o SELF MOTIVATION

The principle behind the $25 million motivation game is simple. If people have:

a) more clarity about their longer-term aims and life goals;

b) an understanding that life is a journey and achieving life purpose takes time and training;

c) a realisation that their role on your team has longer-term benefit and significance to their personal life journey;

are they going to be more or less personally motivated when they wake up each morning?

If you can turn on someone's spirit passion by enlarging their frame of reference to encompass their life journey – against which they assess today's role on your team – you are moving them towards self-motivation.

o LEADERSHIP STEWARDSHIP AND MENTORING

For all of us, the spirit needs to be enthused. The spirit intelligence key is to ensure that there is a balance, an exchange, both giving and receiving.

Certainly you want the people around you to give enthusiastically, to achieve the vision that they have helped you co-create, but what is it they are receiving in return? What is it you are giving them for their life journey?

As a leader, you have a stewardship and mentoring responsibility to the people around you. They arrive as a metaphysical number 5 (on a scale from 1-10), a metaphor for the personal growth they have achieved so far on their life journey.

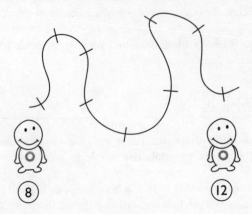

At a deep spirit level, irrespective of whether you are making railway engines, delivering merchant banking services or administering government policy, the fundamental purpose of any organisation is to ensure that the people under your care grow. So having arrived as a 5 they eventually move on as a metaphysical 8, as more experienced, more capable and more mature life journeymen.

> *'Character develops itself in the stream of life.'*
> GOETHE

Arnold Schwarzenegger builds his physical muscles by working against physical resistance, lifting weights. At a deep spirit level, the purpose of any enterprise is for the people to develop metaphysical 'muscles' by working on and solving home, community and work challenges and growing through the process.

> *'Life is a series of experiences, each of which makes us bigger, even though sometimes it is hard to realise this. For the world was built to develop character, and we must learn that the setbacks and griefs which we endure help us in our marching onward.'*
> HENRY FORD

o A PERSONAL GROWTH CONTRACT

If you are in a management position, consider developing a personal growth contract with each of your people to absolutely clarify their life path, your contribution to their personal growth and to maximise their enthusiasm.

The chances are that they will have never experienced this with any other organisation. Once they can see that there is a healthy spirit exchange and that you are concerned about their longer term life journey and their growth for that journey, then their spirit passion will fire up.

Some people may play the $25 million game with unexpected consequences. A client of mine realised she was out of exchange and off her life track and promptly left her highly successful sales career in telecommunications to pursue the joint challenge of a new career in photography and running sailing expeditions to Antarctica! If people are off track, they are going to know it at some deep level. They may not have had the courage or the clarity to face it without the $25 million game but they will know. They may have been going through the motions for years on about five cylinders. They lose, you lose.

Now if they can fire up, leave and get back on their life track in a new organisation so they can keep growing from metaphysical 5 to 8 what does that leave you? A gap or vacancy for someone to join you as a metaphysical 5, ready to be in exchange and to give and to gain as they grow by working with you, bringing your vision into reality.

'I think that most of us are looking for a calling, not a job. Most of us ... have jobs that are too small for our spirit. The challenge, then, is to make your own job big enough to give you what your spirit needs.'
NORA WATSON

Once people have played the $25 million game, they have three choices:

1. See their current role in a new light and fire up.

2. See they have stopped growing in their current role and either re-define that role or seek an expanded role.

3. Leave and find a new role and a new training challenge which opens up a vacancy for the 'right' journeyman on your team.

One of the toughest jobs of leadership, as we run our 21st century companies with flat organisation structures, is to see bright young people leave and move on because we just can't expand fast enough to keep them challenged and on that steep learning curve in our organisation. But they leave with our blessing. If we all understand the life journey metaphor, they can always come back in the future if the right slot appears.

In the meantime the metaphysical 5 new start needs your help.

Some organisations view leaving as an act of betrayal and would never countenance a return. That is an interesting stance. A master craftsman would always welcome back a high performing journeyman to help the team. Time away on the journey in the interim period can only have enhanced the breadth and depth of experience.

If someone comes to you and announces they are not enjoying anything like the balance they are looking for and they are leaving your organisation, then counsel them to review the opportunities on your team before they just walk out the door. Maybe they are not seeing all the areas from which they are gaining growth. Could it be they need to ask for an internal transfer within your organisation?

However, if they see they cannot achieve that balance on your team, then they must leave. Let them go in search of a team that gives them a renewed sense of balance and the personal growth they need.

Be careful in demanding loyalty. Loyalty is earned. You can set up a team. You can offer the growth apprenticeships. People show up and stay because it is the best place for their journey. When it isn't any more, you expand their game or they leave.

Is someone on the production line, who says they work shift just for the money, going to relate to this approach? Possibly not, but everyone has a spirit within. It's just that many people have shut down years ago, surviving life on three or four cylinders. Sure they do a passable job. Your challenge is to fire them up, even the 'shut down' ones, on 16 cylinders using these passion tools.

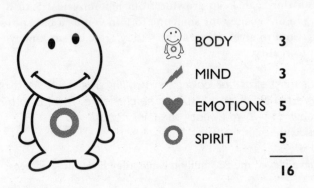

BODY	3
MIND	3
EMOTIONS	5
SPIRIT	5
	16

They say some organisations carry more passengers than British Rail! You can't afford to carry 5 five cylinder passengers in the 21st century. So turn them on or out.

o THE DYNAMICS OF BALANCE

Not everyone has the same goals. Right now, most people around you are working for money as part of the 'contract', but money is not everything and people have different areas of focus and priorities.

The following model may further help you and them understand their priorities and focus and thus assist you in turning on their passions, by empowering them to make better spirit intelligence choices.

The model is called the dynamics of balance and postulates that our life is focused across a number of areas of responsibility and interests. Life can place us under tremendous pressures and stress. However, for long-term health, there must be a dynamic balance between the various areas of our life. These dynamics have a logical sequence or hierarchy, although we may individually place differing emphasis on individual dynamics.

Understanding the importance of these dynamics to the people around you provides another spirit passion key.

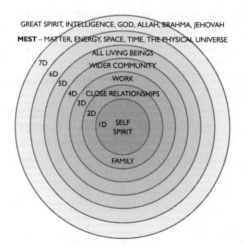

First dynamic — your spirit

The first dynamic is your spirit. You are the most important person in your life. It is absolutely critical that you look after the interests of your own spirit within. For optimum motivation, the spirit must be in exchange with a balance of giving and receiving.

You are no use to anyone else if you are shut down at the spirit level, just going through the motions. You must be clear what you need for spirit health. You already have some spirit intelligence guidelines from our review of clear vision and something significant yet to do. (We will cover more spirit empowerment keys when reviewing team culture in Chapter 12 and persistence keys in Chapters 16 and 17.)

Second dynamic — family & close relationships

The second dynamic is family and close relationships. You are of no use to your family and close relationships if you are sick, miserable or depressed with your spirit shut down. So your spirit comes first. However, life on your own can be very lonely. Looking after family and close relationships is the second important part of a balanced life.

The challenge is significant, but the second dynamic is a powerful motivator and a source of significant passion.

Third dynamic — work

The third dynamic is work, an important part of everybody's life. However, in order to ensure the priorities are clear, let's review the first two dynamics.

Most of us have had experience of working with someone going through a divorce. Divorce throws the second dynamic of family and close relationships way out of balance. Everyone involved suffers and it has a very negative affect on the first dynamic, the person's own spirit.

This in turn brings problems into the third dynamic – the workplace. A person in the midst of a divorce can sometimes turn into 'scrambled egg' for a while.

It seems clear that the first dynamic and first priority is indeed to look after ourselves, our own spirits. The second priority and responsibility is to our family and close relationships. Work, in fact, pales into third place. You are no use at work if your first and second dynamics are chronically out of balance.

For long-term 16 cylinder performance, you need to respect the balance and priorities of these first three dynamics.

We have to emphasise the word 'dynamic' because life can go out of balance in the short term. Sometimes we have to tell the family we will be away a month or working the next five weekends. Or we have to tell the boss that our son has broken his leg playing football at school and we need to visit him in hospital from 9am to 10.30am and come into work late at 11am.

That's why the model is called the dynamics of balance. You put the dynamics out of balance long term at your peril. Remember no one lies on their death bed saying — 'I wish I had spent more time at the office!'

Don't go home late just one last time from work and find the locks changed and the family gone. It happens. Aim for balance.

Fourth dynamic — wider community

The fourth dynamic is the wider community. Some people spend a significant part of their time helping in the wider community. It could be serving as a member of the local council, helping with the scout or guide movement or running local charities. The fourth dynamic is important because it can motivate people around you. It is not possible to make a significant long-term contribution to the community if you are dis-spirited and down, your family life is a mess and you are out of work. Which is why the wider community is ranked fourth.

By showing sincere interest and building rapport with the people around you, you can help them, where appropriate, to optimise their contribution to the wider community and thus increase their motivation and passion.

Fifth dynamic — all living beings

The fifth dynamic covers all living beings. The first four dynamics are principally concerned with the metaphysics of life — across self, family and relationships, work and the wider community. The fifth and sixth dynamics cover the physical aspects of life. It is important we look after our bodies and it is important that we care for all the other living things on this planet. Some people become very involved in caring for the environment. Greenpeace plays an active role in looking after the fifth dynamic. People around you may have a strong interest in the fifth dynamic. This is a source of passion for them.

You need to recognise and respect that interest and incorporate it in your dealings with people who are very involved in the fifth dynamic when building rapport and motivating them.

Sixth dynamic — matter, energy, space & time

The sixth dynamic is our physical universe – matter, energy, space and time. This is the realm of the toys, the houses, the BMWs, the powerboats, the ski trips and travel holidays.

The sixth dynamic is the realm of money. Clearly for most people, the sixth dynamic is very important.

We respect that many people place great emphasis on the rewards of their labour as a major contributor to their motivation and passion.

Seventh dynamic — great spirit

The seventh dynamic is what the North American Indians call Great Spirit. Others speak of God, Allah, Brahma, Jehovah, Universal Intelligence. It is the spiritual dynamic. In many ways, it is beyond the domain of your influence but clearly of very significant importance to many people. The seventh dynamic of spiritual intelligence, the choices people make in how they relate to 'higher intelligence', is often a very private domain and not open to public debate.

Devout Christians may object to swearing at work. Working on the Sabbath for some people is untenable. Observing the dawn to dusk fast during Muslim Ramadan is tough going. Doing challenging mental work on low afternoon blood sugar is not easy for a whole month. Respect people's seventh dynamic beliefs. They are generally not open to debate and are trashed at your peril.

Discreetly supported, they can be tremendous spirit motivators.

The dynamics of balance as motivators

It is important that you find out which dynamics are important to each of the people around you.

Is it that by working harder, with more passion, they can indeed earn more money on the sixth dynamic?

Is it in fact that their true passion is for their family and that the rewards from working hard, reflect back as a better family lifestyle?

Or could it be that they value the part-time nature of their employment because they wish to make a significant contribution to the wider community on the fourth dynamic or to their church, meditation group or religious affiliation on the seventh dynamic?

'If a man does not keep pace with his companions, perhaps it is because he hears a different drummer. Let him step to the music which he hears, however measured or far away.'
HENRY DAVID THOREAU

You are looking to turn on long-term passion. Understanding what is important for each of the people around you will give you a powerful set of spirit intelligence keys to ensure that what they are gaining from being involved with you is crystal clear to them, framed against their needs across the seven dynamics.

A further source of passion and strength derives from people's values and beliefs. We will now explore additions to the range of spirit intelligence passion keys you have at your disposal.

Eleven

VALUES
A SOURCE OF STRENGTH

'The way is not in the sky, the way is in the heart.'
GAUTAMA BUDDHA

You have mapped the territory, achieved rapport, catered to people's deep needs and inspired their *en theos* — the spirit within.

If we now re-visit the iceberg model of why people behave as they do, focusing on people's values and beliefs will give you another tool to turn on individual passion.

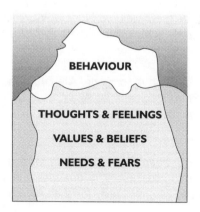

o VALUES AND BELIEFS

Our thoughts and feelings and thus our behaviours are strongly influenced by our values and beliefs.

A belief is an idea or concept that we trustingly accept and easily understand. Not everyone's beliefs are the same, and they can be contradictory. Christopher Columbus believed the world was round when many of his sailors still believed the world was flat. Thus his thoughts and feelings about the behaviour of sailing west across the Atlantic were different from his crew. Without his belief and courage, their beliefs and feelings of fear

The word value derives from the Latin verb *valere* to be strong.

about falling off the edge of the world would have caused them to turn the ship around and sail back home to Spain.

But what is a value?

A value is something that gives us strength, something that is very important to us, something we feel strongly about, something worth standing up for, something that gives our life meaning. Values influence behaviour. We can better understand someone's behaviour by seeking to understand their values.

I have known people with strong religious beliefs unable to attend weekend workshops on their day of worship, even though they were keen to participate and contribute. You may remember the story of Eric Liddell which was chronicled in the film *Chariots of Fire* who was unable to compete in a crucial Olympic heat scheduled for the Sabbath.

The actions of Japanese kamikaze pilots in the Second World War and Palestinian suicide bombers are clearly driven by very deep values that give those people the inner strength to act in a way guaranteed to end their own lives.

"Fight in the way of Allah against those who fight against you, but begin no hostilities. Lo! Allah loveth not aggressors. And slay them wherever ye find them, and drive them out of the places whence they drove you out, for persecution is worse than slaughter.

And fight not with them at the Inviolable Place of Worship until they first attack you there, but if they attack you (there) then slay them. Such is the reward of disbelievers.

But if they desist, then lo! Allah is Forgiving, Merciful. And fight them until persecution is no more, and religion is for Allah."

KORAN SURAH II, VS 190 - 193

"Ye have heard that it hath been said, Thou shalt love thy neighbour, and hate thine enemy. But I say unto you, Love your enemies, bless them that curse you, do good to them that hate you, and pray for them which despitefully use you, and persecute you."

ST MATTHEW 5, 43 - 44

Faced with the above quotes, someone could clearly adopt very different beliefs, values and thus behaviours.

We must respect other people's values even if we can't understand or agree with them. If you can understand and respect other people's values, you hold another powerful spirit intelligence key to their 16 cylinders of passion and enthusiasm.

o VALUES AND BEHAVIOUR ARE CIRCUMSTANCE RELATED

Value driven behaviour can be frustrating and difficult to understand and deal with, because values can depend on circumstances and can change as those circumstances change.

Imagine a very large breakfast bowl full of horrible, brown, live cockroaches. The whole bowl is squirming with them.

In normal circumstances with normal behaviours, would you eat this bowl of live cockroaches for five dollars? Most people would say – 'You must be joking!' Would you eat a large breakfast bowl of live cockroaches for 1000 dollars? You would still probably answer 'No.' What about for 100,000 dollars or for one million dollars? Would you eat a big bowl of live cockroaches for 100 million dollars?

Clearly, there are some people who might eat a bowl of cockroaches for 100,000 dollars and there are some people who would not eat a bowl of live cockroaches for 100 million dollars.

They have strong value judgments on what they will and won't eat — end of story!

But here is the next question. In different circumstances, where you have been in a dungeon for five years in solitary confinement, you are a hair's breadth away from death due to starvation, you know that you are going to be released in two weeks' time, if you can stay alive – would you change your behaviour and eat the cockroaches?

Most people answer, 'Of course, I would do anything to stay alive.'

Values give us strength, but they can also be fluffy and imprecise and loaded with all sorts of emotions and change according to circumstance. What gives your life meaning and thus influences your behaviour in 'normal' situations could be entirely different if you found yourself in the jungle, being hunted by a hostile force, separated from your family and your friends.

Yet values can be very powerful motivators and thus need to be elicited and understood to optimise rapport.

o UNDERSTANDING THE VALUES OF OTHER PEOPLE

If you can understand and respect the values of other people, you have another key to fire up their passion and enthusiasm. This is because people can feel very strongly about the values they hold.

Although values are powerful, they can be hard to elicit because they can operate below normal conscious awareness. The best way to elicit someone's values is to ask them to list what gives their life meaning. In other words, what gives them inner strength.

People can list a wide variety of possible answers to what gives their life meaning — family, relationships, love, understanding, recognition, work, giving, spirit integrity, honesty, fitness, respect, caring, money, possessions, hobbies, helping other people, results, freedom, health, friends, career, being of service, security, quality, challenge, growth, contribution, travel, learning, religion. The list is as variable as the people that write them and can cover all seven dynamics of balance.

However, everyone, given ten minutes, can produce a personal list of what gives their life meaning. It takes a bit of time because some values are deep and usually under conscious awareness until we stop and think about them. Try making your list.

Then rank the value list by numbering each value on the list according to importance. Then re-write the list of the top 5 values from 1 to 5.

1..............
2..............
3..............
4..............
5..............

Then test the relative importance of each value by starting at the bottom of the list and asking:

If I had value 4...................... and no value 5..........................., is that okay?

Try it on your list.

If it is not okay, then reverse the order to ascertain the sequence of personal importance:

If I had value 5...................... and no value 4..........................., is that okay?

If that feels right then re-number values 4 and 5 accordingly.

If that feels okay, then go up to the next pair and test again:

If I had value 3...................... and no value 4..........................., is that okay?

Then proceed to test up the value list.

This tool helps people clarify their number one value. In life, this is what they are striving for.

Knowing this gives them and you a profound spirit intelligence key to a source of their inner strength, passion and drives, especially in turbulent and challenging times.

What's your number one value? What you are striving for? Does it give your life meaning at a deep spirit level?

o COMPANY VALUE STATEMENTS

Many organisations are keen on developing value statements. Value statements are helpful in fostering spirit intelligence and increased performance.

However, as you quickly discover, people are motivated by such different values, and finding common ground in any group of people is always going to be challenging.

By all means try to find a set of common values. However, they will end up as general guidelines which do not appeal to everyone involved but, nevertheless, enhance spirit intelligence and the ability of the organisation to make better choices.

o SUMMARY

Over the last few chapters we have explored spirit intelligence passion tools and approaches to map the territory that surrounds you, to build rapport bridges of communication with the people around you and we have reviewed a range of tools to fire up people's passion by recognising and respecting:

   o their DISC needs and fears

   o their spirit within

   o their values

You can now adjust your rapport approaches and be flexible to match people's needs in all these areas.

These tools call for you to be something of a chameleon as you change style to maximise rapport.

Will people see you as false? My experience is they won't even notice. Why? Because most people are so caught up by what is happening in their own heads, they barely notice the level of skills that you are working to master.

You will build these rapport bridges for the most part below their conscious awareness.

In some regards then, you are a different person for each of the people around you because all the time you are striving to achieve mastery across that bridge of rapport.

You do not need to master these passion keys all at the same time. The goal of being skilled enough to inspire passion, enthusiasm and 16 cylinder performance in the people around you at home, in your community and at work is a vital demonstration of spirit intelligence.

Mastery is a life long journey. You may have heard the quote from the ancient Chinese philosopher, Lao-Tzu:

'The journey of a thousand miles begins with the first step.'

Don't feel overwhelmed. Take one key at a time and practice with it for a month or so. Consider committing to mastery of the passion keys as a life-long journey and goal if you are serious about empowering and inspiring other people.

Our discussion of passion, however, cannot rest here, because as soon as you have two or more people working together, you enter the domain of team culture.

We are all involved with a group of people at home, in our community or at work. Developing high performance teams is a vital spirit intelligence skill because you can rarely achieve your vision on your own.

How do you want your team to play the game? How do you want them to work together to achieve the vision? Chapter 12 will explore the keys to ensuring you keep the passions of everyone involved fired up as they work together as a team.

Twelve

BUILDING PASSIONATE TEAMS

'If we all did the things we are capable of doing, we would literally astound ourselves.'
THOMAS A. EDISON

Now you have the spirit intelligence keys to inspiring the individual passions of people around you, you have to fire them up and motivate them as a team. The key is team culture.

How do you want to care for your team? How do you want them to work together to achieve the vision?

The word culture is derived the Latin noun *cultus* — care.

o TEAM CULTURE

There are two crucial spirit intelligence keys that define the culture of a team that we will cover to ensure you have the tools to develop and sustain a culture of success.

The two keys to a success culture are:

o Trust
o Assertion

In this chapter we will review the keys to trust and assertion and how to apply them to unlock team passion and performance. This will help you maximise harmony and performance at home, in your community and in any organisation.

o TRUST AND ASSERTION

The culture of a team is strongly influenced by how much trust is present between the people on the team, and how much assertion is evident from the people, especially when problems and action choices arise.

Both these behaviours must be demonstrated for long-term 16 cylinder team performance. We will now explore practical tools to help you and your team with these team passion keys.

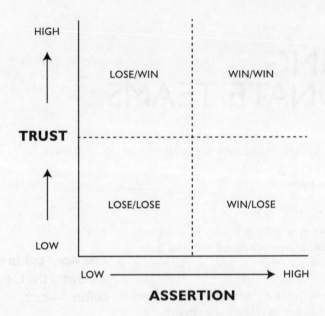

The diagram above has four quadrants for four different approaches to team culture. Each needs to be explored to consider the ramifications.

Low trust/low assertion = lose/lose

If there is very little trust amongst the team members and when problems arise, there is not enough assertion, nobody speaks up and weak decisions or no decisions are made, then the culture spirals down into lose/lose.

Lose/lose means the people feel like losers. They see what's happening, they turn off and their passion cylinders shut down. The team and the organisation also lose because no one is benefiting from the latent passion on the team. Everyone loses.

High assertion/low trust = win/lose

If there is strong assertion — even bordering on aggression — and very little trust, you can enter the domain of dog eat dog, the strong and powerful dominate and the team game that is played is win/lose. I win because I play hard, and you lose. Nice guys finish last. If you can't stand the heat, don't stand next to the fire!

There are two reasons why you cannot allow loud, assertive people to dominate a team with their pushy, potentially win/lose tactics.

First: Team = Together Everyone Achieves More – not just the pushy ones!

Second: The more reserved people have the higher acuity, they see more detail. If you let the strong and powerful assert all the time, the reserved people will fall silent and you and the team will lose their valuable insights.

There is nothing wrong with assertion, it is an essential skill of high performance teams. What you need is a practical tool for assertion that will 'level the playing field' and give the more reserved people on the team an equal voice. We'll come to that shortly.

High trust/low assertion = lose/win

There is great danger if without assertion tools, an organisation encourages trust and team building.

Out there in the real world games of life and business, there are the win/lose sharks waiting to take you out as shark bait. So where there is very little assertion, not enough ability to confront conflict or speak up and raise the real issues that are not being addressed, everyone can end up being too nice. 'NICE' is an acronym:

NOTHING
INSIDE ME
CARES
ENOUGH

Where there is mutual trust and everyone is being nice with no one caring enough or having the courage and assertion to speak up, then your team can wander into the dreadful domain of lose/win. The win/lose sharks are assertive, they couldn't care less about trust, they have a winner takes all attitude and who is taken out as shark bait? YOU ARE!

So lose/win means the aggressors win and the meek, trusting team loses. You've probably seen that amusing graffiti: *The meek shall inherit the earth... if that's all right with you!*

Clearly many people adopt a win/lose approach to life. Spirit intelligence, however, demands a more fulfilling, yet harder to achieve, approach to developing and sustaining team culture — win/win.

High trust/high assertion = win/win

If you are to move towards the resilient culture building combination that is the most fun, empowering, fulfilling and rewarding — the 16 cylinder environment of win/win — you need not only trust and co-operation, but also assertion.

To ensure you have a passionate team, a team that is operating at full strength, through thick and thin, it is important that we review both axes — trust and assertion — and equip you with practical tools for both skills.

Trust

Let us first review trust. Why is it that often in the pressured games of life and business, there is not a great deal of trust evident?

○ OUR WIN/LOSE HISTORY

Look at our history. Where were our ancestors living 4 million years ago, from the time archaeologists have found fossilised remains of primitive man in the Olduvai Gorge in Tanzania? In caves playing the game of survival. When lunch came onto the plain below, if Cave Family 'A' were slow off the mark and Cave Family 'B' grabbed lunch first, often Cave Family 'A' starved.

4 MILLION YEARS — SCARCITY
GRAB AS MUCH AS YOU CAN!
WIN/LOSE

4 Million BC

There was not always enough food to go around and so our ancestors often found themselves living in a world of scarcity, a world of win/lose. The fundamental lesson was – grab it while you can.

Even a few thousand years ago, people were living short, squalid, rough lives. Average life expectancy in ancient Egypt was 17 years! Our ancestors have been playing the game of scarcity for a long time. The game of win/lose, 'grab it while you can' or 'grab as much as you can' has been in our genes for millions of years.

Win/win possibilities

Agricultural experts have calculated that as a result of the recent 'Green Revolution' — the development of hybrid and gene enhanced crops, — we have the capability of producing enough food for everyone.

But that has not meant everyone on the planet today is well fed. About 45,000 children die every day from starvation and malnutrition. Every three seconds, somewhere in the world, a child dies and every three seconds an adult like you has to stop what they're doing, pick up a shovel, dig a hole in the earth and bury a young body. Every three seconds.

The win/win abundance potential

There is potentially plenty of food, water, energy and resources if we were to use them efficiently and effectively. Western farmers are paid not to grow crops. Eighty per cent of the world's urban waste water is not recycled. Solar energy is under utilised. In fact today in theory, the 6000 million people on this planet could play a new game, a game called abundance – win/win.

Scarcity versus abundance - 4 million years versus 30 years

We have 4 million years of win/lose scarcity wired into our genes. How many years of potential win/win abundance practice have we had, even if everybody knew that we had that opportunity? Just over 30 years, since 1970.

Under pressure, most people immediately slip into win/lose behaviour. They play it safe. That could be assessed as a sensible strategy. If it looks like there is going to be a loser here, rather you than me!

That's why 45,000 kids die needlessly every day. That's why we lose the equivalent of a football field of rain forest every five seconds and a species is made extinct every five minutes. At this rate of loss, with only 40% of the world's ancient forest cover remaining, the last tree will be cut down in well under 100 years time, and with about 30 million species on the planet, the last one will vanish in about 300 years. The world is, in the main, ignorant of the win/win abundance that is now theoretically possible and there is a lot of money to be made from the old fear-based win/lose beliefs. Where would the arms makers and traders be in a win/win world?

John Lennon's song *Imagine* expresses the longing for a win/win world, but please don't underestimate the challenge that you face in implementing an empowering culture. Achieving win/win requires spirit intelligence tools for choosing trust-building approaches plus practical tools for assertion, because under pressure your team members can easily revert back to win/lose behaviours.

o TRUST BUILDING TOOLS

What can you do to encourage and build trust on a team against 4 million years of conditioning? Remember, a team has to produce outstanding performance when the heat is on and disagreement about alternative action options is a real possibility.

In Chapter 9 on rapport, we reviewed the four behaviours of trust – reliability, openness, acceptance and straightforwardness.

Clearly, demonstrating those behaviours yourself and expecting those behaviours from your team members is a start.

The trust account

To help you build trust, a useful tool is the concept of the trust account.

All of us are familiar with a bank account. A bank account works very simply. You put money in, (deposits) and you take money out (withdrawals). If you deposits more than you

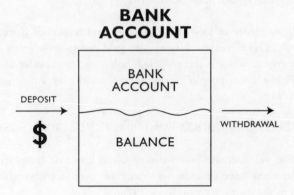

withdraw, you build a positive bank balance. What happens to your bank account if you start making more withdrawals than deposits? Your bank balance goes down. If you persist in this behaviour, it goes down to zero. If you persist further in taking out more than you put in, you go become overdrawn.

If you continue to withdraw, the bank will eventually close your account.

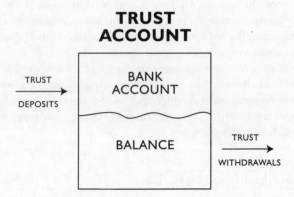

On any team, there is an equivalent concept called the trust account. It is intangible but everybody on the team instinctively knows the trust balance of the team's trust account.

Trust account deposits

To achieve a positive 16 cylinder team culture you need a healthy, positive trust account balance. How do you build up a positive trust account balance?

By making trust deposits.

By ensuring that your trust behaviours are consistent and that your team members are aware and agree to the need for the same trust behaviours.

By making agreements with each other and keeping them.

By ensuring that you and your team all use the spirit intelligence passion keys that we have reviewed to respect and nurture each other:

o their DISC needs

o their *en theos* — the spirit within

o their values

o their dynamics of balance

By aiming for improved understanding and ensuring frequent, high quality communication between team members.

Trust account withdrawals

Why are trust deposits so important? Because for every team, there are going to be trust withdrawals called mistakes. They are inevitable. You know the saying — those that do the work make the mistakes.

Remember the two teams – the winning team and the learning team. How does the learning team learn? By making lots of mistakes. So mistakes are inevitable. Even the more reserved, task focused high 'C' Conscientious people with their need to get it right sometimes stumble.

If a team has built up a strong, positive trust balance in the team's invisible trust account, the team can handle the occasional mistake — a trust withdrawal. The team will rally round, solve the mistake and use the mistake to increase trust deposits in the future through organisational learning.

However, if you make more trust withdrawals than trust deposits, the trust balance goes down and down and down until it reaches zero. The result is a demoralised team, in a constant win/lose scenario, running on only three of their 16 cylinders.

If the organisation then has to ask for extra effort from the people, they are just as likely to tell the organisation where to stick it! Win/lose eventually becomes lose/lose.

What are you going to do to build up the trust account on your team? As mistakes are bound to happen, it could be time to re-visit your Commitments Register and note down some specific trust deposit actions.

o ASSERTION

Having devised strategies to improve your team's ability to establish and maintain trust and cooperation, we now need to review the second crucial aspect of team culture, which is assertion.

In many families and organisations, everybody is being too nice to speak up strongly and address the real issues that should be confronted for success to be assured.

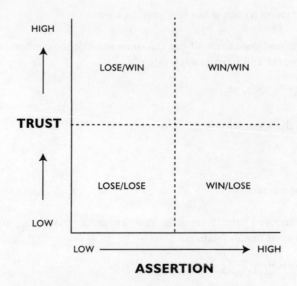

People on the team are just fluffing, super-fluffing or even denying the issues exist. I am sure you have been in meetings that have gone delicately around the problem with everyone being too timid or too nice to face the real alien of resistance.

The challenge is to be able to assert ourselves and our views clearly without becoming rude or aggressive.

This is a tricky. Well meant assertion by more active people can easily be perceived as aggression by more reserved and more sensitive people. You need an assertion tool that everyone on your team can use irrespective of their height, gender, loudness or nature.

An essential element of spirit intelligence is to be equipped with a communication tool of assertion to deal with difficult issues that are a barrier to success.

An assertion tool

The following icon represents one of the best assertion tools.

ASSERTION TOOL

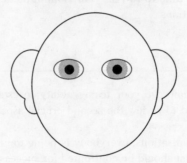

You can see the icon has two big eyes, two big ears and how many mouths? None. That's a clue! The words that accompany this icon are *'I feel like saying'*. It is a powerful tool of assertion.

ASSERTION TOOL

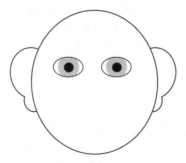

I FEEL LIKE SAYING

Using the assertion tool takes practice and introduction. In a meeting of your team, if somebody says *'I feel like saying'*, then everybody else shuts up and listens to what the person has to say.

Why do you need an assertion tool? Because, as you have seen already, the more active people with high 'D' and 'I' DISC graphic equalisers (with a need for control and recognition) can dominate the conversation.

What then happens to all that valuable input from the more reserved people? Remember that they have higher acuity. They see solutions the others miss. The problem is that by their nature, they are more reserved and so they are not going to speak up, especially when conflict is present in the team. If you allow this to happen, then your choices may well be sub-optimal and spirit intelligence is reduced accordingly.

The use of an assertion tool is great for spirit intelligence.

○ CONFLICT

Remember what they say about conflict: if two people always agree on everything, one of them is not necessary! Conflict is healthy, conflict is good, disagreement is good. You need conflict in your team if you are going to achieve quality answers.

If you place iron ore and coking coal in a crucible and warm it with a candle for several hours, you will end up with warm iron ore and coking coal. However, if you replace the candle with a white hot flame, you produce steel.

It is the same with developing vision, plans and team culture. You sometimes need the white hot heat of conflict and disagreement to hone steel-like responses and action plans from your team.

○ I FEEL LIKE SAYING

The *'I feel like saying'* tool is designed to engender balance. It gives everybody a chance to assert their ideas in a non-aggressive way. Once the *'I feel like saying'* words have been spoken, everybody else shuts up and listens.

The assertion tool is easy to introduce to your team. It is a great equaliser of rank, providing that the tool is respected. It needs explanation and practice like any other new tool.

In many cultures and organisations around the world, regrettably there is still a tendency towards male dominance. A tool like this can give women a chance to input quality data.

You can easily blunt or misuse this *'I feel like saying'* tool. If a carpenter takes out a sharp chisel from his toolbox and uses it as a hammer, the tool is blunted and can never be used again as a chisel. It is the same with this assertion tool. If you use the *'I feel like saying'* tool to open up a space in the team dialogue and then misuse the space by being rude or personal, you can wreck the tool forever. No one will respect or trust it.

○ AN EXAMPLE OF ASSERTION

I once had a very good sales rep called George and an outstanding technical support person called Bill as part of my team. Bill, the support person, was very reserved by nature, a classic high 'S' / 'C' mixture. He came into my office one morning, very distressed and upset:

> *'David, David, what was that phrase we're supposed to use — I thought I felt?'*
> *'I feel like saying, Bill.'*
> *'That's it.'*

Off he went down the corridor to George's office. I then heard him say in a very agitated voice, *'George, I feel like saying.'* That was it, the words were out, the tool utilised.

Now George could have said something like, *'Not now Bill, I'm busy on this proposal'*. But he didn't. He respected the use of the assertion tool. He shut his mouth and opened his eyes and ears.

I then heard Bill say, *'George, I am so upset. I have spent the last three weekends at the client's site. I have worked long hours and not seen my family. In one short meeting this morning, I understand you have undone all the work I put in. We can't go on like this.'*

Now George could have interrupted and said something like, *'Look Bill, the name of the game is selling. If we have to change, we have to change. Life's tough.'* But he didn't.

When the *'I feel like saying'* assertion tool is used with respect, it opens up a communication bridge between people that isn't normally there. Many communications are biased and distorted by people's emotions. No wonder communication in times of stress, is so challenging. That's why you need an assertion tool – to break old patterns and create a new medium of communication.

When Bill had finished his emotional outburst, I heard George say, *'Bill, I feel like saying. I am so sorry. I just didn't realise. We can't keep working like this. I too am under pressure. We simply have to discipline ourselves to have regular review meetings. Maybe every Monday morning for an hour till this current client crisis passes.'*

Away they went, benefiting from a balanced dialogue of communication, involving assertion and at the same time building trust and cooperation. Win/win.

Other uses for the 'I feel like saying' tool

The *'I feel like saying'* assertion tool has other uses. You can use it at the start of a meeting, because often when you have your team meetings, you will find that even though team bodies are sitting round the table, the team minds can be anywhere.

They might still be grappling with yesterday's problems, or worrying about tomorrow's problems, or be anywhere but in the room. So one of the uses of *'I feel like saying'* is simply to use it as a tool to make sure everybody is mentally present in the room, to ensure a quality meeting follows.

o RITUALS

Using the tool like this becomes a ritual. Rituals are important to any tribe or society. Rituals are glue, they bind the culture of the team. Using *'I feel like saying'* is a great ritual.

You can close your meetings with the same *'I feel like saying'* tool. It becomes another ritual. Then it can give everyone a final voice letting everyone leave the meeting with reasonable consensus. Usually people make some sort of positive closing statement that often includes a personal commitment to action. The tool forces them to clarify their summation thoughts before leaving the meeting.

o BEING NICE

Assertion is a vital tool. In most organisations people are too nice to be assertive. Remember, the word 'NICE' is an acronym.

If *Nothing Inside me Cares Enough* to be assertive, then the passion will die. Stop being nice! Start encouraging more assertion from your team.

o SUMMARY

Now you have a vision, preferably co-created with other people. You also have at your disposal keys to understand both your own sources of passion and those of the people around you. Everybody on your team is different. You have to ensure that your team members are all firing on 16 cylinders with maximum burning desire to succeed and passion to optimise your chances of success.

However, any team with a powerful vision, fired up with maximum enthusiasm and passion is not going to get very far unless you have the third success key from *Think and Grow Rich* — clear plans of action.

Part Four

PLANS

Making it Happen

The world is dangerously full of spectators and gonna do's.

Spectators are at their best at football matches. Screaming advice and comments at the players and abusing the ref.

If they were really that good, how come they are not down on the pitch playing the game.

It's the same in the game of life and business. If you create a challenging vision and game plan for your life and your business, the spectators will undoubtedly show up to critique your performance and explain where you are going wrong.

Gonna do's are the ones with the dreams but no action.

To live your life with passion and enthusiasm, spirit intelligence demands that you have plans to enact.

Thirteen

CLEAR PLANS OF ACTION

'The task of the leader is to get his people from where they are to where they have not been.'
HENRY KISSINGER

You have the vision and you have the individual and team passions fired up. What are you going to do?

The third success key is developing clear plans of action. Note there are two parts — plans and action. You have to plan and then act. The challenge of planning is to find the quality time as we all seem to be constantly pressured by important and urgent matters that have to be handled. You know plans are important but as they are not always urgent they can be relegated to 'tomorrow'. Carving out quality time for planning is a discipline that you and your team must master. Unless you do, you will continue to be swamped by urgent matters. Then your choices may be sub-optimal and spirit intelligence suffers.

Most organisations seem to operate in a consistent culture of urgency. Without plans, you can't tell which urgent matters are important and which are in reality un-important.

Good planning is a vital spirit intelligence key.

'We always have time enough, if we will but use it aright.'
GOETHE

'We have left undone those things which we ought to have done, and we have done those things which we ought not to have done.'
THE BOOK OF COMMON PRAYER

o PLANNING TRAPS

There are three keys to planning that can be traps for the unwary. Let's cover them now so you and your team can avoid them and succeed.

Planning trap number one — Fear of the future

The first trap of planning is fear of the future. Because the present is relatively known and the future is relatively unknown, many people have an uneasy fear of the future and so they find looking ahead to be challenging. They prefer to focus on living in the now.

That's why so many people enter old age financially under prepared.

'Those who cannot tell what they desire or expect still sigh and struggle with indefinite thoughts and vast wishes.'
RALPH WALDO EMERSON

Because most people seem to have a deep-seated, usually unarticulated fear of the future, you must have a planning method that avoids this first planning trap.

The planning tool we are to work with in this chapter handles this fear.

Planning trap number two — What's the next step?

The second trap of planning is slightly more insidious because it is not obvious and can snare you so quickly. Let us assume that you have, with your team, overcome any fear of the future and co-created a powerful vision of your team's future.

You stand now in present time, looking into the future at your inspiring vision. Somebody then asks what becomes the second trap of planning — the wrong question — 'What's the next step?'

Why is — 'What's the next step?' — the wrong question?

Because you have intelligent people on your team, they will all come up with plenty of good ideas on what should be the next step on your team's journey to achieving the vision. The issue is that all of their ideas have a little bit of personal 'ego' attached to them.

'Of course Jane's idea is a good one, but it's not as good as my idea!'

Everyone will have a slightly different view of what to do and the end result can be that everyone's ideas of action will want to head off in different directions, like the light from a light bulb.

To succeed you need a set of plans that are focused like a laser beam and that everyone agrees on.

The planning tool we will work with in this chapter neatly avoids the planning trap of *'what's the next step?'*.

Planning trap number three — The Merlin factor

Merlin was the wizard at King Arthur's court and this third planning trap is known as the Merlin factor.

In 1200 AD Robert de Boron described in his verses how Merlin was conceived when a devout maiden was visited at night by an evil demon. Her son Merlin inherited awesome knowledge of the past and present from his evil father and to recognise the goodness of his mother, God gave him the ability to foretell the future.

Merlin explained to King Arthur's knights that the reason he was so wise was that he could see into the future.

Furthermore, he explained, there was something that made it very difficult for the knights as they struggled forward in present time. Not only were they not able to see into the future but they were also dragging something really heavy behind them — the past.

We are all dragging our life journey past behind us and the third trap of planning shows up in the phrase *'that won't work!'*

Your team wants to move forward towards its vision with plans of action. Someone comes up with a good idea of what to do next. You can't see into the future like Merlin to know if the idea will work. However your team has lots of past experiences from their journeys through life and it is so easy for someone to say — 'No, that won't work' and then give reasons from the past to explain why.

No one on the team knows whether the criticism is justified or not, but the idea is crushed by negativity. I'm sure you've experienced this in meetings. Good ideas are crushed before they are given a chance.

This is a serious planning trap that can erode spirit intelligence by reducing choices and you must avoid it.

Quality planning

If you are to succeed in firing up the 16 cylinders of your team, you have to have a planning methodology that avoids these three traps of planning:-

1. Fear of the future — *'Let's just focus on today'*

2. The wrong question — *'What's the next step?'*

3. The Merlin factor — *'That won't work.'*

The planning solution

Fortunately this challenge of avoiding the three planning traps has been solved for all of us. There is a delightful story told by fellow trainer and facilitator Blair Singer. Parts of it are apocryphal and have been embellished along the way but it is a great story and essentially true.

The story describes the origins of a very powerful planning tool that will allow you to produce outstanding, high quality clear plans of action.

Back in 1961, a certain president went on world radio and television and announced to the world that his nation would put a man on the moon by the end of the decade. The nation was America, the president was John F. Kennedy. Kennedy did not personally know how to build a rocket to take the Americans to the moon.

At the time of Kennedy's announcement, one of the senior men on the American space program was a German, Wernher von Braun. He was Director of Development Operations for NASA. During the war, he had been one of Germany's top rocket scientists.

By the end of the Second World War, the Germans had a large weapons base on the North East coast of Germany, on the Baltic Sea, at a place called Peenemunde. They had improved on the early V1s and A3s and were successfully firing V2 rockets, flying bombs, across the English channel each night to bomb London. Work was rumoured on ideas for a V3 which would have flown nightly across the Atlantic. You can imagine how impressed the Americans would have been to have V3 rockets raining down on New York and Washington.

The Russians and Americans both knew that whatever the post-war era held, rockets were going to be an important part of the scene. So at the end of the war, they both made a grab for the German rocket scientists. The losing team received a one-way ticket to Siberia to work on the USSR space and missile programs. The winning team, including Wernher von Braun, won a one-way ticket to Cape Canaveral (as it was called until 1963).

When it came to rockets and space flight, young Wernher knew his stuff. So after Kennedy's speech, Wernher contacted the White House staff and suggested the President went back on the world television to explain he was only kidding. Reaching the moon by the end of the decade was not possible. It couldn't be done! The White House staff told him in no uncertain terms that the challenge lay with him and his colleagues unless they all wanted a one-way ticket to Siberia that same afternoon!

Fortunately the US Navy Special Projects office came to Wernher's rescue. After the war, it was very clear that not only were rockets and missiles going to be important, but if you had your rockets on land, they would also be sitting ducks for the enemy. It was necessary to have the rockets moving around on the water or better still, under the water. So in 1958 the navy formed the Polaris Weapons System Program with the highest military priority.

In developing Polaris, they developed a powerful new planning methodology.

The Navy told Wernher that to succeed, he had to avoid the three traps of planning. To do this, he had to go forward into the future. The Americans will be on the moon by the end of the decade, the President has said so. There is no point in being frightened of that future, it is a fact.

The second planning trap for Wernher to avoid was for him to ensure that he and his team did not ask the wrong question — 'what's the next step?' As the team members probably all had IQs of 160+, he would have hundreds, if not thousands of bright ideas, all with a little bit of 'ego' attached to them, all potentially heading off in different directions.

Thirdly, he had to be careful to avoid the Merlin factor cutting in — 'That won't work. We tried that in Peenemunde in 1943.'

The navy explained to Wernher that his planning approach had to be to work back from the desired future, from NASA's vision of success (a man on the moon), by asking one question repeatedly:

'What happened just before that?'

So was born the planning methodology called PERT – Program Evaluation and Review Technique.

Clearly we are all faced with multiple possible futures. The use of graphical vision enables us to choose our desired future and the PERT planning tool allows us to work back from that envisioned success. This is vital when linked with the reality creation tools used with the deeper parts of the mind. We'll cover this in Chapter 14 on the power of the mind.

o PERT EXPLAINED

The PERT planning method is a very simple and powerful tool. It requires you to start in the future with your vision of success and then plan by working back to present time by continually asking that one question:

'What happened just before that?'

Example — The Apollo mission

As an example to see the PERT planning process in action, let's review the case of the American moon landing. The success vision was Neil Armstrong standing on the surface of the moon.

What did he say on that momentous occasion on July 20th 1969 — *'That's one small step for man, one giant leap for mankind.'*

With Neil Armstrong standing on the moon, the PERT planning tool demands one question:

'What happened just before that?'

The ladder was lowered by the lunar lander, the Eagle, to the lunar surface.

'What happened just before that?'

The Eagle landed.

'What happened just before that?'

The Eagle undocked from the Apollo capsule orbiting the moon.

'What happened just before that?'

The Apollo craft went into orbit around the moon.

'What happened just before that?'

Mid-course correction.

'What happened just before that?'

Blast-off from Cape Kennedy.

The PERT planning technique works from an agreed future vision, planning in incremental steps, back through time.

Was NASA's ultimate goal to have a man standing on the moon? No. The ultimate goal was to have the astronauts back on the deck of the aircraft carrier in the South Pacific.

The astronauts are on the deck of the carrier.

'What happened just before that?'

The astronauts are retrieved from the capsule, floating in the sea.

'What happened just before that?'

Splash down.

'What happened just before that?'

Main parachutes open.

'What happened just before that?'

Re-entry.

'What happened just before that?'

All the way back from the moon.

PERT planning is effective

PERT as a planning tool is effective because it avoids the three traps of planning:

1. Fear of the future.
Your team starts planning out in the future with the vision they have already developed.

2. *'What's the next step?'*
Working back from the future produces more focused planning. People function well as a team when working back from their agreed future vision that has already inspired them. 'Ego wars' are avoided.

3. The Merlin Factor — *'That won't work.'*
Working back from an agreed future vision is a positive experience and does not bring up negativity.

You will have to try the technique for yourself but my experience with clients all over the world has shown that that this is a very powerful tool for enhancing spirit intelligence, facilitating better decision making and better choices.

Of course as time goes by, the external environment can throw up unforeseen challenges. Life is a game and the opposition are always plotting strategy.

When the unexpected occurs, the first question is — does the vision have to change? If so, so be it. If not, then — do the current plans need modification in the light of the new challenges? If so, then start with the agreed vision and plan back through the new challenges to avoid falling into the three planning traps we have discussed.

o PERT AS A GRAPHICAL PLANNING TECHNIQUE

Using a graphical planning approach to the PERT planning tool is powerful with team planning because it involves all the senses and produces plans that are visually striking and clear. Again the picture (graphical plans) is worth a thousand words (written plans). Let me explain.

You will need to set up large sheets of white paper on the wall and then give your team members post-it notes and pens.

PERT is a planning language based upon only two components, events and relationships. It is very easy to learn and use.

o EVENTS

An event occurs at a specific point in time and is described by a noun (a thing) and a verb (a doing). Let's clarify this with some examples:

The event is: Mount Everest conquered. Mount Everest is the noun (the thing). Conquered is the verb (the doing).

EVENT

**NOUN
&
VERB**

Each event is written on a post it note as a point in time and will be stuck up on the sheets of paper as you build the plan. More event examples could be:

o New ferry operating

o New bridge opened

o New product launched

o Book published

o Budget target achieved

An event is a point in time described by a noun + a verb.

o RELATIONSHIPS

PERT plans are made up of a series of events, linked by relationships.

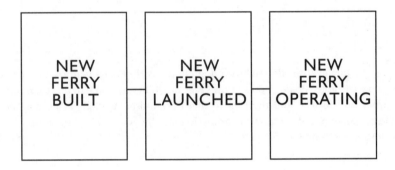

Before the ferry could be operating, it had to be launched. Before it could be launched, it had to be built.

Each event must be linked by at least two relationships to give the event a link to 'before' and 'after'. This is graphically shown in the diagrams.

o THE SEVEN STEPS OF GRAPHICAL PERT PLANNING

A graphical PERT plan is produced in seven simple steps.

Step 1 — Define major events

The first step is to review your vision and decide what key events must have occurred just before the vision becomes reality. These key events might be:

o New sales force succeeding

o New computerised customer database operating

o Market share of 25% achieved

o London office operating

In each case, the key event is defined by a noun and a verb. Each event (noun and verb) is written on a post-it note. Post-it notes allow great flexibility as you can put them up on the planning paper on the wall and then move them around as needed as the plan develops through the seven steps we are now covering. Eventually you will end up with a graphical plan that looks something like this:

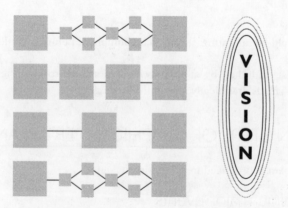

The first step is to establish the key events that occur just before the vision is finally a reality.

Agreeing on the key major events

The first part of Step 1 is to ask each of the people involved to write out (with one event per post-it note), all the key events that in their view have to have occurred just before the vision became a reality. Then ask them to stick them all up on a white board for sorting.

What tends to happen is everybody has similar ideas on the key events. The team groups and summarises all the post-its. Most visions tend to be supported with between six to ten key events.

They generally summarise functional areas:

o New computer system working — (systems)

o New plant commissioned — (manufacturing)

o New advertising campaign succeeding — (marketing)

o Sales force training completed — (sales)

o New office facilities opened — (admin)

o New product launched —- (innovation)

The first step, as the picture shows, is to establish your vision on the right hand side of your field of view, with time flowing from left to right. Then decide the key events that underpin that vision, the major strategic areas.

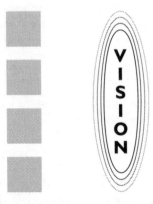

Imagine each PERT planning chart is like a rope bridge across a river with the events connected by the relationships. Your vision is on the far bank of the river. The river is raging and as a metaphor, represents all the problems and challenges of daily life. Some people are happy just to jump into the river of life without planning and the river sweeps them away to mediocrity.

If you want to secure the future vision that you and your team have co-created, you have to have planning rope bridges that link the near river bank of 'now' to the far river bank of the future where your vision exists.

Rather than weave planning rope bridges forward into time, which will bring up the three planning traps we have reviewed, start on the far bank of the river in the future and weave the PERT planning ropes back towards present time.

The key events underpinning the vision are like the pegs on the far bank of the river to which your PERT planning rope bridges are going to be attached.

Then you work back in time, asking that same question – *'What happened just before that'* but just concentrating on the major events back across 'the river' of time.

Step 1 only focuses on the major events. There are usually about four or five major events, which form stepping stones back from the future vision to now, present time.

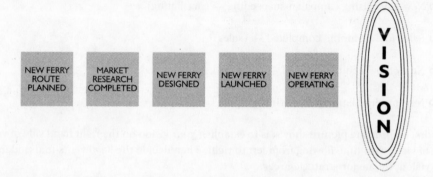

Clearly there are many issues to be confronted, such as the demand for ferry services, the inclusion of new technologies in ferry construction and conforming to possible new harbour regulations. However these are handled in Step 2 when planning the detail.

At this stage we are only concerned with the major events. So if you were planning —

o New Ferry Operating

You would take a large step back in time back by asking — *'What happened just before that?'* – and you might create another major event:

o New Ferry Launched

Clearly there is a great deal of commissioning and training work to be done between launching and operating a new ferry. But we are only initially dealing with the major events.

Then taking another large step back asking the same question — *'What happened just before that?'* — might lead you to a major event:

o New Ferry Designed

The question, again — *'What happened just before that?'* — another large step back —

o Market Research Completed

The question again — *'What happened just before that?'*

    o New Ferry Route Planned

The end result of the seven PERT planning steps will be to have your vision out in the future, on the far bank of the river, linked to this present time bank of the river by a set of detailed PERT planning rope bridges.

    When all the rope planning bridges are in place, the whole team can see that the vision can be achieved.

    All they have to do is take action across each plan rope bridge by going forward towards the vision, one step at a time. Having planned back in time from the future to avoid the three planning traps, the plans are enacted forward from present time.

Step 2 — Define minor events

Taking the simple planning rope bridge, currently outlined with four or five major events, the next step is to define the minor events. The same principles are involved. The minor events are still defined by a noun and a verb and you work backwards in time, inserting the minor events between the major events already established on the planning sheet of paper on the wall.

| NEW FERRY LAUNCHED | EQUIPMENT TESTING COMMENCED | EQUIPMENT TESTING COMPLETED | ALL EQUIPMENT COMMISSIONED | NEW FERRY OPERATING |

Start out in the future with the major event 'New Ferry Operating' — followed by the question:

    'What happened just before that?'

This defines the first minor event.

'All Equipment Commissioned' – followed by the question:

    'What happened just before that?'

This defines the next minor event.

'Equipment Testing Completed' – followed by the question:

'What happened just before that?'

'Equipment Testing Commenced'

This leads back in time to the next major event. In this case – *'New Ferry Launched.'*

You use the same principle in Step 2, asking the same question – *'What happened just before that?'* — just filling in the gaps with the minor events between the major events that you defined in Step 1.

In a marketing example, you might have — 25% market share gained — preceded by —— promotional campaign succeeding — preceded by — promotional campaign launched — preceded by — new product launched — preceded by — new product designed — preceded by — new product specified — preceded by — market research completed — preceded by — market research undertaken — preceded by — possible customer need identified.

Step 3 — Sequence the events

You will find this is a very powerful spirit intelligence tool to choose the best course of action to achieve the vision. As you use the tool, you may find that your thinking can tend to be very linear and sequential. You initially think about the events coming back in time in a single step by step process. That is OK.

Step 3 is to now sequence the events, after having established them, because much of your plan can probably be carried out in parallel.

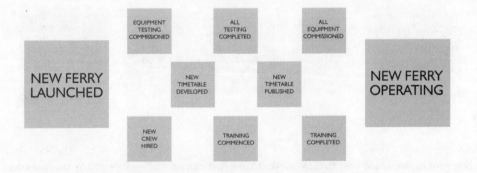

Planning the equipment testing could easily be done in parallel with training the new crew and developing a new timetable.

By using post-its on the paper on the wall, you can move the events around and work to achieve as many parallel activities as possible. It is this part of the seven step process that takes the time but it is the most rewarding. Remember at this stage you have not introduced any relationships into the PERT rope bridge to link the events.

As you work with the events to put as much activity in parallel as possible, gaps will become clear and because the tool is so graphical and so flexible, you can easily write up more minor events (noun plus verb) on additional post-it notes and insert them where necessary. This is easy because the outline of the rope planning bridge has already been created by the sequence of major events from Step 1.

Step 4 — Draw in relationships

Gradually the events, major and minor, which are part of the planning rope bridge, start to take shape. After a while when the plan has started to settle down, Step 4 is to draw in the relationships.

That is done by starting out in the future on the right hand side of the plan with the key event supporting the vision achieved and working back —

'What happened just before that'

and drawing relationships between the events. Working back from the future tests the logic flow of the plans you have developed.

Any event has to have a minimum of two relationships, one joining it to the previous event and one joining it to the next event. There can be more than two relationships linking any one event as the diagram shows.

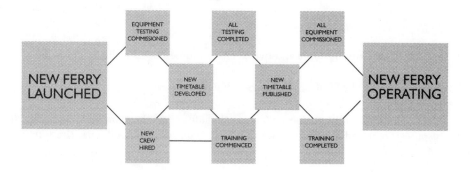

As the relationships are established, the reason for taking your time on Step 3 of sequencing the events before moving to Step 4 of establishing relationships becomes clear.

Because as you work on establishing and drawing in the relationships, working back from the future, sequencing distinctions are made and events continue to move around on the paper. There is nothing worse than drawing a relationship on the paper and then a few seconds later, moving the event to an improved parallel sequence and having to white out the relationship just drawn! So do not hasten to Step 4.

Eventually the relationships start to stabilise and as you develop the plan, you start to see why the metaphor of a rope bridge is so apt for graphical PERT planning.

Step 5 — Allocate resources

Once the graphical planning rope bridge is in place with both events and relationships, Step 5 is to allocate resources. As events are achieved points in time, the resources are allocated to the relationships. People, time and money are the main resources involved. A relationship can require people, time and money to complete.

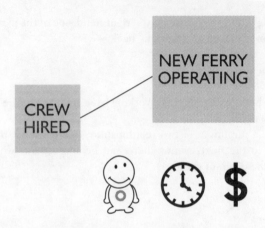

This one might take three people and two weeks resource between the two events.

Step 6 — Calculate resources required

Once the resources are allocated, Step 6 is to calculate across the planning rope bridge, the total resources required — the number of people required, the total cost, the total time involved.

Step 7 — Establish deadlines

The seventh step is to establish any deadlines.

There may be deadlines, such as a point in time defined by which you know something has to be achieved. The sales targets achieved event may have to be by 31 October.

The new ferry must be operating by 15 June .

There may be points on the PERT rope bridge before which an activity cannot commence. Maybe a new release of software, with the new features you need, will not be available till next April so you can't start work till then.

If you are climbing Mount Everest, you can't start till the monsoon season finishes in October. Then you must be off the mountain before the monsoon starts in the following May.

So deadlines and start times begin to define, both the resource needed to cross the PERT rope bridge and what has to be done by when if the planning rope bridge is to be successfully crossed.

Review the plan

The power of graphical PERT plans developed using sheets of paper and post-it notes and mounted on the wall, is that the whole team can be involved, working on separate planning rope bridges. At the end of the planning exercise, the whole team can visually (because it is all up on the wall in front of them) review the vision, the key events underpinning realisation of the vision and the PERT planning rope bridge attached to each key event.

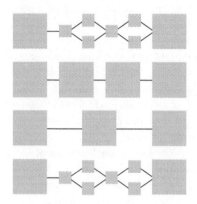

o ACTIVATING THE PLANS

Once the planning rope bridges are in place and the three traps of planning have been avoided, you can then activate the plan from current time into the future.

The power of both the vision and the graphical PERT plan combined is that the people on your team can see, not only where you and your team are heading towards the vision but also the plans that have to be enacted to make the vision a reality.

> 'What men have seen, they know.'
> SOPHOCLES

The PERT planning rope bridges combined with the vision provide a daily sense of direction. When the 'builders' (ie your team) show up, they can now see exactly what they are creating and what to do, day by day. The picture is indeed worth a thousand words.

You will find this is a very powerful spirit intelligence tool. You and your team can make the optimum choices. Enthusiasm and motivation are inspired when a way forward towards the vision is clear to all.

The war room

If you can, it is best to set up a war room. A war room is a meeting room that is dedicated to planning. You've probably seen the military ones in movies, where they have a big sand table in the middle of the room for planning manoeuvers. All relevant data is put up and left up on the walls of the room. Why a war room? Because a large vision attracts large aliens of resistance and you will need to be really well organised with strong flame thrower response strategies to defeat them and succeed.

As time goes by, critical data emerges and joins the growing visual data base on the war room walls. Discussion and decision quality improves considerably as your team can visually access a vast array of pertinent data.

You may be short of space at home or in your office but some of our clients have used this war room tool to great effect. It is worth the effortand it doesn't have to be fancy. A disused workstation or on the walls of a corridor could be a good start.

Clearly the graphical vision and PERT planning rope bridges form crucial war room basics.

PERT is a very powerful graphical tool. The whole team can clearly see the deadlines to be met, when various actions must be started and how different group activity within the team is linked to a common destiny, the vision achieved.

If you have a major vision and set of plans which will take months if not years to enact and achieve, you may choose to take the graphical plans and put them into a planning software package such as Microsoft Project.

Using a software planning product forces the discipline of allocating resources. However, this is a secondary benefit and much time can be wasted endlessly updating computer based PERT plans. The game is out on the field of life, not in the computer.

The key learning from my experience of working with groups in many industries around the world is that people are motivated once the graphical PERT planning rope bridges can be seen to be crossing the river of challenges to achieve the vision.

The spirit within realises the game called 'let's achieve the vision' can be won. That is when spirit intelligence really fires up with initiative, creativity, passion and persistence.

○ TEAM DECISION MAKING

The great advantage with a war room displaying both your co-created team vision and the graphical PERT planning rope bridges is you have created a visual framework for high calibre team decision making.

Spirit intelligence is about making quality choices. Graphical PERT is a very powerful, practical and easy-to-use spirit intelligence key.

When a problem shows up, action options can be reviewed and decisions made using the vision and graphical PERT plans as reference guides.

○ SUMMARY

A vision is 'out there', inspiring your team forward. Now it can be linked to the present by a set of graphical PERT planning rope bridges giving you and your team clear plans of action.

Progress can be visually ticked off as time passes. You already have the passion keys to motivate and inspire enthusiasm.

In the next chapter, we will increase the woo-woo factor and explore how understanding the power of the mind can significantly improve the quality of your planning. We will also explore the nature of reality creation and why graphical vision and graphical PERT planning are so vital in utilising the full power of the mind to achieve success.

This knowledge will give you the spirit intelligence edge to consistently achieve outstanding results.

Fourteen

THE POWER OF THE MIND

'Chance favours the prepared mind.'
LOUIS PASTEUR

Your goal has been to achieve a vision with your team by enacting clear plans of action. This chapter will show you how to use the power of the mind to gain an additional spirit intelligence edge in your planning and why the use of graphical vision and graphical planning are so vital to optimising the mind and achieving success.

o THREE TOOLS OF PLANNING

The 16 cylinder BMES model of body, mind, emotion and spirit has three body cylinders that are physical and the 13 cylinders of mind, emotion and spirit that are metaphysical. Here lies the clue to higher leverage planning because there are three tools that you have at your disposal in developing and then enacting your clear plans of action to achieve the vision. Two involve just the physics of the body, the third is much more powerful.

Tool 1 – Your body
The first planning and enacting tool is your body. You can develop a clear plan of action, then run round 24 hours a day enacting that plan.

Just using your body to run around doing the work is the way to an early grave. It is low leverage and very tiring. The game is 'business', not 'busyness'.

Tool 2 – Your team

You can quickly figure out that you can obtain more leverage by enlisting the help of a team. You could then encourage more 'busyness' by having your whole team running around 24 hours a day getting the job done! The statistics are indicating most people are working longer and harder, complaining of stress and reporting insufficient time for balanced quality of life. It's not surprising that working longer and harder in response to a changing, uncertain world is not producing fulfilling lives.

As only three of the 16 BMES cylinders are physical, having you and your team physically running around 24 hours a day developing and enacting your plans is also low leverage activity.

Tool 3 – The mind

High leverage planning and action must involve the 13 cylinders of the metaphysics of mind, emotions and spirit but as soon as we venture into the area of metaphysics, the woo-woo factor can increase for some people because Western school and business education does not encompass any understanding of metaphysics.

The power of the mind is, however, starting to be recognised as these quotes demonstrate:

'Today's successful business leaders will be those who are most flexible of mind.'
TOM PETERS
Thriving on Chaos

'Leaders of the future are likely to be more dependent on intuitive sensitivity.'
ALVIN TOFFLER
Power Shift

'The empires of the future are the empires of the mind.'
WINSTON CHURCHILL

To give you and your team the best quality plans possible to ensure you get the results you need, we will now explore a set of simple metaphysical planning tools that you can use to increase spirit intelligence and ensure better choices.

o KEYS TO THE MIND

The mind is a very powerful bio-computer. Everyone on your team possesses one. Unfortunately, our education system does not teach us how to access its full power.

This chapter will help you and your team access the power of your mind to improve your ability to succeed at home, in your community and at work. For the detailed metaphysical guidance you need to harness the full powers of the minds of your team, a path ahead has already been laid out in the book *Think and Grow Rich*.

Remember Napoleon Hill interviewed 504 of the world's most successful people last century – people like Henry Ford, Thomas Edison, the Wright brothers, Rockefeller, Woolworth, Gillette and Firestone.

Their keys to success lay not in physical planning but in metaphysical planning. In fact the book *Think and Grow Rich* is really a manual to explain the power of the metaphysics, the power of the mind, linked to the power of the emotions and the spirit. The people interviewed by Napoleon Hill were true spirit intelligence pioneers.

There is always a danger of slipping into a bias for action rather than planning using your under-utilised bio-computer of the mind. You will always have plenty of people around you chanting — *Just do it!*

> *'A man is not idle because he is absorbed in thought. There is a visible labour and there is an invisible labour.'*
> VICTOR HUGO

The metaphysical planning approach is nicely summarised by the eccentric inventor and genius, Nikola Tesla:

> *'My method is different. I do not rush into actual work. When I get a new idea, I start at once building it up in my imagination, and make improvements and operate the device in my mind ... When I have gone so far as to embody everything in my invention, every possible improvement I can think of, and when I see no fault anywhere, I put into concrete form the final product of my brain.'*
> NIKOLA TESLA

You see the 'bias for action' trap all the time as senior management work longer and longer hours, moving efficiently from physical meeting to physical meeting, using their journeymen experience to battle the ever present sense of urgency and crisis, never pausing to optimise the metaphysical leverage of themselves or their people.

Buckminster Fuller explained that the leadership leverage challenge is a generalised principle that he called *ephemeralisation* – doing more and more with less and less.

In the physical world, you see this generalised principle of *ephemeralisation* all around us. The change from valves to transistors to silicon chips is a classic example of doing more with less, as is the communication evolution from smoke signals and drums to letters to Morse code telegraph to fax to Internet and e-mail. We have improved telecommunications from using chunky copper cables to hair-like strands of glass fibre, doing more and more with less and less.

Using more mind energy in thinking and planning rather than using the physical energy of action and doing is clearly a major *ephemeralisation* step. This is a critical spirit intelligence skill of choosing a more efficient approach.

Let's now explore how to use the bio-computer of the mind.

A BIO-COMPUTER USER'S MANUAL

Think and Grow Rich provides operating rules for working with the highest leverage planning tool of all, the human mind. It is a user's manual for a bio-computer so powerful, it could never be reproduced with current technology.

We will explore planning, creativity and original thought using the bio-computer of the mind to assist you get the results you want and, in business, move way ahead of your competition and achieve your success vision.

These quotes from *Think and Grow Rich* present a structured approach to high leverage, metaphysical planning power and thus increasing spirit intelligence:

QUOTES FROM THINK AND GROW RICH

Thoughts are things
'We move towards our Dominant Thoughts.'

Desire
'There are no limitations to the mind except those we acknowledge.'

Faith
'All thoughts which have been emotionalised (given feeling) and mixed with faith begin immediately to translate themselves into their physical equivalent or counterpart.'

Auto-suggestion
'For amazing results, get the deepest part of your mind to go to work for you. Back this with emotion power and the combination is terrific.'

Specialised Knowledge
'You find the knowledge that takes you where you want to go.'

Imagination
'Imagination is the workshop of your mind, capable of turning mind energy into accomplishment and wealth.'

Organised Planning
'It is necessary to plan and to organise in order to get rich. Staying poor is easy, poverty needs no plan.'

Decision
'Lack of decision is a major cause of failure. A made up mind attunes itself to tremendous extra power.'

Persistence
'Persistence is an essential factor in the procedure. The basis of persistence is the power of will.'

Power of the Master Mind
'Great power can be accumulated through no other principle.'

The Subconscious Mind
'Your subconscious mind waits like a sleeping giant to back up every plan and purpose.'

The Brain
'You find amazing new powers in every part of your mind.'

The Sixth Sense
'Inspirations and Hunches no longer pass you by.'

Exploring these concepts will give you and your team practical tools to harness the extraordinary bio-computing power of the mind that every organisation is paying for and very few are using. You will start to see the metaphysical spirit intelligence keys to success are already in your possession as we proceed.

In this chapter, we will review and explore each of the previous quotes to see how you can use the wisdom and knowledge they contain to optimise your vision achievement.

o THOUGHTS ARE THINGS

Thoughts are things. Thoughts – in the realm of the metaphysics of the mind – are just as real as things in the domain of physics.

Your vision and PERT plan events or milestones can be held as powerful thoughts amplified as pictures. As we shall see, the mind is very visual and the full power of graphical vision and graphical PERT planning will become apparent.

o WE MOVE TOWARDS OUR DOMINANT THOUGHTS

We move towards our dominant thoughts. As thoughts are metaphysical things, if you program those thoughts (your vision and PERT milestone events) into the human bio-computer, the mind becomes a goal-seeking device.

We have already discussed that significant vision has significant metaphysical mass and thus activates the law of metaphysical gravity to attract the people and resources you need for success.

You too are drawn forward by that same metaphysical gravity pulling you towards the vision and goals that you have created. You do indeed move towards your dominant thoughts — your vision and goals.

This chapter shows you how to access and program the deeper parts of your mind to harness metaphysical gravity and benefit all aspects of your life.

> 'Life is what happens to you while you are planning your life!'
> JOHN LENNON

Despite John Lennon's amusing contribution, life in fact presents a fundamental choice of viewpoint. Either reality happens to us from 'out there' and as potential victims we respond as best we can, or in some way, as victors, we create our own reality.

Spirit intelligence requires us to take responsibility for our current circumstances and our life journey and accept the latter idea — that indeed we do create our own reality from what we think about.

In the realm of thought, your graphical vision and PERT plan events (the milestones) are your goals — statements of what you want to achieve in the future. These goal thoughts can be energised by the passion and desire of your emotions and the enthusiasm and commitment of your spirit.

Programming these vision and PERT event goal thoughts into the deeper parts of the mind is like broadcasting them into an intelligent metaphysical universe because, as countless philosophers have told us, at a deep level we are all connected as one.

The intelligent universe then responds like a giant feedback machine giving you indications of progress and encouragement if you are on the right track (we call these ticks) and little taps on the shoulder if you are 'off track', allowing you to take corrective action towards your vision.

The advantage and power of these mind tools means you do not have to have all the answers to start with. Often the universal intelligence feedback system comes up with unexpected alternative solutions on the journey towards the vision. We'll cover this later in this chapter when reviewing the power of the mastermind.

To optimise contact and alignment with your own reality creating mechanism, you need to understand how to use the deeper parts of your mind to broadcast the strongest possible signal of what it is that you want.

A common problem for individuals, families and organisations with a weak vision or no vision is that they are so vulnerable to others' visions, goals and thoughts. Just as an asteroid is drawn to the larger physical mass of the sun rather than the Earth, strong visions, goals and thoughts exert more pulling power than weak ones.

The word mortgage derives from the old French words *mors* and *gage* pledged till death.

Whatever your vision and goals are for your life, there will always be other people and groups with their counter visions and goals of what they want for and from you. These counter visions and goals of others may act at right angles or be diametrically opposed to your own aspirations.

As an example, it seems the banks' mortgage vision for you may not completely align with your personal and family vision of financial independence, security and freedom!

To counter-act this cross and counter vision and goal 'noise' from others, you need to broadcast the strongest possible vision and goal signals for what you want. Otherwise you may not be influential enough to achieve your vision of success. That is why in earlier chapters we first covered the tools to develop strong graphical vision anchored with comprehensive graphical PERT plans.

This chapter shows you how to access and use the deepest parts of your mind to send out the strongest vision and goal 'signals'. Imagine the signal strength if everyone on your team used these powerful mind tools.

Let's start by looking at the structure of the bio-computer of the mind. This will provide you with the keys to program your mind and those of your team for maximum power.

o THE STRUCTURE OF OUR BIO-COMPUTER — THE MIND

There are three parts to the bio-computer of the mind, the conscious mind, the subconscious mind and the superconscious mind.

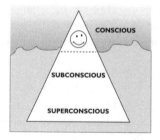

'The mind is an iceberg.
It floats with only one seventh of its bulk above water.'
SIGMUND FREUD

The conscious mind

The conscious mind is the part of your mind that you are aware of. If you have never observed your conscious mind, just pause here. Close your eyes for a couple of minutes and just observe. Go on! Have a go!

What was happening in your mind? Was it spinning along, only partially under your control, with many thoughts just appearing? Was it blank! If your conscious mind is like mine, it is a speedy place, where thoughts spin around endlessly. Some you control, some just seem to appear and disappear. If you pay attention for long enough, you may come to the frightening conclusion that you are not totally in control of the thoughts that stream into your conscious mind. That is not a criticism, but for most people, an observable fact.

Your bio-computer seems to be generating output (thoughts) from programs that you are unaware of. Some of the outputs seem disjointed, almost random. A bit worrying really.

If you had a 10 million dollar mainframe computer that kept ceaselessly pumping out random output, you'd probably call the IBM service department pretty quickly. However, we let our conscious bio-computers run like this, seemingly unchallenged!

The subconscious mind

Beneath the surface of the conscious mind, lies the subconscious mind, which is where early psychiatrists such as Sigmund Freud spent such a lot of time exploring. The subconscious mind is, as the word suggests, below your conscious awareness. It is a very powerful part of the mind. It runs multiple programs that keep you as a functioning, thinking, problem solving being.

The more you pause to wonder at the complexity of your digestive system or your liver or your self-healing abilities, the more you start to realise the power in your subconscious bio-computer. If it's clever enough to figure all that out, don't you think it is a bit silly not to involve it in helping to achieve your team's plans and vision?

The superconscious mind

Deeper still in our minds lies the realm of the superconscious, which fascinated psychiatrists such as Carl Jung in his exploration of the collective unconscious. The superconscious is very high woo-woo terrain for most of us. Imagine being able to access wisdom and intuition from universal intelligence to improve your plans and realise your vision. Now that is real bio-computing power and planning leverage – optimising spirit intelligence.

Maximum bio-computer leverage

If you are to use the full leverage power of your bio-computer, you need to understand how to access not only the conscious mind but also the subconscious and superconscious. If we were to use a computer analogy, the conscious mind can be thought of as the personal computer. It has a reasonable processing power, but limited nonetheless. Researchers have shown that most of us can hold about five things in our conscious mind at any one time. It is not a powerful computer compared with the subconscious mind.

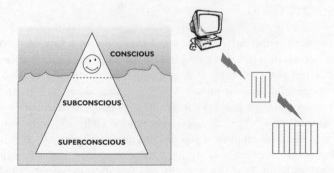

Continuing the analogy, the subconscious mind can be viewed as a mainframe and the superconscious is like a supercomputer.

If you want to have excellent plans that harness all of the available intelligence of you and your team, where would you run the programs to analyse your planning options? In the relatively small work station of the conscious mind or would you put the challenge of achieving your vision into the mainframe or the supercomputer?

The answer is very clear. If your vision is the stretch that it should be — something significant yet to do — then you need maximum bio-computer processing power. You need to know how to access the super bio-computers of you and your team.

You have probably read that large geological survey analysis computer programs can take hours if not days to run, even on a supercomputer. You need this sort of processing power too. The power of your superconscious dwarfs the processing power of the conscious mind, the PC.

In essence, *Think and Grow Rich* is about how to program the awesome power of the superconscious, your super bio-computer. How do you think people like the Wright brothers, Henry Ford and Andrew Carnegie achieved such success? Were they really so much smarter than you and your team? Or were they accessing some 'unfair' advantage? As Henry Ford left school in 1879 at 16 to become a machinist apprentice in Detroit, he didn't have the privilege of a full education, so he had to figure it out for himself. Andrew Carnegie had no formal education. He went to the US from Scotland in 1848 at the age of 13 and started work in a cotton mill. He never went to school.

The business masters from *Think and Grow Rich* uncovered the principles of metaphysical success from experience. So let us now have a detailed look at their instructions and make comments on each so that you can maximise the use of your mind and those on your team to achieve optimum spirit intelligence.

o REVIEWING THE QUOTES FROM *THINK AND GROW RICH*

Thoughts are Things
'We move towards Dominant Thoughts.'

If you set up your graphical vision and PERT milestone events as clear thought goals, they have a metaphysical reality, exerting metaphysical gravitational attraction and your bio-computer starts working out ways to achieve these goals — to bring them from the metaphysics of thought into the physical reality of results.

Desire
'There are no limitations to the mind except those we acknowledge.'

This sentence is so simple and yet so powerful. You and your team own unlimited bio-computer processing power. You just need to learn how to harness it.

Faith
'All thoughts which have been emotionalised (given feeling) and mixed with

faith begin immediately to translate themselves into their physical equivalent or counterpart.'

This sentence is also almost unbelievable in its statement that our metaphysical thoughts create our physical reality. Thought (three cylinders of mind) plus emotion (five cylinders of emotion) plus faith (faith is the domain of spirit – five cylinders) means harnessing the 13 cylinders of metaphysics.

> 'Faith is to believe what we do not see, and the reward of this faith is to see what we believe.'
>
> SAINT AUGUSTINE

The power to realise your team vision lies in the metaphysics of your team.

Auto-suggestion

'For amazing results, get the deepest part of your mind to go to work for you. Back this with emotion power and the combination is terrific.'

The language from 1908 is interesting: 'amazing', 'terrific.' Use the super bio-computer is the clear message.

Specialised Knowledge

'You find the knowledge that takes you where you want to go.'

This is just common sense.

Imagination

'Imagination is the workshop of your mind, capable of turning mind energy into accomplishment and wealth.'

This is the same message – changing the metaphysical mind energy of planning into physical accomplishment and results.

> 'We are what we think. All that we are arises with our thoughts. With our thoughts we make our world.'
>
> GAUTAMA BUDDHA

Organised Planning

'It is necessary to plan and to organise in order to get rich. Staying poor is easy, poverty needs no plan.'

No comment!

Decision

'Lack of decision is a major cause of failure. A made up mind attunes itself to tremendous extra power.'

Decision is another term for commitment. We will explore harnessing this 'extra power' shortly.

Persistence
'Persistence is an essential factor in the procedure. The basis of persistence is the power of will.'

The will is located in the solar plexus. You must learn to contact and use your will power. It is a vital leadership skill. Will power is demonstrated by the power of intent.

The word intent is derived from the Latin *in tendere* to stretch towards — your vision.

Power of the Mastermind
'Great power can be accumulated through no other principle.'

That is why we will cover this mastermind principle in depth in this chapter.

The Subconscious Mind
'Your subconscious mind waits like a sleeping giant to back up every plan and purpose.'

If the subconscious bio-computer is sleeping, it won't process your vision plans. That's why this chapter shows you how to wake it up and use it.

The Brain
'You find amazing new powers in every part of your mind.'

As most people know so little about using their bio-computer, the new powers probably will amaze you.

The Sixth Sense
'Inspirations and hunches no longer pass you by.'

This is when the metaphysics really start to work for you and your team because you are using them consciously.

You can start to see the scope of *Think and Grow Rich* and the spirit intelligence messages and tools that Andrew Carnegie wanted to pass on to you when he sponsored Napoleon Hill back in 1908 to interview the 504 successful people and write the book as we discussed earlier.

o PROGRAMMING THE SUPER BIO-COMPUTER

Now you understand that everyone on your team has a super bio-computer, how do you access and program it? It is very simple. The method of programming the supercomputer is done initially by goal setting. You may have come across goal setting before.

> *'If we could first know where we are, and whither we are tending, we could better judge what to do and how to do it.'*
>
> ABRAHAM LINCOLN

There are a number of key rules that are essential for goals to be used correctly in programming the mind.

○ BIO COMPUTER PROGRAMMING — GOAL SETTING

Goals are defined as events that you wish to occur in the future. The important key to goal setting is to be clear on what the goal is. Don't worry too much about how to achieve it – that is the job of your super bio-computer, to figure out the 'how.'

Your vision achieved is a goal. Any event on the graphical PERT planning rope bridges can be a goal.

Goal setting rule 1 — facts and feelings

The first rule of goal setting is that the goals must involve facts and feelings.

> *It is April 15th, I am taking delivery of our new mark 4 research spectroscope and the whole team is feeling really excited.*

Why is it important that the goal involves facts and feeling? Because, as you've probably read, research has shown that our brain can be thought of as functioning in two halves — a left brain and a right brain. The left brain is the domain of facts, logic, numbers, data and quantitative analysis. The right brain is more intuitive, involving feelings, qualitative information and pictures. Including both data and feelings in the goal means it can be worked on by both the left and the right sides of the brain. This is a sensible approach. You might as well use all the bio-computing power available.

Goal setting rule 2 — present tense

The second rule of goal setting is that goals must be written in the present tense. This is because time is a construct of the conscious mind. In the subconscious and the superconscious mind, time does not exist — there is only the eternal 'now'.

A goal, when inserted into the bio-computer as a program, can only be run in the subconscious and superconscious if it is written in the present tense.

To continue our computing analogy, if you write the goal in the future tense — *'I will be driving a Porsche by the end of next year'*, the super bio-computer scans the future tense 'will' and nothing happens.

If you write your goals in the past tense — *'I have bought my new Porsche, I did it'*, the super bio-computer scans the past tense 'have' and again does nothing.

As Napoleon Hill says, our super bio-computer waits like a sleeping giant. So to wake it up, the second rule is that the bio-computer programming language is present tense.

It is (present tense) October 20th, our new radio astronomy dish is being (present tense) commissioned and made ready for use. We are (present tense) all so excited at the new possibilities before us.

Many people find it really challenging to write goals in the present tense. After all, you knows that the goal is not yet achieved, it is clearly a future event. So watch that the future tense 'will be' or the past tense 'have' do not creep in to your bio-computer goal setting programming.

Goal setting rule 3 — visualise the goal achieved

The third rule of goal setting is that you must be able to shut your eyes and visualise the goal. Clearly if you and your team have done the work on the visuals of a vision and graphical PERT plans, this should be easy.

Visualising pictures is required because the right brain thinks in pictures. Our education system tends to emphasise the left brain — the facts and data. It pays less attention to the qualitative and intuitive visual power of the right brain.

Goal setting rule 4 — goals must be yours

Goals must be yours. You must really want them. No one's bio-computer is going to be fired up by goals imposed by someone else. The passion of the emotions and the commitment and enthusiasm of the spirit must be real. The power of your emotions and spirit are keys to your bio-computer power.

Goal setting rule 5 — short-term and long-term goals must be logically consistent

For the bio-computer to compile your goal programs they must be logically consistent.

My long-term goal is achieving financial independence over the next five years and my short-term goal is spending more time with my family than ever before.

This sounds highly unlikely as a logical strategy and may not run successfully as a bio-computer program.

Goal setting rule 6 — goals must be consistent with your values

Your goals must align with your values.

My long term goal is being financially free and working for Greenpeace on a voluntary basis. In achieving that income, I am becoming sales man of the year selling large numbers of anti-personnel land mines for my company.

These are not consistent goals and again may not run on the bio-computer as they are contradictory in terms of spirit integrity.

○ BIO-COMPUTER PROGRAMMING
INSERTING THE PROGRAMS

It is not enough just to set the goals. You have to learn how to install them into the super bio-computer. It is possible just to read or affirm the goals over and over again to insert them into the PC of the conscious mind. There is, however, a much more powerful, yet very simple technique that you can teach yourself to program the super bio-computer so it can work on your goals and give you additional ideas on how to achieve your plan and vision.

Just as in the case of the supercomputer running huge analysis programs, you may not receive an answer immediately because some of the goals need to be run for maybe minutes, hours or even days, but you will receive answers. Sometimes they come later as flashes, hunches or intuitions. Have you ever gone to bed worrying about a knotty problem and woken up at 3am with the answer? It's the same process that you are now harnessing for you and your team to use at will.

The technique is very simple. You can also teach your team. Imagine harnessing every super bio-computer on your team. That is spirit intelligence in action.

The technique is designed to imprint your goals on to the surface of the subconscious mind. First, you need to understand a little more of the way the mind functions. You may have seen biofeedback machines where researchers hook up electrodes to the surface of the skull and read the frequency of the brainwaves being generated.

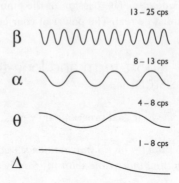

Beta waves

Normal conscious thinking shows up as relatively high frequency brain waves, between 13 and 25 cycles per second. Researchers call these Beta patterns. If you have shut your eyes and observed your conscious mind, you will relate to the fact that the conscious mind is a high frequency, speedy place most of the time.

Alpha waves

Below the level of conscious thinking is the realm of dreaming, the domain of alpha waves. These have a frequency bandwidth of between eight to 13 cycles per second. This is in fact the threshold of the subconscious.

Theta waves

In deep sleep, our brain emits theta waves. These are slower, longer frequencies in the range four to eight cycles per second.

Research shows that we go down into deep sleep and enter a dreaming state several times a night. So we go down into Theta, up into Alpha, down into Theta. Our brain patterns change. While we are in Alpha we dream — and we dream in pictures.

You can see the eyes of a sleeping person move under their eyelids as they literally watch the dream pictures in their mind. Researchers call it REM — rapid eye movements.

Delta waves

Below the realm of Theta waves are Delta brain waves, one to four cycles per second — unconsciousness.

Inserting the goal program

The goal program insertion technique is a method of deliberately slowing your brainwaves down from their normal speedy Beta to the calmer, slower Alpha state, the doorway to the subconscious and the superconscious.

The way to do this is to close your eyes and in sequence, imagine the colours of the rainbow:

RED
ORANGE
YELLOW
GREEN
BLUE
PURPLE
VIOLET

The colours slow the brain waves because each colour affects mood and thus our mental state. Folklore associated colours with emotions — red rag to a bull, Green Peace. Religions and royalty have been well aware of the power of colours on our mental state. High church ministers wear purple robes, Buddhist monks wear saffron clothes. Researchers have simply confirmed this knowledge by measuring our brain waves using biofeedback.

First, imagine yourself surrounded by the colour red. Some people prefer to imagine a red flower in front of them. The colour red in fact induces a certain level of physical relaxation in the body so stay with it for a couple of minutes.

Then visualise yourself immersed in the colour orange, then yellow, then green and on through the colours of the rainbow — blue to purple to violet. Stay with each colour for about half a minute.

What you will notice as you observe each colour in sequence is that your mind will start to slow down. It may take a little while at first and you may only notice this because your breathing becomes shallower. Most people find the technique very easy and very relaxing.

After imagining violet, drift in your imagination to a peaceful scene, a scene of your choice. Some people choose a favourite countryside spot — a deserted beach, sitting on a cloud, the garden of your childhood. It doesn't matter. It's your mind, your peaceful scene. As you do this, you will find that your mind relaxes.

You do not necessarily fall asleep, but be aware this is a great relaxing tool as well as a mind programming tool. If you have a sleep deficit — and most of us in our busy lives do —you may initially drift off to sleep. There is nothing wrong with that. However, with a little practice, you can find yourself comfortably imagining a peaceful scene.

You are now accessing your imagination. You are going to build and utilise an imagination workshop of the mind. To do this, the next step of this goal and vision program insertion process is simply to clear a space in your peaceful scene and build a stage and a cinema screen, much like the old drive-in movie screens.

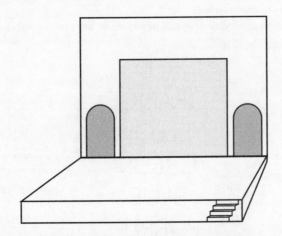

You can build your stage and cinema screen with whatever materials you want to. It is your mind and your imagination workshop. So in your mind, build a stage and stairs leading up on to it, with a big cinema screen at the back of the stage. On the right hand side of the screen build a green door and on the left hand side, a blue door.

Goal projection

In your imagination, project your goal or vision, the result you want, on to the cinema screen as though you are running a movie.

You can see the technique is very visual and as you play out your goal movie, feel the emotions of success. As you watch your vision or goal succeeding on the screen of your mind, by all means have the date up on the wall. There is the calendar, whatever date you want your goal achieved by, in the future. There are all your team mates, there is the customer signing the contract, the car salesman giving you the keys to your new Porsche or you and your family moving into the new house.

This is the way to insert your goal programs into the subconscious bio-computer.

The second part of the process is to imagine that instead of a flat cinema screen, it is actually the entrance to a huge holographic three dimensional image and you can actually walk into this goal achievement scene.

Imagine being there when your success is achieved. It is happening all around you. Feel it. Sense what is going on. See the calendar with your own eyes, even taste the champagne at the victory celebration. Listen to your colleagues chattering excitedly at the success of the goal or vision achieved.

It does not take long, maybe half a minute or a minute. In doing this second exercise, the goal is re-emphasised onto the surface of the subconscious. Remember thoughts are things and we move towards our dominant thoughts.

By clearly inserting the program of the desired goal into the subconscious, you activate the programming for the powerful parts of your mind to start moving towards the new dominant thought – your vision being achieved. The metaphysical gravity pull of envisaged success is activated.

The tense is now — present. Even though the calendar says it is in the future, you are behaving as though you are there now. So in the eternal 'Now', the supercomputer can work on it as all the details of the goal achieved have been imprinted on the mind.

You can sequentially run a number of goals, simply by stepping back out of the holographic image, back on to the stage and allowing the screen to become blank again between goal projections. It is your mind, your imagination — you can do what you like.

In this way you can activate the deeper and more powerful parts of your mind to help you achieve a number of goals and get the results you need — a classic example of spirit intelligence in action.

o PROGRAM OUTPUT

To repeat, the mind will provide solutions over time. Some solutions will arrive as good ideas, sometimes you will have hunches or an intuition. Sometimes somebody will say something to you. They may not realise the power of what they just said, but you will. The Universal Intelligence feedback machine has multiple communication channels. Follow up the feedback provided in your planning and actions.

o THE MASTERMIND

At this point, it is important to mention the section of *Think and Grow Rich* that covers the power of the mastermind, because the green door in your workshop of the mind has special significance for using the principle of the mastermind.

Remember:

'Great power can be accumulated through no other principle.'

The mastermind principle has two applications — physical and psychic. Napoleon Hill explained that the economic or physical mastermind is a relatively simple concept to understand and use, whereas the psychic mastermind can be more challenging to comprehend.

We'll first review the physical mastermind as this tool can assist you greatly in your planning. We will then explore how to use the psychic mastermind to guide you and your team to maximum effectiveness.

The physical mastermind

The physical principle of the mastermind is quite simple. The physical mastermind is described as two or more people gathered together regularly as a team, putting their minds on to solving or achieving the common challenge. Their journeyman experience is thus focused and you can achieve more with a set of focused minds than you can on your own. This makes sense.

> 'He that walketh with wise men shall be wise.'
> PROVERBS 13:20

I am sure that you have found on your journey through life that having two minds or more focused on a subject can be very powerful. Different people give you different aspects, different ideas.

Who is on your physical mastermind? Who are you calling together on a regular basis to discuss the plan and the vision? As you go forward over the PERT rope bridges, the enemy – resistance – is bound to show up. Even the best visions and PERT plans need regular mastermind meetings to track and discuss progress and obstacles.

You may say that your physical mastermind is all of your team. That is great, but the key to a successful mastermind is that it has to meet regularly. So how regularly does your whole team meet? Do you ensure quality time for your planning? Or do you have people interrupting, taking messages and phone calls? What sort of physical mastermind are you regularly running? Be honest.

Before we move on, write down who is really on your mastermind, who meets with you regularly in a focused review and planning environment.

As our children were growing up, we always held regular, clearly identified family mastermind meetings with our boys to discuss everyone's goals and plans. We sometimes went out to lunch as a family to make it special for them and us.

Harnessing the power of other minds as a well-chosen physical mastermind to help you with your planning is simply spirit intelligence common sense.

> 'Every man is like the company he is wont to keep.'
> EURIPIDES

Don't surround yourself with wimps and nice yes men. Surround yourself with people who ask more of you than you do, people who will be straight with you and face the truth, people playing win/win, people with courage, 16 cylinder people.

If you have listed your current physical mastermind members, check them out for these qualities. Should there be any deletions or anyone who should be added? This is not about position or status, it's about the qualities they bring to help you.

'Keep away from people who try to belittle your ambition. Small people always do that, but the really great make you feel that you, too, can become great.'
MARK TWAIN

If you don't have a current physical mastermind, take the time to draw up your ideal list of people, then go and approach them, explain the principle and ask them to join you.

This is critical for optimising spirit intelligence. You must be very careful whom you surround yourself with. It can make or break your chances of success.

The psychic mastermind

The psychic principle of the mastermind is explained in *Think and Grow Rich*:

'The psychic phase of the mastermind principle is much more difficult to comprehend. You may catch a significant suggestion from this statement. No two minds ever come together without thereby creating a third invisible, intangible force which may be likened to third mind.'

Just read that sentence again. 'No two minds ever come together without thereby creating a third, invisible, intangible force which may be likened to a third mind.' This is a remarkable sentence. The Bible says:

'Where two or three are gathered together in my name, there am I in the midst of them.'
MATTHEW 18:20

When you focus on a challenge with more than one mind, additional mind power kicks in. It is almost as though you need two PCs to really tap in to the super bio-computer. 'Where two or three are gathered together in my name, there am I in the midst of them.' It does not say – 'If you show up, I'll show up.' 'Where two or three ....' and that is why you need to have a mastermind group to help you with your planning.

The Christian Bible has some interesting insights on how to use the bio-computer power of the mind. Eastern religions also understand this power. The same concepts are reflected in the Koran and the Hadith – sayings of the Prophet Mohammed.

'Your Lord is best aware of whatever is in your minds.'
KORAN SURAH XVII VS 25

Read Matthew 6:6:

But when you pray, go into a room by yourself, shut the door, and pray to your Father who is there in the secret place, and your Father who sees what is secret will reward you.'

I am not a theologian, but I think the secret place is the workshop of the mind, the doorway to the subconscious and the superconscious. Note the verb — 'and your father who sees' — it is visual. Even though we usually 'say' our prayers — audio. The bio-computer works better with pictures. What are prayers but dialogue with a psychic mastermind some choose to call Father.

o FAITH

Faith is an interesting state of mind. FAITH can be an acronym —

Father and I Together Here

As you work with the awesome potential of your bio-computer and the untapped bio-computers that you are paying for on your team, have faith that higher power exists and you can consciously call on it.

Christians call it Father and speak of divine intervention. North American Indians speak of Great Spirit. Others talk of Brahma, Allah or Universal Intelligence. We are working with superconsciousness. Are these different subjects or just different labels?

The psychic principle of the mastermind is illustrated in *Star Wars* – '*may the force be with you.*'

The power of the psychic mastermind works best if you ensure you have an empty chair at your planning meetings. I would not dream of running a corporate workshop or a public presentation without two chairs up on the stage with me. Why two? If I sit down on one during the workshop, there is always an empty chair for the third mind to join the minds of myself and the audience.

'*Where two or three are gathered together*' – the psychic mastermind shows up. The chair is a visual metaphor, a reminder of that.

Is the concept of a psychic mastermind, a third mind force available to help you, too woo-woo and stretching the bounds of credibility? Possibly. But if it was good enough for earlier generations of highly successful people, maybe using it can help you and your team.

Certainly the mastermind concept is very powerful and you should consider exploring the ramifications of using it if you wish to optimise your spirit intelligence.

o THE IMAGINARY MASTERMIND

You can use the power of the psychic mastermind in your imaginary workshop of the mind.

Once you have projected your goals on the screen of your workshop, you are now ready to use the power of the green door. Behind the green door waits the person that you would like to bring in to be your psychic mastermind — a wise being with whom you can mentally discuss your goals and plans. Using the mastermind principle works best at this deep level of the doorway to the super bio-computer.

Clearly the wise being is an iconic representation of your own superconscious. Some people decide to bring in Einstein, or Shakespeare or Aristotle. Some choose to bring in their mother or father. Napoleon Hill reports bringing in a whole boardroom of advisers. It really does not matter — it is up to you.

This is just another spirit intelligence tool to gain further access to your superconscious. Why have you and your team running around when you can use the high leverage, higher woo-woo techniques of accessing the super bio-computer.

Read Matthew 7:7-8 as a mind manual:

> *'Ask, and it shall be given you. Seek, and ye shall find, knock, and it shall be opened unto you. For everyone that asketh receiveth, and he that seeketh findeth, and to him that knocketh it shall be opened.'*

How do you think Einstein developed his theories of relativity? Certainly not by sitting at his desk using just his conscious mind. He was lying on his back in a field, in the sunshine, looking up at the blue sky and daydreaming. He wondered what it would like to be a sunbeam radiating out from the sun into space. As he did this, he found himself as an imaginary sunbeam on a curved trajectory. What a jolt that was to his left-brain logical conscious mind. The rest, quantum theory and relativity, as they say, is history.

Now back to the technique. Decide who you want to invite in to give you wise council.

In your imagination workshop view your goals on the screen and experience them happening around you, and let the screen fade blank. Then imagine walking across the stage to the green door.

Open the door and invite in your psychic mastermind guest. Some people see vivid pictures of Einstein or Shakespeare or whoever they have chosen. Some people just have a sense that someone is there and some people see and sense nothing. There is a spectrum of ability with visual imagination but it does not matter if you only have a vague sense of a presence or no sense at all. Quality of visualisation is irrelevant.

In your imagination, invite the person in, thank them for coming, explain your goals and then ask them if they have any advice or guidance. Then listen. You may be amazed at the calibre and quality of the mental advice that you receive. It may be completely outside the normal logic sequences of what you would expect. Alternative ideas and strategies may be presented. You may only have some vague feelings. You may receive nothing at all at the time. That is okay.

Even on a supercomputer, some of the programs take hours or days to run. When you have finished explaining each goal and asking for feedback, then ask your wise mastermind being or beings if there is anything else you should know at this point in your life and work activities and again, listen. You may or may not receive clear, immediate communication.

Then thank them for coming, ask them if it is okay if you can invite them again in the future and then, gently and firmly, usher them back across the stage and out of the green door and close the door.

It is okay if you want to scribble some notes on a pad, keeping your eyes closed.

The mastermind being is just a representation of the deeper part of your mind to help you more consciously access your superconscious bio-computer. Most religions encourage the power of prayer. This technique enhances the same principles.Goethe sums it up:

'Whatever you can do or dream you can, begin it. Boldness has genius, power and magic in it. Begin it now.'

The words dream, power and magic take on new significance with these metaphysical planning tools at your disposal.

o THE BLUE DOOR RECHARGE

Now once again, you are alone on the stage of your imaginary workshop. The final step is to imagine walking across the stage to the other side of the screen to the blue door.

The word idea derives from the Latin
id deo
that from the god.

Open the blue door, step over the threshold and find yourself drifting into the colour blue. You will find that drifting in this state, into the colour blue, is deeply and powerfully relaxing – a great way to refresh spirit intelligence.

Once you have drifted through the colour blue for up to 20 minutes, in your own time and at your own speed, come back to full conscious alertness by surrounding yourself with the rainbow colours in the reverse order, from blue to red. In your own time, wiggle your toes, stretch your fingers and open your eyes.

The colour blue has deep significance and power. We say to each other, where did that idea come from? I don't know, it just came out of the ...? The blue!

o YOUR ACTIONS NOW?

So what are you going to do now you have the option of enhancing your planning and spirit intelligence by using the power of the mind? You could just run your team using the vision you have co-created and the PERT rope bridge plans you have developed and remain low leverage, just you and your team working hard.

But we are moving faster and faster in the world of the new millennium. Our telecommunications are literally moving down glass fibre at light speed and product life cycles and competitive response times become shorter and shorter.

In this accelerating world, the only sustainable differential that you and your team may have will be in the quality of your service and your relationships, which at the end of the day comes down to the quality of your people.

You may be satisfied to hire high calibre people, let them run using the PCs of their conscious minds and leave it at that. However, if any of your competitors decide to methodically and systematically access the power of their super bio-computers and the psychic power of the master mind, who is going to come up with better creativity? Who is going to come up with better plans? Who is going to come up with a higher quality of originality and innovation? Who will get the gold medal results?

That is the issue.

o THE MIND-PLANNING TOOL IN ACTION

The senior marketing management team of a large client organisation was intrigued by our discussions about high leverage planning using the power of the mind and we ran a psychic mastermind session to elicit the key competitive differentials for their organisation into the future.

The way that we did this was to discuss the technique of going down through the colours of the rainbow, setting up the stage and screen in the imagination workshop of the mind, visualising the goals and then inviting in the psychic mastermind.

Before we initiated the activity, we agreed on a set of questions that they wanted to ask their collective psychic masterminds. What were the advantages available to their organisation, how should they use them, were there any pitfalls, what were the biggest problem areas and how should they overcome them, etc? Their list covered those sorts of questions.

When the marketing team had agreed the set of questions and each individual had decided who they would invite into their workshop of the mind as their personal psychic mastermind, we started the exercise.

They shut their eyes and I guided the entire management team down through the colours. They created their own individual peaceful scenes and imaginary workshops. They ran their company goals and vision individually on the screens in their minds and entered the 3D holograms of success achieved.

Then each person welcomed in his or her psychic mastermind visitor. I slowly read the questions aloud one by one, and they asked their psychic mastermind guest the question and made notes of the answers received on a pad in front of them, with their eyes closed.

At the end of the session, each person had a few minutes of private dialogue with his or her mastermind icon asking for personal guidance. They then asked the mastermind icon to leave and after some minutes behind the blue door drifting in deep relaxation, the group came back up through the colours.

They then broke into small groups of two or three to discuss the experience. It was not your average corporate strategic planning meeting of the 20th century, but it might well be in the 21st and 22nd centuries.

What amazed the team was, first, several of them had been visited by the same icon (an old Tibetan monk) and secondly, in the group of 14 people, the answers, received independently, were very similar.

The answers they received may not surprise you but they certainly surprised them. Even though the company is a high technology company, the answers were that the sustainable differential advantage did not lie with their advanced use of technology; it lay with their people, their culture and their level of customer service.

There were many more distinctions. Indeed, the managing director of their advertising agency was present at the session and the agency went on to make a very powerful TV advertisement that incorporated the themes from that session including the Tibetan monk! The ad generated huge response and the company continued to grow.

I have facilitated similar planning sessions to explore areas that are really challenging for just the logical mind. Are there specific mineral deposits in a certain rock structure? What is the best way of tackling customer service? How to best market accounting services in the 21st century?

Using the tool takes courage. The technique is not infallible. It is a powerful spirit intelligence tool that you can add to your tool kit – vision creation, PERT planning, keys to passion and now use of the super bio-computer. Try it. What have you got to lose?

○ BIO-COMPUTER TIME STORAGE

To ensure you have the best planning capability possible, there is one more tool that we should review while covering the power of the mind to optimise spirit intelligence. The tool checks how you and the members of your team use and store time in your own bio-computer. This tool is easier to use if you have a partner.

This approach can have a profound effect on the planning capabilities of some people if their storage of time in their bio-computer is not well organised. As you don't normally check it out, you have no idea how you are doing it.

In our workshops people sit in pairs. One person closes their eyes. Their partner then asks them to physically point to 'Now' with their outstretched finger in the space around them.

They have to identify in the physical space around or in their head, where 'Now' is. Some people point to a spot inside their skull, some people point to a location just in front of their nose or their eyes or between their eyebrows. Some people point two feet in front of them.

Then the partner asks them to point to where tomorrow is, then next week, next month, six months out, a year out, five years out, ten years out. Each time the person has to identify where in the physical space around them, they are literally storing time, the direction, distance out and elevation from the horizontal plane.

The partner asking the questions maps their responses:

They ask them to point to where yesterday is in their minds, then last week, last month, last year, five years ago, ten years ago.

Some people find it extraordinary to learn that we actually store time in physical space and that our mind space extends beyond our skulls, into the space around us.

The feedback can be equally astounding at first. Some people store all of time in a sphere of a metre around their head. Some people store 30 years ago 100,000 kilometres behind them. Fifty years in the future is stored 1 million kilometres in front of them.

When someone says they are storing 30 years ago 100,000 kilometres behind them, is that a metaphor or is it true? In my experience, it is true. Our metaphysical mind space is absolutely enormous and extends out into the physical realms in all directions. So there is an immediate distinction between the brain, the physical entity and the mind, the metaphysical powerhouse.

In mapping time storage, you will find that some people program time as a line passing through them. Their future is in front of them in a linear straight line ahead. Their past is behind them in a linear straight line and so time flows through them.

Some people choose to represent time as a left to right line in front of them, with their past out to the left and their future to the right.

When you ask people who have a time line passing through them, why they chose to program past time behind them, they usually do not know. They may then reply that it is logical because their past is behind them and they are looking into the future. People who program their time line in front of them, from left to right, often say that they like to keep an eye on the past because the experience of the past guides them in the future.

People employ different time storage strategies, usually adopted unconsciously. All have merit. For some people, time curves.

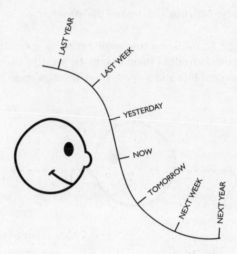

It really does not matter how and where you store time, as long as it makes sense for you.

You will occasionally find people on your team who have time stored randomly. Tomorrow may be in front of them, the day after that may be exactly behind them, five years ago may be six inches in front of them and next month is off behind them at an angle of 40 degrees.

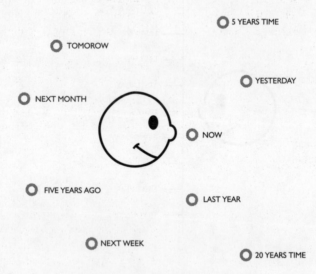

If you program time irregularly all over your bio-computer in a confused and disorganised way, it is not likely that your plans are going to be logical and smooth flowing. Spirit intelligence – the ability to make better choices — can be diminished.

Even if you did not consciously plan where you programmed time storage originally, it is very easy to reorganise your time planning. You can simply reach out, with your eyes closed, grabbing tomorrow and literally placing it where you want it to be in physical space.

o REPROGRAMMING TIME STORAGE

People who have a disorganised time storage system can actually rearrange their spatial time storage system to re-program their bio-computer. Does this sound a little strange? Maybe, but it can be a very useful tool to improve planning ability and thus spirit intelligence.

If either you or people in your team have a poorly organised spatial representation of time, use this tool to reprogram it.

When I first came across this tool, I found that my future went up in front of me as though I was climbing a mountain and my past was down behind me. I realised that life was bound to be tough if I programmed time like that because every day I set out into the future climbing uphill. So I chose to move my time line. Instead of every day waking up and facing a mountain, every day I now face a down hill ski run future with my past time going up the slope behind me. No more climbing.

The general manager of a large mining company found to his amazement that he too was climbing up a time mountain. He too agreed that he preferred to move his future downhill and to balance it with the past time going uphill behind him. He rearranged the time storage system in his bio-computer by closing his eyes, reaching for the future in the physical space in front of him and moving it to a downhill position as we have discussed. He rang me three months later to tell me how much easier his job had become in the three months since that activity!

Some people protest at this saying — *'No, no. Life would not have any meaning if it was not a struggle.'* Well, if they choose to struggle uphill every day that is their choice. You at least now have a choice in how you program time in your bio-computer to optimise your spirit intelligence.

We have covered the keys to purpose and vision, to passion and now planning to ensure you have clear plans of action. You now have the tools for using the power of the bio-computer of the mind to achieve your plans.

In the next chapter we will review the keys to managing people. Optimising the performance of other people so they are empowered to make the best choices and decisions is a vital spirit intelligence key as you can rarely succeed on your own.

This is equally true at home and in your community as well as at work.

Fifteen

MANAGING PEOPLE

'In the last analysis, the individual person is responsible for living his own life and for finding himself. If he persists in shifting his responsibility to someone else, he fails to find out the meaning of his own existence.'
THOMAS MERTON

In this chapter we will review a simple management system to ensure that the people you are called upon to manage are crystal clear about what is required from them as part of your high performance team. This will make it so much easier for you to attract, hire, manage, praise, counsel, correct and appraise each team member.

You may also find this management approach useful when working with other people in your community or even trying efficiently to run a house full of kids or teenagers!

Spirit intelligence requires that as the manager, you make the right choices in dealing with people to empower them and sustain them on 16 cylinders and then focus their efforts appropriately.

o THEIR CONTRIBUTION CONTRACT

The key to managing people so they achieve outstanding performance lies in developing a contribution contract with each of them. The individual contribution contract defines what it is that you expect each of them to contribute in achieving personal and team success.

To fire up their 16 BMES cylinders, it is crucial that everybody on your team has 'something significant yet to do'. Their contribution contract provides a format to define that.

At work, this tool is essential. Most homes would also be far more harmonious if contribution contracts were hammered out at the start of each year so everyone knew what was expected of them to keep the home show 'on the road'.

There are five steps to developing a contribution contract:

Step 1 — Define their customers

The first step is to identify the customers to whom each of your people are in service. These may be external customers. They also include internal people within your organisation. You, as their manager, are certainly one of their internal customers.

For a housemaid in a hotel, the hotel guests are her external customers. The hotel manager, hotel maintenance and room service supervisors would be her internal customers.

Miners drilling at a rock face have their team leader or mine captain as their major customer. They also have geologists as customers who require specific survey samples.

A priest has customers in the form of his parish. A conductor of an orchestra has customers, the audience who come to hear the orchestra play and the musicians who look to him for guidance and instructions. An army sergeant has customers — the nation he is charged to defend, his senior officers above him and the men looking to him for direction.

The first critical point of a contribution contract is to make sure that it is customer focused because everybody, everywhere, is working to satisfy a customer.

When you feel sea sick, where do they tell you to focus your eyes? On the horizon. Why? The horizon is a stable reference point despite the rough seas. The customer is just like the horizon, a relatively stable reference point during business turbulence. So a customer-focused contribution contract will give your people stability and resilience during challenging times.

For example, a telephone receptionist may have four major groups of customers:

o Visitors to reception

o In coming callers

o The organisation's staff

o His / her manager

CONTRIBUTION CONTRACT

1   DEFINE THEIR CUSTOMERS

2   THEIR CUSTOMERS' VALUE CRITERIA

3   VALUE CRITERIA — GOLD MEDAL PERFORMANCE STANDATDS

4   WORK TO BE DONE

5   TWO SIGNATURES

THEIRS — ACCOUNTABLE & RESPONSIBLE
YOURS — TO EMPOWER THEM
16 CYLINDERS

Step 2 — The criteria by which their customers assess value

The second of the five contribution contract steps is to clarify the criteria by which each of their your customers are assessing value from your team member's contribution.

If your staff member has a number of customers, it is likely each customer or group of customers may have different value criteria.

In the case of the receptionist, the customers may have the following value criteria by which they are assessing service and thus performance:

Contribution Contract with our receptionist (Robin)

Your Customers	Their Value Criteria
o In coming callers	speed of response in answering the phone friendliness of voice tone skill in directing the call to the right department clear articulation of any problems or delays to the customer's call
o Visitors to reception	speed of service friendly, helpful manner knowledge of company personnel
o Our staff	outstanding service ethic knowledge of company personnel
o Your manager	punctual work habits outstanding service ethic acceptable dress sense technical capability with telephone switchboard

Step 3 — Standard of performance evaluation Gold medal performance

The third of the five steps is to clarify the standard of performance for each of the customer's value criteria. What level of performance will ensure a 'gold medal' from the customer?

In the game of business, there are only two medals – gold and lead. If the customer is happy, you win the gold. If the customer is not happy and goes somewhere else, there is no silver medal. You win the lead medal. Its heavy and worthless.

The question is – what does your staff member have to do to achieve a score of 10 out of 10 in the eyes of the customer?

For the telephone receptionist example, a gold medal / 10 out of 10 performance for each of their customers' value criteria may be defined as follows:

Contribution Contract with our receptionist (Robin)

Your Customers	Their Value Criteria & Gold Medal Performance Standards
o In coming callers	speed of response in answering the phone o *Phone answered in three rings or less is a gold medal performance. Four rings or more is lead medal – unacceptable* friendliness of voice tone o *All calls must be answered in a friendly tone with the words – 'Good morning, Top Team Company. This is Robin. How may I be of service?' Unfriendliness, irritability or brusqueness equala lead medal performance.* skill in directing the call to the right department o *All calls directed to the correct department first time is gold medal performance. Passing customer calls from department to department represents lead medal performance.* clear articulation of any problems or delays to the customer's call o *Clear articulation of any problems or delays to the customer's call. Call transfer problems must alwaysbe explained to the customer. For a gold medal performance, the procedures of call on hold must be explained to the customer every time:'I will be back to you within a maximum of 30 seconds.' Delays of more than 30 seconds response back to the customer represents a lead medal performance.*
o Visitors to reception	speed of service o *Personal attention as soon as possible. Eye contact within 30 seconds if busy* friendly, helpful manner o *Warm, friendly, helpful attitude under all levels of pressure and stress* knowledge of company personnel o *Complete mastery of company phone directory and organisation chart*

o Our staff

outstanding service ethic
- o *Total commitment to providing speedy, accurate service under all levels of pressure and stress*

knowledge of company personnel
- o *Complete mastery of company phone directory and organisation chart*

o Your manager

punctual work habits
- o *Gold medal performance is on time, every time – arrival, breaks, departure. Lateness at the reception desk is a lead medal performance, no excuses.*

outstanding service ethic
- o *Recognition that the customer is always important whether they are angry, rude or unfriendly. How may I be of service?' is the only acceptable response. Personal irritability, lack of courtesy, smart remarks are lead medal performance.*

acceptable dress sense
- o *Presentable business attire is vital. No tattoos or chewing gum.*

technical capability with telephone switchboard
- o *All facets of switchboard equipment understood and demonstrated at all times. No mistakes, no surprises.*

Yes, some of these criteria are subjective, but that's the point. Value is perceived by the customer. Value is subjective. If the customer assesses value around the criteria of a welcoming smile and friendly voice tone then that is what is required — every time.

Management by objectives is a wish for a logical, predictable world. Regrettably customers make emotional evaluations and decisions. Their value criteria define the rules of the games of life and business. They are the customers!

Arab Bank Australia came to the conclusion that 10 out of 10 / gold medal performance from their tellers was to make eye contact with the customer within 20 seconds of their joining the queue at the counter. It is possible that the tellers might be busy serving someone else, but it is important to make eye contact with the person in the queue and say — 'I will be with you shortly.'

If they did that, the customer would wait patiently in the queue for some time. If they did not, some customers became impatient and upset and demanded to see the manager.

Think back to your early jobs. Would you have found it useful to have a contract with your boss that helped you understand who your customers were, how they would be judging your performance and how you had to perform to consistently win gold medals? Young people and inexperienced people especially need this help.

Step 4 — Work to be done

The fourth step in developing the contribution contract is to summarise the work to be done by your staff member to achieve gold medal standards in the eyes of their customers. How much detail needs to go into this section on work to be done? At the very least, there needs to be bullet points summarising the work to be done. For a younger, more inexperienced team member, it can be quite useful to lay out in some detail the work to be done.

Contribution Contract with our receptionist (Robin)

Work to be done

o Arrive 8.25am

o Take your place at reception with headphones on by 8.30am

o Switch off the overnight answering machine

o Play back messages and forward to relevant staff

o Balance the demands of phone traffic and reception arrivals

o Always ensure relief staff are in place before taking a break

o Notify manager of sickness or absence by 7.30am

o Activate answer machine before leaving reception at 5.30pm or at any other time when no relief is available

o Report switchboard malfunctions immediately to manufacturer's service provider

o Issue visitor passes and record all visitor arrivals in the visitor register

Having contribution contracts defined makes it so much easier to manage the induction of new people as they understand the basic rules of the game, what is expected of them and how they will be assessed.

At home these can be posted on the fridge door.

Step 5 — Two signatures

The fifth step in developing the contribution contract requires two signatures.

First, your staff member signs that they are accountable and responsible for satisfying their customers' value criteria to the gold medal performance standards in the contribution contract.

You then sign that as their manager you agree to support and empower them to help them achieve success.

Staff Signature — I agree I am accountable and responsible to achieve gold medal standards for each of my customers' value criteria:

....

Manager Signature — I agree my role is to support and empower you to sustain 16 cylinder performance:

....

Before we review these tools to assist you in supporting and empowering your people to sustain 16 cylinder performance, it is necessary to explore the history of management and to explain the crucial paradox that managers now face in developing contribution contracts with their people.

o THE HISTORY OF MANAGEMENT

To understand current management and leadership dilemmas, we might review the demands on management from the Agrarian age through the Industrial Revolution and on into the Information age which has brought with it the quickening pace of change.

The Agrarian age

During the Agrarian age our ancestors worked first as hunters and gatherers and then as farmers. Most people lived on the land and the rhythm and pace of life were defined by the seasons. They planted in the Spring, their crops grew in the Summer, they harvested in the Autumn and then they ploughed and the land remained fallow in the Winter. Skills were passed down through families. Trade skills were learned under the apprentice/journeyman/mastery system we have discussed.

AGRARIAN AGE

HUNTERS & GATHERERS

↓

90% ON THE LAND
LABOUR INTENSIVE
PACE — RHYTHM OF THE SEASONS

The Industrial age

The Agrarian way of life was changed forever when in 1763 James Watt invented the steam engine. The power of the steam engine and Bessemer's development of steel production significantly increased our ability to produce goods and thus ushered in the industrial revolution. The higher tensile strength of steel beams enabled the construction of large factories that housed the manufacturing machines that were driven by steam power.

The machines were designed to produce goods but needed people to operate them. So where did the labour come from? The labour came from the land. People flocked from their farms to work in the factories and so towns grew larger and larger. These people coming from the farms were mainly poorly educated farm peasants.

The capitalists who owned the machines and the factories required a new type of worker — the manager. The manager was needed to tell the poorly educated workers what to do.

In the Agrarian age, the seasons defined the pace of life. Once you have a steam engine, you can run a factory 24 hours a day, seven days a week. The pace of the games of life and business was changed forever.

INDUSTRIAL AGE

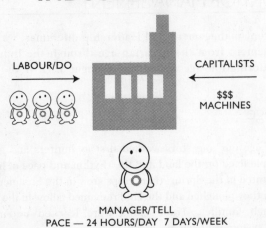

LABOUR/DO   CAPITALISTS

$$$
MACHINES

MANAGER/TELL
PACE — 24 HOURS/DAY 7 DAYS/WEEK

In those early days of what the poet William Blake labelled 'dark satanic mills', labour was exploited and the union movement was born to fight injustice. If a group of labourers didn't perform or complained about harsh conditions, it was easy to get rid of them. There were plenty more where they came from.

The fundamental principle behind the industrial revolution was that managers needed to be intelligent and trained to direct worker activity. They understood what needed to be done in the factory. So managers directed and workers worked. The Western education system developed to supply workers with basic primary skills and managers with secondary enhanced skills.

That was the central idea — that managers know what to do. They tell the workers and the workers do it.

The Information age

This is often no longer true. We have now moved rapidly beyond the industrial revolution into the Information age. We no longer rely on steam power and electricity. Much of our information is moving down glass fibres at light speed.

The pace of change is quickening. Manufactured goods account for far less than they used to in world economies which are now more service driven. The endless range of choice has shifted the game of business to a customer focus, customer value, customer loyalty and the creativity to differentiate yourself from the competition.

INFORMATION AGE

COPPER CABLE ⟶ GLASS FIBRE
LIGHT SPEED

PACE INCREASING

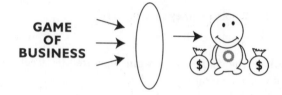

GAME OF BUSINESS

o THE NEW MANAGEMENT DILEMMA

These changes have created a subtle management dilemma that you must be aware of and know how to handle if you are to optimise spirit intelligence.

In any enterprise your people spend more time with your customers than you do. They know more about your customers on a day-to-day, hour-by-hour basis.

Classical management theory says that you as manager are supposed to tell your staff what to do. In this Information age, it is not possible for the manager to draw up a staff member's contribution contract in isolation. To tap their more detailed knowledge of what the customer wants, it is critical that the contribution contract is jointly worked out between you and your staff member.

o INVOLVE THEIR CUSTOMERS

Not only must you talk about customers with your staff members to achieve clarity on their customers' value criteria and gold medal performance standards, you will also have to talk to their customers to ensure clarity.

You can then work with your staff member in defining Step 4 — the work to be done.

By the time the contribution contract is signed, all parties are clear on what the contribution has to be. When your staff member signs that they are accountable and responsible for achieving the results, they are signing with their eyes wide open.

You, in turn, can then say to them with integrity – *'We both understand the task ahead of you. My job is to now empower you on 16 cylinders to ensure you win gold medals for both of us.'* Win / win.

○ SUPPORTING AND EMPOWERING YOUR PEOPLE

How do you, as the manager, work to support and empower your people to sustain 16 cylinder performance? Once the contribution contract is clear and both parties know the value criteria and what is a gold medal/10 out of 10 performance, then supporting and empowering your people is simply a question of management focus to assist them in three areas:

1. Able to

   Are they *able to* do the job with adequate skills and abilities?

2. Want to

   Do they *want to* do the job, are they motivated?

3. Chance to

   Are you giving them the *chance to* perform supported by excellent systems and a success oriented win/win culture?

This system of management is summarised in the following diagram. The contribution contract defines what is expected.

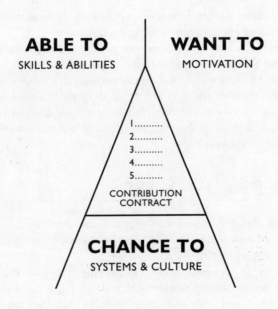

This is important. Spirit intelligence requires that you make the right choices. When faced with a person who is not performing, there are only five questions to ask:

1. Do they understand the game – 'let's achieve the vision'?

2. Do they know the rules – their personal contribution?

3. Are they *able to* play the game to win – skills and abilities?

4. Do they have the *chance to* play the game – supported with good systems and culture?

5. Do they *want to* play the game – are they motivated?

With these five spirit intelligence keys, we can now explore approaches to assist you support and empower each person on your team.

Want to

Do your staff members *want to* work on your team and achieve your vision? Are they motivated? You already have available to you the motivation keys of trust and rapport, their values, their DISC needs and fears, their dynamics of balance, their journey through life and enthusiasm.

Do they have a clear sense of their personal journey through life? Have they worked out the dynamics of the exchange working on your team? What are they giving and what are they gaining that is preparing them for their longer term life journey? Making sure that they understand with clarity their journey through life is the first key to *want to*. Do they have an explicit personal growth contract with you as we discussed in Chapter 10?

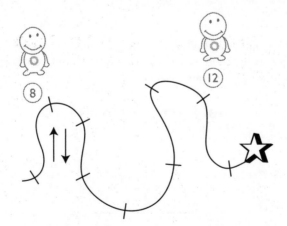

WHAT IS IT THAT I AM GETTING FROM WORKING IN
THIS CURRENT "POTTERY" THAT IS TRAINING ME,
DEVELOPING ME, STRETCHING ME, GROWING ME
FOR THE BIGGER JOURNEY THAT LIES AHEAD TO
ACHIEVE MY LIFE VISION?

Do you and do they understand their preferred DISC graphic equaliser settings, so that you can reach out and consistently press their needs button and avoid pressing their fears button?

Do you and do they understand their priorities across the seven dynamics of balance?

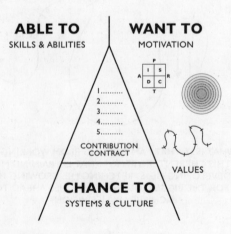

Do you and do they understand their values and the number one value they are striving for?

All these keys are available to you to turn them on and keep them motivated as they work towards achieving your team's vision.

Chance to

Ensuring your people have the *chance to* perform is about systems and culture. It is not fair to ask somebody to do a job and not give them the systems and culture to support them. Denying someone the *chance to* play the game to win is treason to the spirit within and thus demonstrates low spirit intelligence.

Review the keys from Chapter 12 on team passion and the culture tools of trust and assertion. Are you giving your people a *chance to* perform? Many performance problems are caused by sloppy, inefficient systems but because we are not trained in systems analysis, we miss the root cause of the sloppy system and blame the effect, the person making the mistake. (We'll cover this further in Chapter 16 on persistence.)

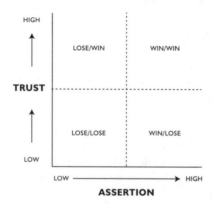

Do your people have well organised systems supporting them so they can be flexible and creative in their work? It is possible you may not be aware in detail of how your systems support or do not support your people, because you may not use them every day.

Sit down with each of your people and say to them:

'Now we have the contribution contract clear and we have both signed it, my job is to support and empower you. I am going to do that by using three questions at all times.

Are you able to, do you want to, and do you have the chance to perform to the gold medal standards we agreed?

In the area of want to, when we do have performance issues to discuss, I will be using the keys to passion to make sure I can help you stay motivated.

When we analyse chance to, let us jointly review the support systems. I want to make sure the systems are there to support you to achieve gold medal performance.

We need to be clear which of your support systems are well organised and efficient and which are sloppy and need improvement.'

List of Support Systems for our receptionist (Robin)

- o Reception desk — efficient

- o Switchboard — efficient

- o PC / Printer / Fax — efficient

- o High Quality Reception Chair — efficient

- o Phone Directory — sloppy & out of date

- o Organisation Charts — sloppy & out of date

- o Paging system — efficient

- o Rostering system — efficient

- o Training system — sloppy

- o Appraisal system — sloppy

Once you both have a clear understanding of the support systems and their current state, there must be a set of action plans to improve any sloppy, inefficient systems to acceptable standards.

Are you going to be able to wave a magic wand and solve all your system problems tomorrow? That is highly unlikely, but as long as your people are aware of that and you know where the systems may let them down, then you can adjust your contribution contract expectations accordingly. As the systems improve, the gold medal performance can be achieved every time. With the *chance to* secured, spirit enthusiasm increases markedly.

Able to

Having monitored and used your *want to* and *chance to* empowerment keys, that leaves you with the third area of managerial support. If they want to and they have the chance to perform, are they *able to* perform? Do they have the skills and training?

You need a good approach for reviewing current and required skill levels. It can sometimes be challenging when you are trying to explain to people that they are not quite as able to do the job as they think they are. They need the feedback but spirit intelligence demands that you must maintain their self-esteem. No one likes implied criticism.

Known strengths

The best approach for reviewing skills, as the table shows, is to talk to team members first about their known strengths. That is a good way to start an *able to* review because it boosts ego and people feel good.

'Martin. Let me explain the strengths you have that I think you already know. They are formidable so let us list them out here on the white board.'

A KNOWN STRENGTHS	**B** UNKNOWN STRENGTHS
C KNOWN IMPROVEMENT OPPORTUNITIES	**D** UNKNOWN IMPROVEMENT OPPORTUNITIES

Unknown strengths

Once you have covered their known strengths, it is then a good time to talk about their unknown strengths.

'There may be an area, Martin, where you are not aware how strong you are. I want to make it clear that the sense of integrity that you bring to this team is highly valued by both myself and senior management and your co-workers. I am not sure if you realise how strong your sense of integrity is Martin, but it is important that we list it.'

It is possible that people do not understand some of the strengths they have. Bringing them out in the *able to* review also boosts their feelings of self-worth and self-esteem. This can prepare them to be more open for the next two review areas.

Known improvement opportunities

'Martin. We have talked before about leaving the workbench tools in a mess for the next shift. You know the procedures for shutting down a shift. You attended a workshop on the new lathes four months ago. So Martin, let us talk through the actions we agreed upon last time and find out why it is you are not responding to these Known Improvement Opportunities.'

It is possible that their performance is being undermined because of a genuine reason in the area of *want to* or *chance to*. You now have the skill or ability gap out in the open for continued discussion and correction.

While on the subject of counselling and mentoring, remember the golden rule — praise in public and correct in private. Never correct in public. In some cultures, even praise needs to be in private.

Unknown improvement opportunities

'Martin, over the last three months, there is an area of your performance that I need to bring to your attention. Your configuring errors are really starting to annoy the engineers and they have been making snide comments to me in the corridor.
You may not be aware of this problem, so that's why I'm bringing it up under our heading of Unknown Improvement Opportunities here on the whiteboard.'

Because you have dwelt first on their strengths to boost their self-esteem, will they be better or less able to handle a 'need for correction' discussion? It is better to be prepared.

Remember that the voice of ego in their heads is always chattering to defend them — *'Stupid twit, she should try doing what I have to do. I'd like to see her configure our processors with sales people screaming about deadlines. I've got enough to do without worrying about those guys on night shift.'*

Everyone has the voice of ego. The ego's job is to defend us so our self-esteem is not crushed into oblivion.

There is a communication hierarchy: *truth, justify, blame, deny, quit.* Knowing this may help you and them focus on the truth of the situation and short circuit long digressions into justification, blame and denial of the performance issues.

Talk through the *able to* review using the grid to draw out the unknown improvement opportunities. Emphasise the gold medal performance that is required and with them analyse the action needed to bring them up to strength and keep reminding them:

'Martin, my job is to empower you. You have agreed this is the contribution you want to make to our vision achievement and this is the performance level that you have to achieve, the gold medal / ten out of ten performance.

*If you have the motivation Martin, the **want to** and the systems and culture are there to give you the **chance to**, then as you know we agreed that we need to look at your **able to**.*

These are the Unknown Improvement Opportunities that I needed to discuss with you today, Martin. They stand between you and gold medal performance. I signed your contribution contract to support and empower you and make you a winner, so we have to talk about them even if it's tough to do. Does that make sense, Martin?'

Of course, once you have talked to your people using the model, it is bound to make sense, however uncomfortable they may be in facing it.

○ MANAGING PEOPLE

Clearly your people will have a range of abilities and levels of motivation. To draw the best from each of them will require flexibility in your management approach.

The diagram shows how to vary your management emphasis:

	TELL	DELEGATE
HIGH	LOW ABLE TO	HIGH ABLE TO
	HIGH WANT TO	HIGH WANT TO
WANT TO	TELL & ENCOURAGE	ENCOURAGE
	LOW ABLE TO	HIGH ABLE TO
	LOW WANT TO	LOW WANT TO
HIGH		

LOW   **ABLE TO**   HIGH

CHANCE TO

If you review the diagram, you can see *want to* on one axis, *able to* on the other axis and *chance to* underpins everything. Without well organised, efficient systems, your people will not be able to consistently perform to gold medal standards. So *chance to* indeed underpins everything.

The diagram provides four defined quadrants which represent the four types of people you may need to manage. Spirit intelligence requires a different management approach for each type of person.

Low able to / high want to

A person may be very low in terms of *able to*, because they are lacking the skills and abilities. Yet they have very high *want to*, because their motivation is strong. Your team member certainly has enthusiasm, but it can be misdirected because they are not very *able to*. These people need significant, regular attention. You need to train them and show them what to do. They are really enthusiastic apprentices.

Section 4 of their contribution contract, work to be done, needs to be quite detailed. Ensure you keep them on a relatively short leash with frequent check points. Ask them to tackle the current problem, define an action plan and then come back to you for discussion and approval before proceeding.

Training and mentoring these people can be a time consuming responsibility. They are your apprentices. Yet it can be really rewarding as you watch them grow.

Low able to / low want to

People like this are neither *able to* nor *want to* do the job. In today's turbulent work environment, they can be a real problem for you. They need to be managed with detailed instructions on how to do the job and you also have to give them constant support and encouragement to motivate them. This can be a real drain on your own energies and enthusiasm, but remember, everyone has the potential. They could easily prove to be a real gem. It may be poor management or a traumatic life journey in the past that has shut down their 16 cylinders.

Your support and empowerment responsibility is to help them fire up again. So give them a chance. Set up their contribution contract. Give them a detailed Section 4 on work to be done. Analyse with them their training gaps and an action plan to close them. Work through the *want to*, the motivation passion keys from Chapter 10 to help them turn it on. Make it clear you have a team vision to achieve and you need a motivated team to achieve that vision. You can't afford to carry any passengers.

High able to / low want to

These people are quite *able to*, but they are not motivated, they don't *want to* perform to gold medal standards. With the passion keys you now have, you can confront their difficulties. They need a supportive, encouraging management style to help them.

Either you can support and help them re-motivate themselves or clarify if indeed they are a square peg in a round hole. Maybe they are in the wrong job and needing to find another team.

Again you need to make it clear to these people that the vision will only be achieved with a motivated team. You may be challenged by some very able people carrying huge chips on their shoulder. They think life owes them something. They want to play the game of victim, designed to avoid personal responsibility for personal motivation. Don't tolerate the victim game, it is too expensive to maintain the excuses these people carry. Help them, because the spark of spirit can be rekindled. So give it everything you've got to help them fire up and re-motivate themselves.

High able to / high want to

With the people who have both ability and personal motivation, you can delegate more. Because they are capable, experienced self-starters, Section 4 in their contribution contract on work to be done needs only be a few summary bullet points.

Then you have to agree when you are going to have regular check point meetings with them to review progress. Delegation does not mean abdication. You need to have agreed progress meetings and the other sections of the contribution contract are just as important. The old hand needs to be as clear on gold medal performance as the young apprentice.

Some managers find the old hands very resistant to the introduction of the discipline of contribution contracts:

> *'Come on Kim. We've been doing this with our eyes shut for years, Why do we suddenly need contribution contracts? You know I can deliver. Trust me and spend your time on the younger ones. They need your help and some fancy contract. Not me.'*

Your answer is simple —

> *'Robert, you know every competitor is after our gold medals, so unless we improve our systems and formally focus on the customers as a team discipline, yesterday's*

gold medal standard only qualifies as lead medal tomorrow. The bar keeps going up. And anyway, I need your help as an opinion leader so everyone can see we're serious about gold medals. These contribution contracts are a critical part of our gold medal approach. I really need your active support on this one.'

○ APPRAISALS

Another important use of the contribution contract is at appraisal time. Clearly you must hold a major appraisal with each of your team members, at least once a year, and in this era of rapid change, you probably have to do a second shorter appraisal every six months.

You can now appraise against the performance agreed in the contribution contract. With the *able to / want to / chance to* support and empowerment model in place, you can talk that through with your team member.

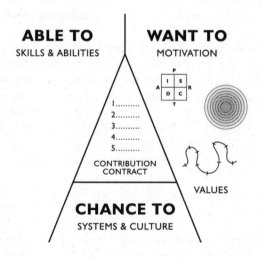

A contribution contract with Section 1 listing the customers (internal and external) provides the format for 360 degree feedback. This involves feedback on performance from internal customers who may be subordinates, peers and superiors and from external customers. The contribution contract focuses the input away from fluffy generalisations to specific gold medal winning feedback. It is so much easier to review strengths and improvement opportunities against this framework.

○ HIRING PEOPLE

Hiring the right people can be a real challenge and take significant time from a busy schedule. Having a clear contribution contract for the position makes advertising the job that much easier. You know the type of person you are looking for. A contribution contract is far more powerful than a job or position description or a series of objectives or key result areas (KRAs) and key performance indicators (KPIs).

Why? Remember the quote from Einstein — *'Sooner or later, we realise that the highest calling on the planet is to be of service to our fellow man.'*

A job description rarely speaks to the service enthusiasm of the spirit. Remember, nobody is looking for a job, everyone is looking for a game. A contribution contract provides the rules of your service game – satisfying the value criteria of the internal and external customers to achieve your organisation's vision.

When hiring people, finding out what they would like to do in the long term can be very useful. The key is to develop a personal growth contract with the candidate so that they can link the motivation of joining your team and helping realise your vision with the motivation for their own life journey. Remember the $25 million game to clarify life goals.

Say to the candidate – *'If you had 25 million dollars what would you do with your life?'* The reason for asking the candidate is to develop a sense of where they are heading. Do they have a really powerful sense of life direction? This knowledge serves two purposes. First, it tells you the calibre of person, the spirit within you are dealing with. Secondly, it gives you a hiring hook.

I remember one candidate who said, 'If I had 25 million dollars, I would move to the country and grow avocados.'

I thought to myself, 'Oh well, she seemed a good candidate, but she is not for my team. There is no powerful motivator to encourage a personal growth contract.'

To test her out before ending the interview, I said to her, 'Just assume you had been living in the country for ten years. Is that where you really want to live for the rest of your life?'

She said, 'Oh no, I wouldn't stay there all my life.'

So I asked her what she would do then and she said, 'I would come back to the city' and she then gave me a detailed description of the way she would like to be of service to humanity.

I asked her, 'What sort of qualities will you need if you are going to achieve that long term goal?'

She thought about it and we discussed her future growth needs to be the person worthy of attaining her life journey service goals.

I then said, 'Here is the deal. If you join us (because don't forget, good candidates usually have a number of alternative job offers), I will expect you to put in a 150 per cent effort to achieve gold medal performance in the areas specified in your contribution contract. I will support and empower you to make sure you achieve consistent gold medal performance standards. I will also further empower you by increasing your skills in the areas that you will need on your longer term life journey. That is the exchange.'

That is a Personal Growth Contract offer that your competitors (who are also trying to attract this candidate) are unlikely to make because they do not know how to talk to the spirit within.

Using these empowerment models can be very powerful in attracting the right people to your team. Most people want to play the games of life and business on 16 cylinders and there are relatively few 16 cylinder opportunities currently out there.

Offering them a 16 cylinder environment coupled with life journey growth (explicitly stated) will give you a great edge to attract and retain the best people.

o USING THE LAW OF GRAVITY
TO ATTRACT CALIBRE CANDIDATES

To assist you in understanding how to attract the right people to your team, there is a generalised principle of physics that we can use here to explain a powerful law of metaphysics.

Newton's law of gravity states that the force of attraction 'F' between two physical bodies is a function of 'G' the gravitational constant multiplied by 'M1' the mass of one body multiplied by 'M2' the mass of the other, divided by the square of the distance 'd' between them.

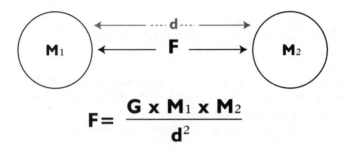

$$F= \frac{G \times M_1 \times M_2}{d^2}$$

Because this law of physical gravity is a generalised principle, it holds true throughout the physical universe. Gravity is the force that holds the physical universe of planets, stars and galaxies in place.

Equally, there is a force of metaphysical gravity that is always present as a metaphysical generalised principle. Everyone has metaphysical mass related to the state of their mind, emotions and spirit and the way they live.

Someone with limited, fearful thinking who is disassociated from their feelings and living with no integrity will have a small, unattractive metaphysical mass. Conversely someone who is sharp and alert, emotionally alive and living to high standards of integrity and service will have larger metaphysical mass.

Because you, your team and your vision have a certain combined metaphysical mass, you need to explore the effects this law is having on your business. What sort of people are you attracting? The laws of gravitational metaphysics affect the type of people and customers you will attract.

You can see that the law of gravity shows that the stronger the mass of one body, the stronger the force of attraction. A mass of 100 has more 'pulling power' than a mass of ten.

So the larger, the shinier, the brighter you make your team, work environment, culture and vision, the more likely you are to attract the calibre candidates you need.

Additional metaphysical gravity observations

You can also see from the law of metaphysical gravity that the closer you and your people are to your vision, the force of attraction increases proportional to the square of the distance still to go across your PERT planning rope bridges.

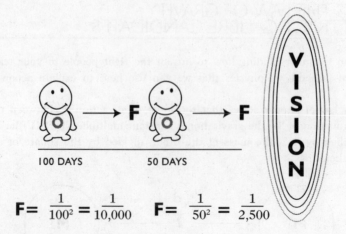

$$\mathbf{F} = \frac{1}{100^2} = \frac{1}{10,000} \qquad \mathbf{F} = \frac{1}{50^2} = \frac{1}{2,500}$$

The weakest force exerted by your vision on your team is the day you first draw it. After that, every day of action brings you closer and the metaphysical gravity of attraction between your team and the vision increases.

Managing people who are excited by an organisation's vision is so much easier.

The metaphysics of leaving

The law of metaphysical gravity also shows that the toughest step in walking away from an unhappy job (or a relationship!) is the first. One metre out the force pulling the person back is one over one-squared and equals one. Ten metres out, the force pulling back drops to one over ten-squared and is 100 times weaker.

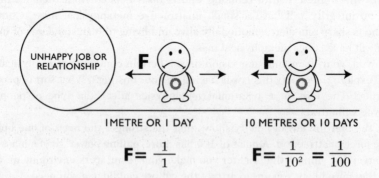

$$\mathbf{F} = \frac{1}{1} \qquad\qquad \mathbf{F} = \frac{1}{10^2} = \frac{1}{100}$$

It's twice as tough because the pull towards their preferred future (or new partner) is the weakest with the first step as the above diagram shows.

If one of your people really wants to leave your team to expand their life journey but is finding the decision hard, show them this diagram. If they really do need to move on, help them leave. Like the journeymen in the Middle Ages, they can always return later on with a whole world of new experiences to bring to your team's vision achievement.

o SUMMARY

Now you have tools to provide your people with:

- o purpose and vision

- o passion, motivation and enthusiasm

- o plans of action

With their contribution contracts, you also have a systematic approach to managing them to high performance by ensuring at all times the:

- o are *Able to*,

- o *Want to*,

- o and have the *Chance to* perform.

In the next chapter, we need to explore the fourth critical key to success — persistence. This is a vital spirit intelligence key because the aliens of resistance will show up and the spirit within must prevail and succeed. Giving people the power of persistence is essential.

Part Five

PERSISTENCE

Winning the Game

Arnold Schwarzenegger builds his muscles by lifting weights.

Spirit intelligence is developed by overcoming obstacles and gaining experience in achieving worth while vision and goals.

Newton's third law of motion states that for every action there is an equal and opposite reaction.

For any vision or goal that you create and then try to achieve, you are bound to encounter forces of apathy and opposition.

That is why you need the keys to persistence to overcome these forces.

Sixteen

THE POWER OF PERSISTENCE

'What this power is I cannot say, all I know is that it exists and it becomes available only when a man is in that state of mind in which he knows exactly what he wants and is fully determined not to quit until he finds it.'
ALEXANDER GRAHAM BELL

If you want to achieve consistently outstanding results, the ability to demonstrate the fourth success principle seems to be the great divide between the gold medal winners and the rest. It is summarised in one word — persistence — from the Latin — *per sistere* — to stand firm throughout.

Persistence is the fourth success key from *Think and Grow Rich*.

o DEFEATING THE RESISTANCE

Why is this? Because the enemy out there is called resistance — from the Latin — *re sistere* — to stand against you. On your life journey so far, I have no doubt you have already met the enemy — resistance.

Robert Burns said:

> *'The best laid schemes o' mice and men gang aft aglay.'*

Rough translation — shit happens!

At work, resistance can come at you in the form of an off-spec product for a crucial customer, unscheduled machine down time when trying to meet a contractual commitment, an unexpected competitor price drop, the resignation of key staff, failure to meet deadlines. At home or in your community you can be hit by unexpected power cuts or storms or sickness. The list of possible challenges that can wear down people's enthusiasm and staying power is endless.

The enemy is alive and well. The issue with resistance aliens is not whether they are going to show up to stop you. The issue is what you and the people around you are going to do when they do show up, because show up they will. The qualities of persistence are vital and you must ensure everyone has powerful strategies to beat the enemy.

> *'The boy who is going to make a great man ... must make up his mind not merely to overcome a thousand obstacles, but to win in spite of a thousand repulses and defeats.'*
> THEODORE ROOSEVELT

Remember you can't kill a resistance alien by tickling it with a feather. In the *Alien* movies, the heroine, Sigourney Weaver, has the mother of all flame throwers to do the job!

The purpose of this chapter is to explore the tools that you and your team will need to make sure that you minimise the chance of encountering resistance aliens.

Remember the Army maxim – *time spent in reconnaissance is never time wasted*. Reconnaissance to spot resistance aliens is certainly never time wasted. When they do show up, your flame thrower strategies must be sudden and intense, because as you know aliens grow very quickly by devouring their prey – US!

o SYSTEMS

Your primary weapon to ensure your team has the power of persistence is a focus on systems. Many resistance aliens can be defeated by increasing your awareness and understanding of the systems that are supposed to support and empower your people.

Examples of systems

What is a system? In the 1660s, accountants in Venice invented the general ledger as a systematic way of recording business transactions. Traffic lights and white lines on the road are systems for controlling the flow of traffic. In Australia, we drive between the white lines in an orderly flow of traffic. When the traffic light is green we go, when the light is red we stop, and when the light is amber we put our foot to the floor to go as fast as we can to get through!

Traffic lights and white lines are systems designed to move the traffic around without too many mistakes or accidents. Systems are an organised approach to achieving more efficient and effective activity.

You have systems designed to support your team — computer systems, quality control systems, telecommunication systems, machining systems, appraisal systems, communication systems. Everywhere you are surrounded by systems.

At home you may have the laundry basket, the pantry where you keep the food, the refrigerator. They are all systems, designed to make your life easier.

The need for good systems

Probably one of the best proponents of systems analysis was W. Edwards Demming. Demming was an American and after the Second World War, his view was that the key to competitive advantage in the post-war global market was going to be systematic measurement, communication and cooperation.

He first visited Japan in 1946 under the auspices of the Economic and Scientific section of the US Department of War. Over the ensuing years, he made a tremendous contribution to Japanese industry as they worked to rebuild and develop.

Consider product quality from post-war Japan. If you bought a transistor radio from Japan in the early 1960s and you turned it on, what came off in your hand? The knob! Their product quality was generally appalling.

Demming showed the Japanese that in a world market, competitive advantage can be derived from quality and the way to consistent quality improvement is systematic analysis and organisation.

97 per cent of mistakes and problems originate from poor systems

Demming is reported to have said that in his view, 97 per cent of mistakes and problems originate from sloppy, inefficient systems. We know that a mistake — in the Japanese example, the customer holding the radio knob in his hand — is a withdrawal from the trust account. So much for any chance of customer loyalty, which is a measure of the customer's trust account with the supplier.

Usually a mistake initially looks as though it is caused by somebody on the team. John or Louise has made a mistake. Although the cause of the mistake looks like a person, the real cause is almost always in the systems supporting or not supporting the person. So the poor performance of the person is the effect from the root cause of a sloppy support system, a resistance alien within the organisation.

If you've ever tackled a blocked drain, you will know that the blockage is the effect. The cause can be a root from a tree many meters away.

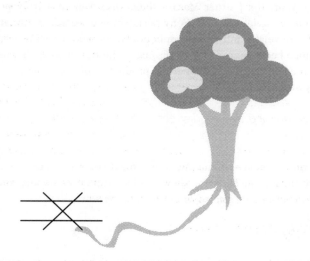

To maintain a high performance team, when mistakes or problems occur, always review the systems that are supposed to be supporting your team. Ninety-seven per cent of the time, the root cause of the problem will lie in your systems.

Systems education

The problem for us in tackling systems is that the Western education curriculum gives us very little training in systems analysis and understanding. Most people, on thinking about it, conclude they have had minimal or no formal education on this critical subject of identifying or developing systems. How about you?

That's why we don't spot the problem. We see the effect, the person apparently making the mistake. We are just not trained to spot the underlying root cause — the often invisible, sloppy, inefficient system. That was Demming's point.

Spirit intelligence requires that you correct this educational omission and start to focus on support systems analysis. Why? Because poor systems are the source of 97 per cent of the aliens of resistance that can crush the enthusiasm of the spirit within.

This is vital at work and equally important at home and in your community.

o KAIZEN

With Demming's help, the Japanese developed the concept of Kaizen — constant and never-ending systems and quality improvement.

> 'Little by little does the trick.'
> AESOP

For instance, the original idea for the Sony Walkman came from Sony co-founder Akio Morita himself when he saw how his daughter Naoko was so keen to have music around her everywhere she went. His partner Masara Ibuka also wanted a truly portable unit and complained about the weight of early Sony portable tape recorders. Initial production of a truly portable, light-weight unit and headphones was quite an engineering challenge. The Walkman has since been improved through many different models, because the Japanese realised that you could not reach the perfect product in one iteration. It was necessary to improve step by step – Kaizen.

> 'Perfection is attained by slow degrees, she requires the hand of time.'
> VOLTAIRE

Kaizen is constant and never-ending improvement. If you want your people to have strong empowering culture and the ability to show resilience and persistence, you have to employ the principle of never-ending improvement to your systems.

Your top six systems

What are the top six systems that your team performance depends on? They might be computing systems, scheduling systems or sales systems. Just take a minute to note them down.

Now asterisk those that are in truth, somewhat inefficient and sloppy and not really supporting your people in achieving gold medal performance.

o FLUID FLOW – LAMINAR VERSUS TURBULENT

To help you gain a better grasp of the importance of systems for your team culture and the resilience of your team and thus the effect on team passion and persistence, let's review another law of physics to provide a guide on the relevant law of metaphysics.

Take the example of fluid flow. Let's look at the difference between lamina flow and turbulent flow. Liquid pumped through a smooth, well formed pipe displays very efficient lamina flow.

LAMINAR FLOW VS TURBULENT FLOW

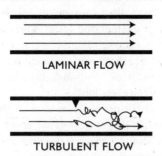

LAMINAR FLOW

TURBULENT FLOW

Lamina flow is defined as when the components of the liquid or gas are moving smoothly and efficiently down the pipe. A laminar flow pattern optimises flow.

If a snag or some sort of jagged edge is introduced on to the inside surface of the pipe, then the liquid will break into what is known as turbulent flow. Turbulent flow is much less efficient.

Flow rates will drop 20 per cent to 40 per cent, once lamina flow breaks down into turbulent flow. You can start to see that for high levels of sustained passion and persistence, it is critical that you ensure as much of the work of your team is flowing in lamina format, proceeding smoothly and supported by excellent systems.

Inefficient, sloppy systems are like snags on the inside of your team energy pipe. The inefficient system causes mistakes and problems, turbulent flow sets in and productivity and morale dives, not just a minor 2 per cent but a massive 20 to 40 per cent.

This law of fluid flow should sound your alarm bells. The effect of inefficient systems on your team can have a massive negative effect on your team culture and their ability to demonstrate persistence and achieve high performance results.

Conversely, working on the worst of your systems can have a major pay back on your journey to hone a resilient, high performance team success culture and the power of persistence.

Systems analysis is just as relevant in your community or at home. Faced with this major source of resistance aliens, spirit intelligence requires a systems focus everywhere.

Check the list of your top six systems and visit your Commitments Register. What can you do to tighten up your sloppy, inefficient systems? If you don't act, it is like feeding the resistance aliens and eroding your team's power of persistence.

You won't need to worry about external competition. Your own self-generated and tolerated competition in the form of home-grown systems based resistance aliens will successfully cripple your team. So what can you do to fix these system problems now? Write it down.

○ AN EXAMPLE OF SYSTEMS BASED RESISTANCE ALIENS

Let's look at an example of mistakes and problems and then explore the systems cause behind them.

Service call out delays

A good example of invisible systems based resistance aliens causing trouble surfaced during a meeting of the management team of the Emperor Gold Mine in Fiji. We were discussing the unacceptably long delays caused when mining work stopped underground because of mechanical failure of the drilling equipment, and how long it took to call out someone from technical services or engineering to go down the mine to assess and fix the problem.

Initially it appeared as though the tech service and engineering people on call-out were to blame and there was a fair amount of emotional discussion about the fact that the call-out people were lazy and not doing their job.

So the effect was clear – the call-out people were slow in showing up at the rock face underground, thus they were to blame. However, because of our discussions in the past on systems analysis, Brad Gordon, the Mine Manager at the time, stepped up to the whiteboard and drew the system that underpinned the call-out process.

Brad drew a picture of the mine and the telephone link to the hut which acted as the central co-ordination point for call-out services. Brad made it clear that the responsibility for call-out staff lay with a different functional area of the mine management structure.

When we tackled the systems operating in the call-out hut, we found that the call-out service people, mainly Fijians and some Indians, had been spending long hours sitting in the hut waiting to be called out. So call-out management had agreed that they could go back to their homes in their villages that surround the mine and be on stand-by to be called out from there.

When they were needed, a truck would be dispatched to fetch them. It would only be a few extra minutes to reach any of the village communities around the mine and they could spend all those hours productively with their family which made a lot of sense.

Further analysis, however, showed that the quality of the radio communication system between the call-out hut and the trucks had been intermittent and generally poor quality. Communication equipment was the responsibility of another functional area within the mine.

You see what is happening here. Functional responsibility in any organisation is allocated and delegated. Systems run locally. No one sees the wider ramifications and the resistance aliens have a field day.

A large mine site always has something that is not working properly. The conditions are relatively harsh. So action was agreed to fix up the radios, but there were still persistent problems. It took a while for further systems analysis to show that in another area of the mine there had been tremendous concern about fuel consumption, so the engineering department had altered the governors on the mine trucks to reduce the fuel consumption.

The problem was that some of the call-out staff lived in villages up fairly steep hills. So when the truck went out to pick them up, the truck could no longer climb the hill to the man's house as the governor adjustment to reduce fuel consumption had also reduced available power! The truck driver had to walk up the hill. Sometimes the man was not in his house, but had gone to visit a nearby friend.

So what started out as a simple problem — call-outs were taking too long — evolved into a quite complex systems analysis and at each point, somebody seemed to be at fault. However, behind the person at fault, it was the systems that were inefficient and sloppy.

An isolated incident? Not at all. Demming would have said — *typical. 97 per cent of mistakes and problems originate from poor systems.'*

The root cause of the problem — the truck governors had been altered in a genuine attempt to reduce fuel consumption. The effects, not 20 yards away (like the metaphor of the tree roots blocking the drain), but a mile away on the other side of the mine site, were horrendous call-out delays. Any savings in fuel consumption were far outweighed by the cost of the mine crews kept waiting, unable to drill precious footage.

So what are you doing with your systems, be they computer systems, machining systems, team systems or leadership systems?

Optimising spirit intelligence suggests that you re-visit your list of the key systems that support your work. Then with your team analyse each one with the ferocity of a flame thrower attitude. Where are the systems inefficient and sloppy? Where can they be improved?

o SYSTEMS ACCOUNTABILITY

In any organisation everybody has a tale to tell of inefficient and sloppy systems. Everybody knows the systems are failing them. Ask them who is accountable for the system and they reply that it is someone in personnel or someone in engineering. Then ask them if they have a person with the name 'someone' on their pay-roll! There is no 'someone', so nothing gets done to fix the problem.

Systems analysis is one step. Finding who is accountable for a system can be a second major challenge, because often responsibility for systems spans a number of functional areas in a company. Because we are not trained in systems analysis in the Western education system, we cannot see the systems for the resistance aliens that they have become. Therefore it is highly unlikely that functional teams in an organisation will easily spot the cross-functional systems problems.

To overcome the aliens of resistance, you must tackle this issue by forming cross- functional systems analysis teams.

If you leave it to 'someone' else, the resistance aliens thrive. You need unreasonable champions to fix your sloppy systems, people who are prepared to take on the aliens of inefficient systems. It can be a real battle needing tenacity and passion.

Boiled frogs

You see the need for the process of systems analysis. You may have heard of the famous experiment of the boiled frog: if you put a frog in cold water in a pot and heat the water up quickly, the frog will jump out. However, if you put a frog in cold water and warm the water very slowly, the frog does not notice and as the temperature rises, the frog drifts into unconsciousness and finally is boiled alive.

We are often blind to our systems issues, the resistance aliens have surreptitiously crept up and are slowly 'boiling us alive'. The spirit within then shuts down in despair.

Alien of the month

With our clients, we often have an 'alien of the month' focus. We run a systems analysis around the principle of – what's not working? You may find that this sounds negative, but I highly recommend it for your next team meeting. You can preface the review of what's not working with an upbeat review of what's working really well.

People may say — *'Well, for months and months when we worked back, the air-conditioning used to go off at 7 pm, but now with that key installed on the wall, we can re-boot the air-conditioning system and work on all night if we want to. That is working really great. Well done team! Got that one fixed.'*

When you have discussed the things that are working, and the mood is up and positive, you can then ask what is not working. This is not a general endorsement for a complaining. This is specifically to find out what systems are letting the team down. List what is not working so well. Make sure you take the analysis time to ensure you are listing root cause systems and not effects.

Spend time putting your team's list of poor systems in order of priority and then pick the highest priority system that is failing everyone. Make that the resistance 'alien of the month' and then develop an alien eradication program and flame thrower strategy to fix the problem system: what has to be done and by whom to improve the target system to gold medal standards. Remember spirit intelligence is about making better empowerment choices.

Use the principles we have already covered and describe the ideal system you need. Then use the PERT graphical planning technique to work back — *what happened just before that?* — to provide a mini plan to ensure the specific system is improved permanently.

Excellent systems avoid the turbulence associated with mistakes and problems.

'When people understand the entire system, there is something about the human spirit that spontaneously aspires to be competent and succeed.'
W EDWARDS DEMMING

o PHYSICS AND METAPHYSICS OF PERSISTENCE

When reviewing your systems, it is easiest to first look at the physical systems that support your team, such as computer systems, call-out systems, engineering systems, priority systems. However, it is not enough to just look at physical systems challenges as a key to persistence. To maximise persistence, you need to look at the metaphysics of what is happening on your team.

Ohm's law

As we have discussed previously, the keys to the laws of metaphysics lie in a review of the laws of physics. One law of physics which is very useful in improving team and personal persistence is Ohm's Law. Georg Ohm worked with electricity and his law is usually expressed as:

$$V = I * R$$

'V' the voltage equals 'I' the current multiplied by 'R' the resistance.

For our purposes, the law is best expressed as:

$$I = V / R$$

Where the current 'I' equals 'V' the voltage divided by 'R' the resistance.

OHM's LAW

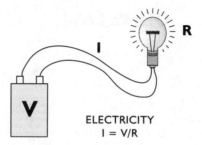

ELECTRICITY
$I = V/R$

In the diagram, the current flowing through the wire 'I' is a function of 'V' the voltage of the battery which is like the pressure in the battery pushing the electrons down the wire and 'R' which is the resistance of the filament in the light bulb.

To increase the current 'I' flowing through the wire, either increase 'V' the voltage, or reduce the resistance 'R' of the filament. Either way there is an increase in the flow of current 'I'.

Ohm's law is equally applicable to the physics of the hose you use to water the garden.

OHM's LAW

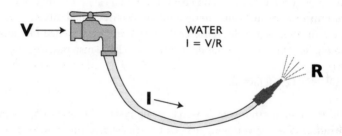

WATER
$I = V/R$

'I' now equals the flow of water through the hose pipe, 'V' is the water pressure and 'R' is the resistance of the spray nozzle.

To increase 'I' the flow of water through the hose pipe, you have two choices: increase the water pressure 'V' or reduce the resistance 'R' of the spray nozzle by changing from a fine spray to a strong jet.

Ohm's Law is a law of physics. It equally applies in the law of metaphysics.

Suppose you have a good team, but there is trouble with their persistence. You have the purpose defined. You have a vision. You have your plans clear. You have produced your graphical PERT planning charts and they are up on the wall in the team war room. You have focused on inspiring team passion to fire up the 16 cylinders and you still seem to be striking a lot of problems. You need more energy, more enthusiasm in your team. They don't seem to be able to sustain their enthusiasm when problems arise, they lack persistence and the ability to stand firm throughout. What do you do?

OHM's LAW

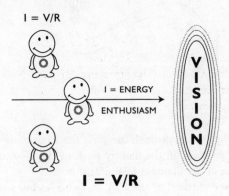

$$I = V/R$$

$$I = \text{ENERGY} \quad \text{ENTHUSIASM}$$

$$I = V/R$$

Apply Ohm's law to the metaphysics of your team. If 'I' equals the energy and enthusiasm flowing through your team, which is a measure of their ability to persist, what is 'V'? 'V' is the power of your team vision. To increase team enthusiasm, you need to increase the power of the vision that is motivating your people to move forwards towards an exciting co-created future.

You might say you can't do that. The vision is about as good as you can do. So what else can you do to improve enthusiasm, energy and persistence capability?

Ohm's law indicates that to increase enthusiasm and persistence further, you have to reduce resistance 'R'. On a team, what does it mean to have resistance in the metaphysics?

The law of entrainment

Here we need to turn to another generalised law of physics: the law of entrainment, because the law of entrainment gives you your first clue to resistance on your team.

In 1665 a Dutch scientist, Christian Huygens, discovered that if two cuckoo clocks are placed side by side on a wall, within the space of a few days, the pendulums start to swing in a synchronised manner, even though they are not connected physically.

'If two rhythms are nearly the same, and their sources are in close proximity, they will always entrain.'

CHRISTIAN HUYGENS

LAW OF ENTRAINMENT

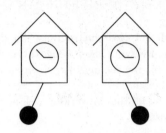

This is quite an extraordinary phenomenon. The law of entrainment is a high woo-woo physical law. A Russian, Itchak Bentoff has done further work on this law. His studies showed that when a mother puts her baby on the breast, within a minute or two the heartbeats of the mother and baby entrain and beat in unison, even though the blood supplies and hearts are separate.

o RESCUING HUG

The picture below is from an article called 'The Rescuing Hug'. The article details the first week of life of a set of twins. Each were in their respective incubators, and one was not expected to live. A hospital nurse fought against the hospital rules and placed the babies in one incubator. When they were placed together, the healthier of the two threw an arm over her sister in an endearing embrace. The smaller baby's heart rate stabilised and her temperature rose to normal. Let us not forget to embrace those whom we love.

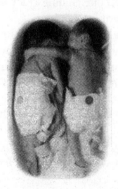

To demonstrate the power of this law of entrainment in our workshops, I ask the team to stand in a circle, shoulder to shoulder, facing in towards the centre of the circle, holding their arms out and down with their hands together so that their arms and hands form a pendulum. Then I ask the team to work together as a team, to swing their pendulums from side to side and achieve entrainment.

Of course everybody independently swings their pendulum from left to right, bumping into the people next to them and it is total chaos. There is no synchronisation, no entrainment. I ask them how it feels and they reply – 'That is how it feels working on our team' — and everybody laughs.

Then I ask the leader to call out clear instructions. So they all lean in with their pendulums – 'left, right, left, right.' Everyone then swings their pendulum to the left and the right in harmony. As they lean in, the feeling in that circle is really powerful. It feels really good to be on an entrained team.

You have probably been on a team that is working well and totally entrained. It feels great yet can be challenging to sustain.

Counter-entrainment

In our team circle example, I then ask a couple of people to act as counter-entrainers. In their own time, once the whole team are swinging their 'pendulums' in harmony and entrainment, the counter-entrainers start strongly swinging their pendulums in the opposite direction.

Well you can imagine what happens. Within a few seconds the rhythm and the entrainment of the whole team falls apart. I then say to the team – 'Cast your mind back into your organisation. Who is counter-entraining? Who is working contrary to the spirit of the team?'

Invariably, almost everybody can identify somebody who is working counter-entrained, working against the team spirit. The problem is you only need one person on your team to be counter-entraining to significantly take the team from the smooth harmony of laminar flow to the 40 per cent drop in efficiency that turbulent flow represents.

It is treason to your team to allow that person to remain unchallenged. You may have the greatest definiteness of purpose and vision in the world. You could be a master of the passion cylinders. You could have outstanding PERT planning rope bridges, but counter-entraining is treason to the team spirit.

People who commit treason during wars are lined up against a wall and shot. Perhaps this may be a bit extreme for your organisation! But counter-trainers must be dealt with.

I once created a challenging situation for myself. I hired a sales manager who was very sharp mentally. He was an exceptionally good salesman with an excellent marketing brain. What I did not realise was his approach to acceptable standards of business was very different from mine. In those days I had to cover a large geographical area so I would be out of the office for days and occasionally a week or two at a time, leaving the sales manager in charge. I would leave the team feeling good and entrained. I would come back a few days or a week later, step out of the lift doors and I could feel something different. What was wrong? The entrainment had gone.

I subsequently found out that as soon as I was out of the office, out came the keys to the drinks cupboard in the boardroom. The sales manager was taking the staff out for long liquid lunches, taking customers to topless restaurants. You have to form your own judgements on what is acceptable behaviour for your business, but as far as I was concerned that was not on.

I called the man in and I explained that I was not impressed and that the mood of the team was down. He said that he understood where he had been going wrong and that it would not happen again. What do you think happened? Yes. It happened again.

How many chances and counselling sessions do you give someone? I restated what was required in terms of acceptable business and team performance standards. Again he contravened my requests, caused counter-entrainment and eventually he left the organisation.

It is treason to allow the rotten apple to flourish because your whole team barrel will go bad. One of the keys to persistence is to identify who is counter-entraining and then take corrective action.

'And if a house be divided against itself, that house cannot stand.'
MARK 3:25

'United we stand, divided we fall.'
AESOP

However, before you remove your counter-entrainers, remember that in chapter fifteen on managing people, we discussed that when faced with a person who is not performing, there are five questions to ask:

1. Do they understand the game — 'let's achieve the vision'?

2. Do they know the rules — their personal contribution?

3. Are they *able to* play the game to win — skills and abilities?

4. Do they have the *chance to* play the game — supported with sound systems and culture?

5. Do they want to play the game — are they motivated?

Are there any counter-entrainers on your team that you need to confront and counsel?

To continue our review of the keys to persistence, in the next chapter we will review keys to improving personal persistence.

Seventeen

PERSONAL PERSISTENCE KEYS

'It is better to conquer yourself than to win a thousand battles.
Then the victory is yours. It cannot be taken from you, not by angels
or by demons, heaven or hell.'

GAUTAMA BUDDHA

The power of persistence is a critical team skill because the resistance aliens will always show up to stand between you and your success.

As we have discussed, team persistence is greatly enhanced by ensuring you have good systems and a supportive success culture.

The power of personal persistence is a key leadership quality because when the going gets tough, people will look to you for guidance, inspiration and sometimes raw staying power.

This chapter will explore the spirit intelligence choices you have so you can improve the power of your personal persistence and deliver outstanding leadership.

We will do this by reviewing the personal resistance aliens that must be confronted if you wish to develop to the full extent of your management and leadership potential. For some people, this will increase the woo-woo factor.

o PERSONAL RESISTANCE

Do you sometimes find that your personal energy and enthusiasm is failing and yet you do not want to quit? Do you find yourself mentally tired at the end of the day and sometimes not able to think as clearly as you would want? Do you sometimes find irritability and stress affecting your judgment and your interactions with people around you?

Sure, we all have good days and bad days, but some of us are confronted with such enormous challenges that extra persistence and clarity could make the difference between long-term success or failure.

As 13 of the 16 cylinders of body, mind, emotions and spirit are metaphysical, most of the high leverage keys to reducing personal resistance lie in your metaphysics.

○ OHM'S LAW RE-VISITED

As we need guidance from the laws of physics to understand the laws of the unseen metaphysics, we turn once again to Ohm's law.

'I' is now the energy and enthusiasm flowing through you and 'V' is the power of your personal vision and your goals. If you want more energy flowing through you and more enthusiasm, you first need to increase the attraction of your personal vision and the power of your personal goals.

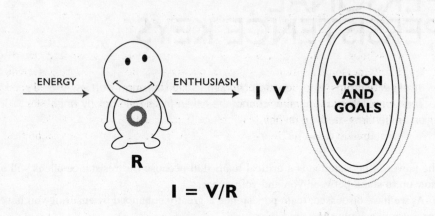

$$I = V/R$$

If you say you have done that to the best of your ability, then the answer that stares at you from Ohm's law is quite clear, you have to reduce 'R' your personal resistance. What does that mean?

○ LAMINAR AND TURBULENT FLOW RE-VISITED

We have previously reviewed resistance within a team. Resistance can come from a number of areas. When we review personal resistance, it is best to re-visit the example of laminar and turbulent fluid flow.

Remember with smooth pipes, the water flows through the pipe in highly efficient lamina flow.

If, however, there is a snag or a jagged edge on the inside of the pipe, when the water flow reaches the snag, it is thrown into turbulent flow. Efficiency is reduced 20 per cent to 40 per cent.

So where are the possible snags in your personal physical and metaphysical 'pipes'? Can you afford this potential loss in personal efficiency and life energy?

To answer these questions we need to review the concept of personal speed and the lack of personal speed caused by personal resistance.

○ BMES SPEED

We can use the 16 cylinder model of body, mind, emotion and spirit to review personal speed, because we are not at rest.

We are all in motion, at speed, in body, mind, emotion and spirit. We move around our environment. Our minds are constantly moving from thought to thought. Our emotions are shifting continually. Our human spirits are tough and resilient, ever tackling adversity and moving along on life's journey.

○ THE RELATIONSHIP LAWS OF METAPHYSICS

In our workshops, we often start this section on metaphysical motion and speed by first reviewing interpersonal relationships and then discussing people at work. Reviewing inter-personal relationships introduces the concepts you need to improve your personal persistence.

This approach allows examination of the relevant generalised laws of physics and sheds considerable light on the metaphysics of relationships, at home and at work.

We have already discussed Newton's law of gravity between two physical bodies:

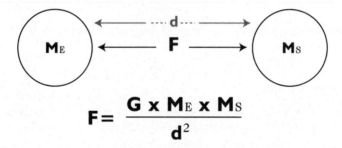

$$F= \frac{G \times M_E \times M_S}{d^2}$$

If 'Me' is be the mass of the Earth, 'Ms' the mass of the sun and 'd' the distance between them, then the gravitational force of attraction 'F' pulling the Earth towards the sun is a function of the gravitational constant 'G' multiplied by the mass of the Earth 'Me' multiplied by the mass of the sun 'Ms' divided by the square of the distance 'd' between the two bodies.

However the Earth is not stationary, it is in motion as it orbits around the sun.

○ THE LAW OF CENTRIPETAL FORCE

Therefore if we now also consider the attraction between two physical bodies in motion, such as our Earth orbiting the sun, or possibly a binary star where the two stars are orbiting each other, there is a second physical law that comes into play, the law of centripetal force.

The law of centripetal force states that the force 'F' required to hold an orbiting body such as the Earth in orbit is a function of 'Me' the mass of the Earth multiplied by the square of 'Ve' its orbital velocity through space divided by 'd' the orbital radius, in this case the distance of the Earth from the sun.

For a physical body in motion, such as the Earth, to orbit around the sun, the force of gravitational attraction between the Earth and the sun provides the centripetal force that keeps the Earth in orbit.

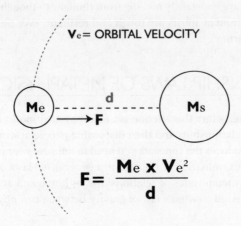

V_e = ORBITAL VELOCITY

$$F = \frac{M_e \times V_e^2}{d}$$

Without that centripetal force of attraction holding the Earth in orbit, the Earth would fly off at a tangent into deep space.

o RELATIONSHIPS

If we look at two people in a relationship, we move from physics into the realm of unseen metaphysics and the same generalised principles of gravity and centripetal force apply.

When two people originally meet they are in motion, going about their daily lives.

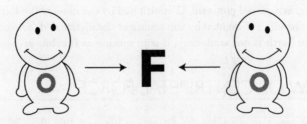

If on meeting they are attracted to each other, the law of metaphysical gravity comes into play.

The strength of a metaphysical attraction between two people depends on the distance between them. It's harder to maintain a relationship separated by a large physical distance because the force of inter-attraction reduces by the square of the distance dividing the two people: the tyranny of distance.

You may have experienced the same problem in managing a distant branch office. In Australia, Sydney and Melbourne are only 500 miles apart but Perth is 3000 miles to the west. Trying to have the Perth branch committed to the same team and the same vision is hard work. The tyranny of distance is true, proven by Newton's law of gravity as the inter-attraction reduces by the square of the distance. The Perth guys are always doing their own thing. It's not their fault. They just don't feel that close to head office.

It will be the same problem for branch offices on any continent because the law of metaphysical gravity is a generalised principle. It always holds true.

Returning to our example of two people who are attracted to each other by the law of metaphysical gravity — because the two people are also in motion with speed, the law of centripetal force is also at work and if they form a relationship, they orbit each other.

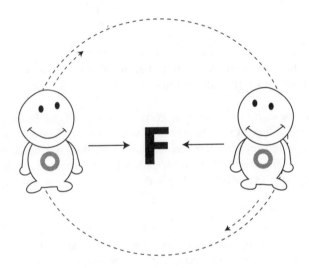

They stay in motion going about their daily lives but now they are in a relationship. They share their lives by staying in touch physically, mentally, emotionally and spiritually.

The force of metaphysical gravity, the attraction they feel for each other, provides the centripetal force to keep them orbiting each other in relationship.

Stable relationships

For a relationship to be stable and last, their orbits must be stable. The two people must have roughly similar body, mind, emotion and spirit speeds.
A fitness fanatic who loves the outdoor life is unlikely to stay happily in orbit with a beer swilling, totally unfit slob. A genius is unlikely to remain in harmonious orbit with someone who is dumb and boring.

An emotionally expressive person is unlikely to remain in stable orbit with a cold emotionless person who is totally withdrawn and dissociated from their feelings. A spiritual person is unlikely to remain in relationship to a liar and a thief.

Two people of similar metaphysical speed will orbit each other in a stable relationship.

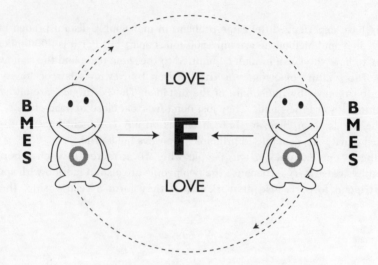

As the diagram shows, you orbit your partner because you both are in motion, physically, mentally, emotionally and spiritually and the space in the circle between you is what we call 'love'.

It would seem clear, from the laws of gravity and centripetal force, that for you to increase the amount of love in your relationship you need to increase the size of the orbit. The laws of physics and metaphysics dictate that to do that you need to increase your metaphysical mass or speed or both. So in a relationship if you want more love, how do you both increase physical and metaphysical speed? We'll come to that shortly.

Relationship break up

A binary star consists of two stars in motion, orbiting each other. If one of the stars were to suddenly pick up speed, the physical law of centripetal force would predict instability and orbital imbalance.

The same is true if one partner in a relationship starts to pick up physical or metaphysical speed. If one partner increases speed and the other does not, the relationship can be thrown into orbital imbalance.

If one of the partners starts to improve physical fitness, they will pick up physical speed. If the other wants to stay as an unfit couch potato, watching television all day, orbital balance may be impossible to maintain.

The same principle of orbital speed change, orbital imbalance and relationship break up similarly occurs if one partner becomes interested in sharpening the mind, emotions or spirit using the keys we will summarise in this chapter, and the other partner does not.

When severe orbital imbalance occurs, the partners fly apart, the relationship ends and they continue in motion on their own, no longer in orbit around each other.

They will then be affected by the laws of metaphysical gravity and motion and be attracted to someone of similar metaphysical mass and speed and form a new stable orbit with their new partner who is at their new speed.

You will sometimes observe in middle age, that either the man or more often the woman in the relationship will start to pick up spirit and emotion speed by going to yoga or

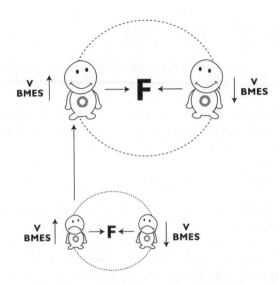

meditation classes or self-development courses. The other partner does nothing, they do not pick up speed and so orbital imbalance occurs. The relationship breaks up with the partner at higher metaphysical speed attracted to someone new of similar metaphysical speed who maybe they met at the self-development class! Goodbye old partner!

Teams in orbit

The same gravitational metaphor applies when examining teams. In this case the vision can be likened to the sun. The team orbit the vision held in orbit by the centripetal attraction of the vision.

Various team members can have different metaphysical mass and speed and thus orbit at different radii to the vision, like the planets orbiting our sun.

With teams, the space in the middle of the orbits is called trust. A weak vision, slow speeds, small orbits and small metaphysical mass produces low trust. Strong vision, greater centripetal attraction allowing larger metaphysical mass, greater speeds and thus larger orbits allows more trust.

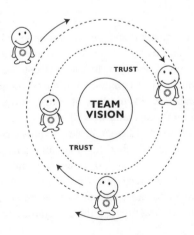

o INCREASING PERSONAL SPEED

Let us now look at what could be slowing down your personal speed and what you can do to increase speed. This in turn will increase your personal resilience, energy levels and persistence.

Because you are in motion, your speed is affected by your internal resistance. To increase speed, you need to reduce internal resistance. Resistance of body, mind, emotions and spirit. What does that mean?

Physical body speed

Body speed is the easiest to start with. If you need to reduce your personal physical resistance and increase physical speed, how fit are you physically?

As we have discussed earlier, you know that you are supposed to do aerobic exercises three times a week for 20 minutes. Do you exercise regularly? Why not make a commitment to improve your physical fitness and speed?

You know that you are not supposed to overdo junk food and drinks, coffee and alcohol. Are you handling the intake to your physical body in moderation and sensibly? You never accidentally put food and drink in your mouth! In improving speed, your physical fitness is an easy first step to reducing personal resistance.

Spirit speed

People with spirit speed are working with integrity, they are not clogged up and crippled by guilt, fear and negativity. Clarify your life purpose with the $25 million game. Take responsibility for your life journey of growth, your plans and your passion keys and your relationships. Live with integrity.

Imagine that universal intelligence is watching over your shoulder so wrong behaviour cannot be hidden! Strengthen your own personal ethics, for example, point out a discrepancy in your bill to your waiter when you are undercharged at a restaurant — play it straight. Value your spirit space and keep it clean. Show spirit intelligence.

Mind and emotion speed

Increasing the clarity and speed of the mind and emotions is about removing the blocks of the mind and the blocks to emotional laminar flow. To understand these concepts, we need a model:

At the core of your being there is your spirit, the real you. As we have discussed, to access that spirit point of awareness, just calm down and observe your body, the thoughts streaming through your mind and the ebb and flow of your emotions. That's the spirit you — the watcher, the calm centre of the cyclone we call life.

All of us have surrounded ourselves with an impressive act as we go through our daily lives. Our act is the front we maintain to the world that shows we know what we're doing and we have it all together. Well, most of the time! We all try and appear cool and in control. That's our act!

However, beneath the surface, we have what is known as emotional baggage. We keep this emotional baggage buried deep down inside our subconscious mind and hidden in our bodies. Here we store all the pain, all the hurt, all the rejections and all the negative beliefs that we have experienced in our lives.

It is as though these negative beliefs are tape recorded loops just below our conscious awareness, whispering:

I'm not good enough

Nobody loves me

It's no use trying

Men / women can't be trusted

I'm angry

I'm scared

I can't make it

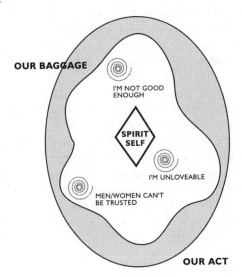

Occasionally our emotional baggage comes up towards the surface of conscious awareness and then we have to make an effort to push it back down again so we don't feel it.

Our emotional baggage clogs our thinking and our emotional resilience. It reduces mental and emotional speed. It is our personal resistance. It is our emotional baggage that hinders our personal persistence.

Our emotional baggage can manifest as uneasy, stressful feelings. That is why some people smoke because smoking cigarettes is, in their experience, an effective way to suppress unwanted feelings and emotional baggage. When they try and give up smoking, up comes their emotional baggage that the cigarettes effectively suppressed. They feel irritable and yucky, they can't think as clearly and so are strongly tempted to reach for another cigarette to suppress the emotional baggage again.

Some people put on extra body weight because body weight is useful for suppressing and holding old emotional baggage feelings that we do not want to feel. They hold the negative feelings safely at a distance in their body mass. Hiding negative emotions in our muscular structure is a wonderful way of not feeling the metaphysical yuck.

That's why losing weight can be such a tough challenge. The excess weight is the effect — the emotional baggage being held is the hidden cause. If some one loses weight, up comes their emotional baggage, they crave relief from feeling uneasy or yucky, they eat, they find relief, their body weight increases again. They are caught in a vicious cycle.

○ REDUCING YOUR RESISTANCE — CLEANING UP YOUR EMOTIONAL BAGGAGE

If you want to reduce your personal resistance and turbulence and speed up your mind and improve your emotional resilience, how are you going to get rid of the emotional baggage? How are you going to ream out the snags on the inside of your 'pipes' to achieve laminar flow? How are you going to clean up your inner metaphysics?

Fortunately, in the last 40 years, the so-called New Age movement has produced a wide range of new answers, and thousands of years ago, the Eastern sages had already developed some simple tools.

We will now review some of the tools available. Does it take courage to tackle your own emotional baggage? Yes. Is it worth it? I can only speak from the personal experience of myself and my associates and the answer is overwhelmingly – yes.

Why would you bother to tackle your own deep subconscious emotional baggage? Because as you systematically clean it out, you feel better, your health improves, your thinking gains in clarity, you have more composure and better emotional empathy. Your powers of personal persistence increase significantly.

In summary, you develop better leadership qualities because the quality of your 'PASS-I-ON' improves. It is that simple. If you want to do the most for your team, you must maximise your own leadership potential. Tackling your own personal resistance and subconscious emotional baggage is the way forward but it does require more personal courage than some people can muster or sustain.

Many people prefer to hide from confronting their personal baggage and either choose to be followers or try and lead from their act. This is not a good strategy as people see through the act even if they pretend they don't. Respect is never gained and the leadership fails when pressure mounts. The resistance defeats the persistence.

To achieve long-term success, you will require persistence, so I urge you to muster the courage and tackle the personal resistance that may be hindering you.

Meditation

Probably the oldest approach to cleaning out your emotional baggage is the simple technique of meditation. There are many schools of meditation. All are designed to progressively clear the blocks and focus the mind. A clear mind operates at speed as there are no blocks. Visualising the colours of the rainbow from red to violet is one way to still the mind as we have learned.

You have probably heard of using mantras, repeating a sound, over and over again to calm the mind. When we slow the mind down from the normally speedy beta wave state to the calmer alpha wave state, this allows the mind to very gently throw off emotional baggage. Does this all happen in a day? No. It takes days, weeks, months and years of regular practice. Your emotional baggage was built up over time, it takes time to clean out. Meditation is a gentle way of clearing out the emotional baggage in our deeper minds.

> 'The man who acquires the ability to take full possession of his own mind may take possession of anything else to which he is justly entitled.'
> ANDREW CARNEGIE

Try it and watch how your mental clarity, calmness and resilience under pressure improve as time goes by.

Yoga

Yoga is an excellent tool for toning the physical body by stimulating your metaphysical energies (the chakras or energy centres as we discussed in Chapter 7 on leadership passion).

Our energy centres support and sustain physical health. By stretching the muscles, yoga exercises 'squeeze out' the emotional baggage held in the muscles. This promotes physical flexibility and clarity of mind.

Re-birthing

The New Age movement has developed many other techniques for reducing your internal metaphysical resistance, the snags in your 'pipes'. Re-birthing is a technique whereby, in the hands of a skilled professional, you lie down and hyperventilate, breathing in and out without pause to hyper oxygenate the blood.

There comes a point when your spirit observes — *'Wait a minute. Let me check this out. I am lying safely on a soft mattress. I am protected. I am with a professional expert. I have more oxygen in my bloodstream and more energy than I have had for many years. Hey, have I got some emotional baggage to let go!'* — and out it comes in the form of anger, crying, shouting, bashing the mattress, or even hysterical giggling.

It really does not matter, because as the emotional baggage blows, it is gone forever.

Is this high woo-woo for some? Sure. It requires courage to temporarily lose it in front of the re-birther while you release your pent up emotional baggage, but ask yourself what do you want. Do you want to operate at slow speed, carrying all your internal emotional baggage? Or do you want to live at high speed, with high resilience, free from emotional baggage? It is up to you whether your reach for your Commitments Register or your shelf!

Bio-energetics

Bio-energetics is an easily learned, simple physical technique for shaking away out of the body, old locked up energies that have been holding emotional baggage.

Rolfing and deep tissue massage

Rolfing and deep tissue massage are other methods whereby a skilled masseur goes deep into the muscles and massages out the negative emotions that are held there.

Other emotional baggage clearing techniques

There are many other emotional baggage clearing techniques available. The Hindus have a saying – *'When the pupil is ready, the teacher appears.'* So if this area of reducing personal resistance to increase your personal persistence and speed interests you, these days in any bookshop there are hundreds of books to guide you.

Go searching and you will find the book or the course or the workshop that is most suitable for you.

In my view, the techniques of removing personal resistance to improve personal resilience and persistence are absolutely essential in business and also in maintaining personal relationships in today's stressful world.

Without reaming out the 'pipes', without clearing your own internal emotional baggage, you may not be able to muster enough persistence to stay the distance. Remember the gold medal standard is getting tougher all the time. All you need is courage and some action to get started.

Fear

Usually the fears of doing something that may plague you are an illusion. FEAR is also an acronym:

FALSE
EXPECTATIONS
APPEARING
REAL

The only real enemy is in your mind. I am sure in the past, you have experienced situations where you have been almost paralysed by fear. However, once you have found the courage to start dealing with the problem, it is never as big as you thought it was. Have you found that?

'One of the great discoveries a man makes, one of his great surprises, is to find he can do what he was afraid he couldn't do.'
HENRY FORD

So if you have fear of tackling your personal emotional baggage, ask yourself — what is the expectation appearing before me that looks so real? Find the courage to act and know that the expectation is probably false.

'Do the thing we fear, and the death of fear is certain.'
RALPH WALDO EMERSON

Can you confront and handle your own emotional baggage? If you do find the courage to do that, then you will have the leadership experience to show the way, to help your team members eventually tackle their personal resistance so the whole team can improve personal speed and persistence.

Clearing team emotional baggage

If you are tempted to encourage your team members to clear their emotional baggage so that everyone can pick up speed, remember the basic market life cycle principles. In a new market for any good or service, innovators will try first. Opinion leaders are exactly that, they influence the opinions of others. The mature part of a market and the laggards will initially say — *'I don't need that'*.

Don't force personal growth on your team.

When launching a new product or concept, the marketing message in a new market is aimed at innovators and the promotional message is — *'you need this'*. Once a market begins to grow, the marketer aims at the opinion leaders with the promotional message — *'it's available'*.

Most of your team will probably initially shy away from this very personal, high woo-woo concept of reaming out metaphysical 'pipes' to clear out old emotional baggage, reduce personal resistance and increase personal persistence and speed.

Lead by example. Then target the innovators on your team followed by your opinion leaders.

'You cannot teach a man anything. You can only help him to discover it within himself.'
GALILEO GALILEI

o INTENT

Another area that effects personal persistence, as we saw in studying *Think and Grow Rich*, is the strength of your intent.

How strong is your intent to succeed, to stretch towards your team vision?

The power of intent comes from down in the solar

The word intent is derived from the Latin *in tendere* to stretch towards

plexus where the will power is focused. Demonstrating intent is easy when times are good. When times are tough and you feel like quitting, the test is how strongly you can get in touch with your will power and summon the intent to reach forward towards your goals and the vision.

'I have brought myself, by long meditation, to the conviction that a human being with a settled purpose must accomplish it, and that nothing can resist a will which will stake even existence upon its fulfillment.'
BENJAMIN DISRAELI

Clearing your emotional baggage improves your power of intent. Sometimes the power of your intent may be all that will carry you through against a full scale aliens of resistance attack at some point on your life journey. Optimising your power of intent and thus your personal persistence is spirit intelligence in action.

o ATTITUDE

Personal persistence is affected by your attitude to big problems. How do you react to the resistance aliens when they show up?

'Whether you think you can or think you can't — you are right.'
HENRY FORD

When the resistance aliens show up, your attitude will define the outcome of the ensuing battle. When you are under attack, strengthen your attitude by controlling your emotional state. If you bend your head and look down and worry, and fear and concentrate only on the problems, everything can overtake you and you can sink down into unhelpful, negative emotions.

To break a down cycle of depression and worry, try looking up at the ceiling and smiling for 30 seconds. Go on, put this book down and try it now! It is very hard to remain depressed and worried when you are looking up at the ceiling and smiling. This is an easy key to emotional state control and personal persistence.

When the going gets tough, maintaining personal persistence means maintaining an attitude of belief in yourself.

'Everything is possible for him who believes.'
MARK 9:23

Hang in there!

'Everything can be taken from a man but one thing: the last of the human freedoms — to choose one's attitude in any given set of circumstances, to choose one's own way.'
VIKTOR FRANKL

You know what they say — if it is to be, it's up to ...? Me! So when it gets down to the wire and the going is tough, guard your attitude.

o RESPONSIBILITY

What is your *response-ability*, especially when tough times and the resistance aliens show up?

With whom does the responsibility lie for improving your personal persistence? It lies with you.

> *'Man must cease attributing his problems to his environment, and learn again to exercise his will — his personal responsibility.'*
> ALBERT SCHWEITZER

o SUMMARY

Developing the power of personal persistence all comes down to alertness, speed and fitness – fitness of body, mind, emotion and spirit. All the tools to increase personal spirit intelligence are out there available to you, whatever your emotional baggage.

It does not matter what emotional baggage you are carrying from your past, these days you can take action, heal and cleanse it. Ream out your internal 'pipes'. As you clear out your old emotional baggage, laminar energy flow replaces turbulent energy flow and your energy and persistence increase significantly. As your energy goes up, you can pass on that energy as charisma, motivation and inspiration to your team. The choice is yours.

Do you have the courage to reach for your Commitments Register? How serious are you in realising your full leadership and team contribution potential?

You will need to be good to achieve long term success in the fast changing world of tomorrow.

Armed with the spirit intelligence keys of purpose, passion, plans and persistence, in the next chapter we will explore tools that will help you analyse and make sense of the changes already happening around you, so you can keep your life and business enterprises focused and successful.

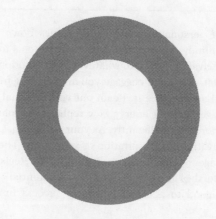

Part Six

PARADIGMS

Your Life Journey

*'I'm the one to die when it's time for me to die, so let me live my life
the way I want to.'*
JIMI HENDRIX

You are not your body, nor your mind, nor your emotions. They are transient tools of your
eternal spirit.

So how are you going to use your time on this amazing planet? That is the ultimate
spirit intelligence question.

Only you can answer if you, like Neo, indeed chose the red pill alternative and claim
your own spirit freedom and integrity.

The blue pill choice appears so much easier.

But if you have read this book this far, it seems the blue pill choice of surrender to
living your life to other people's agendas is not your path.

So now you must start to own your life journey, look around you, take stock,
if necessary regain control and make the changes needed in an already fast changing world.

Eighteen

CHANGE IN A CHANGING WORLD

'If we all worked on the assumption that what is accepted as true is really true, there would be little hope of advance.'
Orville Wright

To achieve consistent results in the turbulent years ahead and make the optimum spirit intelligence choices, you need to understand the changes that are happening in the world around you and how they will affect your life, your family, your community and your business enterprise.

You may find the ideas presented in this chapter to have a high woo-woo factor. If so, remember your shelf for storing currently unacceptable ideas that we discussed in Chapter 1.

The word **paradigm** derives from the Greek word *paradeigma* a pattern.

o STUDYING WORLD CHANGE PATTERNS

You may have heard of the word 'paradigm'.

As a responsible journeyman and leader, you need to look for the patterns in the changes occurring in the world so you can understand the ramifications of those changes and what strategies you need to adopt to ensure success despite the changes.

There are clearly major change forces at work on the world stage affecting people's thoughts, emotions and spirit.

To help you make more sense of it, we will review the history of pattern change. This will help explain and give meaning to the major changes now happening as we move into the new millennium so you can plan to accommodate these global changes and still succeed.

You've probably seen these two famous quotes from outstanding business pioneers that show the difficulty in predicting how change or innovation will affect us:

'I think there is a world market for about five computers.'
Thomas J. Watson, chairman of IBM, 1943

'There is no reason for any individual to have a computer in their home.'
KEN OLSEN, PRESIDENT OF DIGITAL EQUIPMENT CORPORATION, 1977.

o THE HISTORY OF CHANGE

There are clearly significant pattern changes occurring in our lifetime that affect how we live. The rate of change wasn't always so rapid as it is now.

For thousands of years during the Agrarian age, we ploughed, sowed and harvested to the rhythm of the seasons. The pattern did not change much. Most people worked on the land or as tradesmen, under a feudal system.

James Watt's development of the steam engine in 1763 heralded the era of the industrial revolution. Changes continued as a result of major inventions such as Bessemer's development of steel production, the harnessing of electicity, Thomas Edison's light bulb and Alexander Graham Bell's development of the telephone. Each invention in the industrial revolution hastened remarkable shifts and changes in the way people lived and worked.

After the Second World War, the development of computers and global telecommunications heralded the rise of the global service economy and the Information age.

Enormous change continues all around us. The personal computer, the CD, the mobile phone, email, the Internet and e-commerce are all examples of major technology change that are affecting how we live and work.

Technology changes had a major effect in the 20th century and will continue in the 21st century. Where will the next technology break-throughs come from?

It seems incredible that we have only used CDs for a few years. Widespread programmable laser disk technology is now a reality. The common use of video phones by everyone is only years away. There is talk of new generations of planes that allow flights from London to Sydney in less than 12 hours. The first hints of gravitation experiments are being reported. Major research on hydrogen engines that run on water is continuing.

What will it all mean to your life, your vision and your plans? There is no second guessing technology change. It requires vigilance, awareness and mastermind meetings to discuss the possible affects on your ventures.

People changes

Even though technology changes are fascinating, there are deeper changes occurring to people around you that are far more powerful.

If you are to optimise spirit intelligence and achieve success, you must understand these worldwide changes to people and think through the ramifications.

Viewing history on a grand scale can be helpful in gaining clarity on what is happening around you today. This will enable you to make better spirit intelligence choices.

By looking at history as separate large blocks of time, changes can be best understood by using the concept of the astrological ages. This requires a basic understanding of our galaxy and the changing physical position of the stars relative to the sun and the Earth.

Once you understand these blocks of time, we will review the profound people changes that have occurred in the past and the equally profound changes to people now occurring globally that will fundamentally affect the spirit within.

Armed with this understanding, you will see why the spirit intelligence keys in this book are so vital if you are to succeed in the turbulent years ahead.

o ASTROLOGICAL AGES

We don't need to open up into a detailed debate on the methods, validity or relevance of modern astrology, but it is useful to know that the Earth does not orbit perfectly round the sun in a perfect circle, but rather follows the oval path of an ellipse. The Earth's axis of rotation is at an angle to its elliptical orbit around the sun.

This means the sun is only directly above the equator twice a year. These days in March and September are called the equinox – when there is exactly 12 hours of daylight and 12 hours of darkness.

The elliptical orbit is the reason that we have seasons. As you can see from the diagram, at one end of the elliptical orbit, the northern hemisphere points at the sun and enjoys summer. The sun appears higher in the sky. At the other end of the elliptical orbit, six months later, the southern hemisphere has summer. That's when the other hemisphere has winter because the sun is lower in the sky and delivers less heat.

MARCH EQUINOX

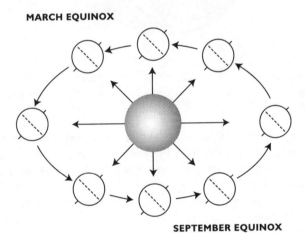

SEPTEMBER EQUINOX

Imagine now looking from the Earth at the sun. Beyond the sun is the backdrop of the stars in our galaxy in their constellations. As the Earth orbits the sun every 12 months, the sun appears against a different backdrop, a different constellation each month. You can see that the sun appears to move during a year right across a 360 degree backdrop of constellations.

Astronomers have names for the constellations. Astrologers divide the perceived celestial backdrop (the zodiac against which the sun seems to move) into 12 segments, the 12 signs of the zodiac. These are named after specific constellations.

If the sun is only directly above the equator twice a year at the equinoxes, then twice a year the equinoxes also define a point in the zodiac, the celestial backdrop against which the sun appears to be.

Precession of the equinoxes

Here's the point. Like a gyroscope, the Earth is not spinning perfectly and the poles describe an orbit of rotation every 25,920 years. This is called the precession of the equinoxes.

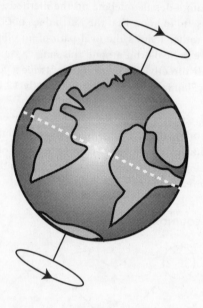

The title doesn't matter. What does matter is that this changes the point on the zodiac against which the sun is backdropped on the equinoxes. Thus astrologers divide up this 25,920 year precessionary cycle into 12 segments of time consisting of 2160 years per segment and call them ages.

Astrologers believe the stars are a physical representation of a fundamentally metaphysical, unseen universe. Much of the universe is indeed invisible. Just as the physical universe is in constant change, so the metaphysical universe changes. We call it evolution.

Astrologers say they can read the swirling forces of metaphysical evolution that affect us by relating to timings and positions of the stars and planets in the physical universe. They may be right, but they've done a pretty poor job of marketing their services to conservative Western business. Eastern businesses tend to be more open to metaphysics.

We can use each astrological age as a way of reviewing large scale spirit changes that have and are affecting us all. Understanding this is especially important for those called to lead other people through turbulent, uncertain times and market forces.

The exact timing of the transition from one astrological age to the next is much debated. There is no definitive boundary point as the effects of the ages merge in to each other. However, the major changes are evident when viewed against the background of time.

Taurus age 4580/4380BC – 2420/2220BC

In the period commencing around 4500BC, the sun at the time of the northern hemisphere spring equinox each year was back dropped against the part of the celestial zodiac named after the constellation of Taurus. Taurus the bull is an earth sign. The major physical symbols of man's religious and political labour reflect the Taurus period and are earth structures — the Pyramids, the megalithic stone temples on Malta, the unbaked brick palaces and early stepped ziggurats of Mesopotamia, the tower of Babel, the hanging gardens of Babylon, the famous walls of Jericho, England's Stonehenge and Neolithic burial mounds.

The symbolism of the Minotaur, half-man, half-bull echoes the Taurus period. Britain's John Bull also originates from that time. The Egyptians mummified bulls as sacred animals and they often depicted Isis, the wife of Osiris, with cow horns.

During this period of time, spirit beliefs and contact with 'higher spirit realms' for the common people were controlled by Pharaohs and Emperors aided by priests.

Aries age 2420/2220BC – 260/60BC

By about 2400BC, the sun at the spring equinox started to move into the sector of the zodiac named after the constellation of Aries. Aries the ram is a fire sign. From this period, we see religious and political symbols that reflect the symbolism of Aries such as cremation of the dead, Zoroastrian fire worship, burnt sacrifices, Moses and the burning bush, Elijah's fiery chariot, the fiery pillar and the sacrificial lamb. King David was a shepherd.

Jesus was called the shepherd, the lamb of God, reflecting the old Aries era. Shepherds showed up at his birth.

During this period, spirit beliefs and contact with 'higher spirit realms' for the common people were still controlled by Emperors and Kings aided by priests.

Pisces age 260/60BC – 1900/2100AD

In the years before the birth of Christ, the sun on the spring equinox moved into the zodiac sector of Pisces. Pisces the fish is a water sign. The early Christians used the fish as their Christian symbol. Christ called his disciples fishers of men. John the Baptist baptised with water. Jesus walked on water. He turned water into wine.

Christ died on Good Friday and on that day Christians are supposed to eat fish. The bishop's mitre is shaped like a fish's head. Devout Muslims wash parts of themselves five times a day. Hindus immerse themselves in the waters of the Ganges.

In this period, mankind explored the world by sailing across the waters, built aqueducts and canals to improve water transport and invented the water powered steam engine.

During this period of time, Kings, Czars and the Church hierarchy controlled spirit and religious institutions for the common people in the Western world, Emperors, chiefs and priests had tight control in the rest of the world.

Aquarian age 1900/2100AD – 4060/4260AD

As they sang in the musical 'Hair', this is the dawning of the age of Aquarius – as the sun now moves into the zodiac sector of Aquarius. Aquarius, the man with the pitcher of water, is an air and mind sign.

The Wright brothers developed Kitty Hawk in 1903 and flew through the air. Teslar and Marconi developed radio across the air waves in 1895. The first public television broadcast also across the air waves was in England in 1927. The launch of the Russian sputnik satellite in 1957 heralded space travel.

The Theosophical and Anthroposophical societies, founded at the turn of this century were the heralds of a huge surge in mind science and the study of the *theos* — the spirit. We have come to know this as the New Age movement. The Information Age is upon us as mind data proliferates.

The man with the water pitcher waters the Earth and we become environmentally aware.

o STUDYING CHANGE PATTERNS

You start to see the point of studying patterns of change. As a leader, you have to understand the spirit forces and patterns swirling around you and your team if you are to optimise spirit intelligence.

What is significant for you and the whole point of this digression into astrological time, is that at the dawning of the age of Aquarius, we are seeing a massive erosion in the control of spirit values by power groups. The authority of Emperors has dwindled. You may have watched the film — *The Last Emperor*. The Russian revolution got rid of the Tsar.

The weekly drama of British and Monaco royalty over the last 20 years has put a big dent in the authority of royalty. Think about the popular reaction to the tragic death of Princess Di, the renegade from the royal system, the queen of hearts, the people's princess. Isolation, loss of authority and irrelevance increases for remaining members of the royal family.

With some exceptions, in the West, Church attendance statistics speak of a generally waning influence of the Church and priestly authority. Respect for politicians is declining rapidly. Business and sex scandals plague the Western political and religious scene. Bribery and corruption are rife in the East. This is hardly the stuff of powerful and inspiring political, religious and business leadership. Traditional authority is losing power and respect everywhere.

o PEOPLE POWER

Thus we arrive at an era best summarised as the era of people power. In the age of Aquarius, the common people are responsible for their own spirit values. There is no one in authority to intercede for us or tell us what to do or believe or access 'higher realms' for us. We are on our own. This is a historical first — and one of major spirit intelligence significance. To be in tune with the age, we have to make up our own minds on spirit empowerment matters.

It was people power that took down the Berlin Wall. Imagine the courage of the first person to take a hammer and chisel to that wall, knowing that most who had challenged it previously had lost their life in the attempt.

It was people power that ousted President Marcos from the Philippines by putting flowers in the soldiers' gun barrels. It was people power that removed President Soeharto in Indonesia. It was people power that stood up against suppression in Tiananmen Square in Beijing in 1989.

The turmoil of Eastern Europe, after the collapse of the Soviet Empire is all about people power, trying to figure out the new era of political, economic and spirit freedom. It can be very challenging. People power is not necessarily easy.

What does this mean for you? Will people power be well served by a 16 cylinder empowering team culture?

During the Spanish inquisition, Church officials might have burned you for encouraging people power by supporting and empowering them to 16 cylinder performance! Not today.

Think through the spirit intelligence choice ramifications. Use the keys in this book to turn on and harness people power on your team. You will be in tune with the age.

What previously might have appeared high woo-woo becomes relevant to the dawning age because we are less than 100 years into a 2160 year cycle.

The ramifications of the loss of power faced by royalty, the church, politicians and secular business leaders will be enormous. If democracy by representation produces falling trust, rising cynicism and dissatisfaction, what will democracy by participation be like?

The rise of the use of the Internet (and some governments' attempts to censure global information) give hints of what lies ahead. So do the recent anti-globalisation and anti-war demonstrations. We all have a great deal of original thinking to do.

So where does this leave you? What of your future?

Ninteen

YOUR FUTURE

'Taking a new step, uttering a new word, is what people fear most.'
FYODOR DOSTOEVSKY

o LUCK AND PREPAREDNESS

They say luck is when preparedness meets opportunity. Who knows the opportunities that your life journey will present to you? All you can do is work on your preparedness.

To achieve mastery of the games of life and business, you have reviewed the need for a definiteness of purpose and a graphical vision at work, in your community and at home.

You have learned about the keys to inspiring passion, motivation and enthusiasm.

You understand the need for clear plans of action, prescribing the success vision of the future with the people around you, then working back using the graphical PERT planning rope bridges and asking — *what happened just before that?*

You have explored the necessity for persistence, both team persistence underpinned by good systems and a supportive culture, and personal persistence which can be improved by reducing personal resistance.

You know you are heading into a new millennium and we all need to be alert to the people power changes happening around us.

All these keys give you better spirit intelligence choices.

o YOUR COMMITMENTS TO CHANGE

Now is the time to check your Commitments Register to change.

You are armed with an array of 175 practical spirit intelligence keys to help you and the people around you at home, at work and in your community to make better choices, to go confidently forward and succeed.

Remember the definition of spirit intelligence insanity is to keep doing everything the same and expect your results to magically improve.

What are your commitments to change? Check them now.

○ THE POWER OF COMMITMENT

This often published quote from WN Murray of the 1951 Scottish Himalayan Expedition may reinforce to you the power of commitment:

Commitment

'Until one is committed, there is hesitancy, the chance to draw back, always ineffectiveness. Concerning all acts of initiative (and creation) there is one elementary truth, the ignorance of which kills countless ideas and splendid plans: that the moment one commits oneself, then Providence moves too. All sorts of things occur to help one that would otherwise never have occurred.

A whole stream of events issues from the decision, raising in one's favour all manner of unforeseen incidents and meetings and material assistance, which no man could have dreamt would have come his way. I have learned a deep respect for one of Goethe's couplets — Whatever you can do, or dream you can, begin it. Boldness has genius, power and magic in it.'

WN MURRAY, 1951 SCOTTISH HIMALAYAN EXPEDITION

Your commitment to change in your Commitments Register is recorded for clarity and future reference.

○ THANK YOU

Finally, let me say how much I appreciate your persistence in working through this book. Its purpose is very clear. You are on a journey through life. You have something significant yet to do and you have something special inside you, something unique, a gift with which you can make a difference.

You can now elect to take the red pill and own the quality and destiny of your life journey and help those around you.

If this book has helped you towards the mastery of spirit intelligence in making better life choices at home, at work and in your community — both in the game of life and in the game of business — it has served its purpose.

As you now continue on your journey, all I can do is offer you my personal best wishes.

It is always best to go where you are wanted. Never try and force yourself in where you are not wanted. It doesn't work out. I have found this maxim useful. It might help guide your life journey.

As a cautionary note, remember:

'Great spirits have always experienced violent opposition from mediocre minds.'

ALBERT EINSTEIN

The enemy of resistance is alive and well. The spirit intelligence journey is always the road less travelled.

Like Daniel you may at times feel you are facing the lion's den. Remember then the well known hymn:

Dare to be a Daniel
Dare to stand alone
Dare to have a purpose firm
Dare to make it known

Remember the empty chair of the mastermind. That superconscious power is always there to help you. In the words of this old Irish blessing:

May the road rise up to meet you
May you have the sun on your face
* and the wind at your back*
May angels lighten your load and
May God hold you in his hand
all through the coming years.

In conclusion — *Carpe diem* — seize the day. Make your life extraordinary. Good Luck!

MY COMMITMENTS REGISTER

MY COMMITMENTS TO CHANGE ARE:

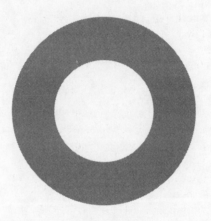

SPIRIT INTELLIGENCE RESOURCES

Contact the Author
To contact the author, please access our website www.spirit-intelligence.com

Market Analysis Tools – Customer Value Management
In any market, you need to know the value criteria that your customer or prospect is using to make the 'buy' decision.

These buy decision value criteria reflect the relative perceived quality of:
- the products supplied by you and your competitors
- the service delivered
- the relationships established
- as well as the relative cost or price

Achieving 'gold medal' service and relationship quality must embrace a whole person analysis. This includes understanding and meeting the unseen needs of your customer's mind, emotions and spirit - a classic example of Spirit Intelligence in action.

Our Customer Value Management software provides powerful, easy-to-use analysis and mapping tools to help you better understand not only your customers but also your competitors and how your customer views your organisation relative to your competitors.

The graphical outputs (the picture is worth 1000 words) are essential for developing 'gold medal' winning marketing and sales strategies.

Full details can be found on our website www.spirit-intelligence.com

Sales Campaign Mastery
If you are involved in selling, you will find our Sales Campaign Mastery analysis and planning software tools to be very powerful aids in improving your 'gold medal winning' sales performance.

You need to bring the Spirit Intelligence approach of analysing the whole person to each relevant contact in your customer's organisation.

Unless you know you are meeting their whole person needs, your sales approach will be sub-optimal.

The powerful graphics (the picture is worth 1000 words) provide exceptional analysis tools in helping you correct and improve your sales campaign after each sales call — another example of Spirit Intelligence in action.

Full details can be found on our website — www.spirit-intelligence.com

Spirit Intelligence

175 PRACTICAL KEYS

1. Powering up the whole person
- Whole person 16 cylinder empowerment (body, mind, emotions and spirit)
- Use the generalised principles of physics and metaphysics
- Understand the woo-woo factor
- Use the shelf

2. The life journey
- Life as a journey
- Life skills inventory
- Life master learnings
- The game of life
- The game of business
- The winning team and the learning team
- My commitments register
- Hard vs easy — a life approach

3. Keys to success
- Four Success Keys
  - A definiteness of purpose
  - A burning desire to succeed — passion
  - Clear plans of action
  - Persistence

4. A definiteness of purpose
- A purpose or mission statement
- Courage
- Comfort zone
- Life journey responsibility
- Fluff / superfluff / specific
- Stakeholder success criteria
- Visual / audio / kinesthetic

5. The power of vision
- o Vision
- o Leadership
  - o Vision over-reach
  - o Vision under-reach
  - o Team consensus
- o Icons
- o Capturing the vision
- o The picture is worth a thousand words

6. Working with vision
- o Vision without action — merely a dream
- o Action without vision — just passing the time
- o Vision with action — can change the world
- o Vision with nations — significant vision precedes significant success
- o Vision with individuals — something significant yet to do
- o Vision inspires enthusiasm
- o Vision with young people
- o Law of compression and tension
- o A compressive vs a positive tension management style
- o Vision stability
- o Metaphysical gravity
- o Unclear vision

7. Your leadership passion
- o The unreasonable champion
- o Pass-i-on
- o Body language
- o Power centres
- o Charisma
- o Physical appearance
- o External and internal zones of empowerment
- o Nexus of influence
- o Zone of empowerment check list

8. Mapping the territory
- o Leadership non-existence – mapping the territory

9. Achieving rapport
- o Rapport keys
    - o Sincere interest
    - o Building trust
        - o Reliability
        - o Openness
        - o Acceptance
        - o Straight-forwardness
    - o Satisfying needs
- o DISC rapport
    - o A mixed team
    - o DISC graphic equalisers
- o Variable rapport styles — DISC
- o Your DISC graphic equaliser profile

10. Keys to the spirit within
- o Life in training
- o The $25 million game
    - o life purpose elicitation
    - o self motivation
- o Spirit exchange
- o Leadership stewardship and mentoring
- o A personal growth contract
- o The dynamics of balance

11. Values — A source of strength
- o Values – circumstance related
- o Ranking the values
- o Company value statements
- o Multi-level rapport

12. Building passionate teams
- o Team culture
    - o Trust
        - o Win / win
        - o Trust building tools
        - o Trust account
    - o Assertion
        - o An assertion tool - I feel like saying
- o Conflict
- o Rituals
- o NICE

13. Clear plans of action
- Planning traps
  - Fear of the future
  - What's the next step
  - The Merlin factor
- PERT graphical planning
  - Events and relationships
  - What happened just before that?
  - Reviewing the plans
  - Activating the plans
- The war room
- Team decision making

14. The power of the mind
- Three tools of planning
  - Body and team
  - The leverage of the mind
- The mind as a bio-computer
  - Thoughts are things — the power of the metaphysics
  - We move towards our dominant thoughts
- Programming the bio-computer
- Goal setting
- Bio-computer programming
  - Inserting the programs
  - Goal projection
  - Power of the mastermind
    - Physical mastermind
    - Psychic mastermind
    - Faith
    - Blue door re-charge
- Bio-computer time storage
  - Re-programming time storage

15. Managing people
- The contribution contract
  - Define their customers
  - Customer value criteria
  - Gold medal performance standard
  - Work to be done
  - 2 signatures
- History of management
- Supporting and empowering people
  - Do they understand the game?

- Do they know the rules?
- Are they able to play the game?
    - Known / unknown strengths
    - Known / unknown improvement opportunities
- Do they have the chance to win the game?
- Do they want to play?
- Managing people — able to / want to / chance to
- Appraisals
- Hiring people
- Candidates - law of metaphysical gravity
- Metaphysical gravity observations — the first step is the hardest

16. The power of persistence

- Systems analysis
- Kaizen
- Fluid flow – laminar vs turbulent
- Systems accountability
- Alien of the month
- Physics and metaphysics of persistence
    - Ohm's law
    - Law of entrainment
    - Counter-entrainment

17. Personal persistence keys

- Personal resistance
    - Ohm's law re-visited
    - Laminar and turbulent flow re-visited
    - BMES speed
- Relationship laws of metaphysics
    - Law of centripetal force
    - Stable relationships
    - Relationship break up
- Teams in orbit
- Increasing personal speed
    - Physical speed
    - Spirit speed
    - Mind and emotion speed
    - Reducing your resistance – cleaning up emotional baggage
        - Meditation
        - Re-birthing
        - Bio-energetics
        - Rolfing
        - Other techniques

- Fear handling
- Clearing team emotional baggage
- Intent
- Attitude
- Responsibility

18. Change in a changing world
- World change patterns — history of change
- People changes
    - Astrological ages
- People power

INDEX